Linguistics Today

Keith Brown is Reader in Linguistics at the University of Essex. From 1965 until 1983 he taught linguistics at the University of Edinburgh and before that he lectured in English at University College of Cape Coast, Ghana. With J. E. Miller he has published two other books: *Syntax: a linguistic introduction to sentence structure* (1980) and *Syntax: generative grammar* (1981).

Fontana Linguistics

Published

Keith Brown

Linguistics
Today

Fontana Paperbacks

First published by Fontana Paperbacks 1984

Set in 10 on 11.7 point Times
Made and printed in Great Britain by
Richard Clay (The Chaucer Press),
Bungay, Suffolk

Contents

Introduction to Fontana Linguistics

In the past twenty-five years, linguistics – the systematic study of language – has come of age. It is a fast expanding and increasingly popular subject, which is now offered as a degree course at a number of universities. As a result of this expansion, psychologists, sociologists, philosophers, anthropologists, teachers, speech therapists and numerous others have realized that language is of crucial importance in their life and work. But when they tried to find out more about the subject, a major problem faced them – the technical and often narrow nature of much writing about linguistics.

The Fontana Linguistics series is an attempt to solve this problem by presenting current findings in a lucid and non-technical way. Its object is twofold. First, it hopes to outline the 'state of play' in certain crucial areas of the subject, concentrating on what is happening now, rather than on surveying the past. Secondly, it aims to show how linguistics links up with other disciplines such as sociology, psychology, philosophy, speech therapy and language teaching.

The series will, we hope, give readers a fuller understanding of the relationship between language and other aspects of human behaviour, as well as equipping those who wish to find out more about the subject with a basis from which to read some of the more technical literature in textbooks and journals.

Jean Aitchison
London School of Economics

1 Language and Communication

Communication of all kinds is like painting – a compromise with impossibilities.

(Samuel Butler)

Language is the most sophisticated and versatile means available to human beings for the communication of meanings. We communicate primarily by the use of language, by the manipulation of words. The principal task of linguistics is to investigate and describe the ways in which words can be combined and manipulated to convey meanings. This is generally labelled 'syntax'.

In this book we shall be primarily concerned with the part that syntactic structures play in this communicative process and how linguists have chosen to model this contribution. Before turning to this particular concern, however, it will be helpful to set the scene in more general terms so that we can see just what kind of contribution syntax has to make. A number of preliminary questions arise. What range of meanings can be communicated through language? What other channels of communication are open to us, and how do they differ from language? What are the particular properties that distinguish language from other systems of communication? The questions are interrelated, and, not surprisingly, there is no straightforward answer to any of them. But we need to have some views on such matters, or at least see what the problems are, before we can proceed to our particular interests. We need, in other words, to have some idea about the objectives of a syntactic description, and of its limitations.

As we shall see, there is some agreement over certain basic facts, but there is also violent disagreement as to the relative importance of some of these facts, and whether and how they should be incorporated into a theory of language. Suppose that it is agreed that language is realized by words, which are constructed according to certain principles, and that words, again in accordance with certain principles, can be structured into sentences which in turn relate to meanings. Clearly, then, we need to establish what these principles are and how they interact, and then describe a language according to these principles. We are immediately confronted with a series of questions. Should we start with a description of how words and sentences are constructed and then see how these relate to meanings? Or should we investigate the properties of meanings, and then see how these might be related to sentences and ultimately realized in words? Or should we perhaps try to develop a semantic description (a description of meaning) and a syntactic description (a structural description) side by side? And what sort of general principles should guide our choice? Each of these positions is adopted by some linguistic theory and the resultant grammars are rather different, and focus on different aspects of language. Nor is this all. Should we draw a distinction between 'language' and 'the use of language', and if so, how? Again the resultant grammars will look rather different, depending on what sort of choices we make. It is a matter of considerable controversy how a description of a language should, as it were, carve up the descriptive cake in order to arrive at an illuminating description of how language conveys meanings, and language, like cake, is not 'naturally' divided into slices!

This leads to yet another series of questions. We will presumably be looking for the best description of the 'facts'. But what *are* the relevant facts? If we are attempting to produce a description that is psychologically 'real', a description that is in harmony with what we believe is going on in the minds of speakers, and what other investigations tell us about the production and comprehension of language, then we will want to call on one type of 'fact'. If, on the other hand, we wish to describe the way in which language is used in society as a vehicle for the expression of our wishes and desires, and as an instrument for interacting with other people, this will call on a rather different set of 'facts'. Or again, we may wish to consider language as an abstract 'calculus', relatively independent of social and psychological issues. This will involve different 'facts' again. Descriptions will differ according to what particular aspect of language they focus on, and linguistics today does not suffer from a shortage of different approaches to language.

1.1 Language and non-linguistic communication

We began with the assumption that using language involves manipulating words to convey meanings, so let us consider briefly the range of meanings that can be communicated through words. These are diverse, and any attempt to distinguish between different kinds of meaning is difficult and controversial. Largely following the taxonomy of Halliday (1970), we will, however, distinguish three.

An obvious use of language is to communicate information about the world about us and to get things done. This 'transactional' use of language is often thought to be in some sense the primary use of language, and when we use language in this way, especially when we use it to refer to things and events in the world, the statements we make are generally susceptible to public judgements of truth and falsity. So, if I say *It is snowing*, you can determine whether what I say is true or false by inspecting the state of the weather. By extension, we can use language to refer to hypothetical states of affairs, to imaginary worlds, and to our own and other people's ideas, wishes and desires, and we know what the world would have to be like for these statements to be true or false. Novelists obviously do this all the time. They invite their readers to enter an imaginary world and use language to refer to events and so on in this world. This use of language to convey information is often thought of as involving the 'literal' use of language and has been called 'cognitive' or 'descriptive'.

A somewhat different, but equally important, use of language is closely tied up with the first. This is our use of language to describe our reactions to events and to regulate our interactions with other people. In this 'interactional' use of language, judgements of truth and falsity are difficult or impossible, since this use is concerned with evaluations and relationships rather than facts, and is often private rather than public. If I say *I am pleased that it is snowing*, I imply that it is in fact snowing, and the truth of this is ascertainable; you cannot, however, always correctly judge whether this does or does not please me. The same is true of the way we use language in our relationships with other people. An obvious instance is the words we use on greeting and parting. Here, what is said is usually conventional and is sometimes factually untrue or insincere or both. Judgements of this sort, however, miss the point since what is most important in this kind of language is the fact of speech itself. When someone says *How are you* on meeting, the function of the utterance is not to ask for a detailed health report, but rather to offer a conventional politeness that indicates goodwill and may serve as an ice-breaker to initiate conversation. This use of language to maintain social bonds occurs all through many verbal interactions and sometimes, indeed, seems to be the sole purpose of conversation: this is certainly the typical caricature of 'cocktail party' chat. More seriously, it can be thought of as the use of language that regulates the function of utterances in interchanges – a question invites a reply, an apology is often responded to with its acceptance and so forth. It has been called the 'interpersonal' or 'social' use of language.

A quite different, but again important, use of language is to signpost the way round communication itself. For example, the introductory words of the preceding paragraph, *A somewhat different use of language*, indicate a new topic and relate it to the preceding paragraph. Other phrases indicate that an example is going to be produced, that the sense of the paragraph is about to be summarized, and so on. This signposting function of language is extremely important, since we clearly need to be shown our way through other people's meanings and to guide them through our own. This use of language is obviously very different to the first and second uses, since its purpose is to structure information carried elsewhere rather than convey information or evaluate. It can be referred to as a 'textual' use of language since it conveys information about the structure of stretches of language.

These types of meaning are clearly not in self-contained

compartments. There are important interactions between them, and a fully comprehensive description would need to take account of them all, and of the interactions between them. In practice, however, linguistic descriptions tend to concentrate on one or the other. Some concentrate primarily on the first, and these tend to focus their attention on the structure and meaning of sentences in isolation. In this case, a grammatical description will concentrate on the rules that govern well-formed sentences, and a semantic description will tend to seek a representation of the 'basic' or 'literal' meaning of sentences, independently of their use in context. And a representation of meaning often involves the use of formulae derived from logic. Other descriptions concentrate on the meaning of language in use. These clearly cannot ignore the first use we mentioned, but are likely to be particularly concerned with the second and third. Here a grammatical description will be interested not only in rules for the well-formedness of complete sentences but also in the ways sentences and fragments of sentences relate to each other in a text. The corresponding semantic description will now be interested not only in literal meanings, but also in 'functional' meanings (the purpose behind the utterance) and in the 'pragmatic' meanings (the meanings that can be directly related to the context of utterance) that can be inferred from sentences in context. To contrast the two approaches, consider again the sentence *It is snowing*. Let us suppose the literal meaning of this is 'It is snowing', and that the truth of this literal meaning can be checked. In context, other meanings no less important from a communicative point of view may also be intended. If I look out of the window and utter the words, my intention may simply be to 'inform', particularly if I think my interlocutor does not know this information and would be interested to have it. If I use the words in answer to the question *What's the weather like?*, my words will not only inform but will have the function of a 'response'. If I use the words to reply to the question *Would you like to go for a walk?*, I may or may not inform my interlocutor. It could be that my interlocutor already knows that it is snowing, and that I know that he knows. In this case the function of my utterance may be to refuse the invitation without actually saying 'no'.

The sorts of meanings mentioned in the preceding section can obviously be conveyed through language, the use of words. But this is not the only way in which such information can be conveyed and when we use language it is inevitably accompanied by other communicative signals. If language is written, then the properties of this medium are themselves communicative: handwriting is said to be an indication of character, and the choice of font, the layout and so forth can be used to effect in printing. Equally, when language is spoken, the acoustic and auditory properties of this medium are communicative, and spoken language is generally also accompanied by visual and gestural signals, some of which are closely related to language, and others hardly related to language at all. We can see that this is so by considering how information is conveyed in a conversation.

When, how, and how often we look at each other is communicative. Lovers are said to 'feed on each other's eyes'. This behaviour is clearly not language, although it may well be more communicative than language, and is indeed often said to 'speak more clearly than words'. Gaze and eye contact are, however, important regulators of language behaviour, and the manner in which they are manipulated in conversation provides important clues to the way conversational 'turns' are negotiated, to the nature of the relationship between speakers, the level of attention one is paying to the other, and so forth. The same is true of gesture. The way we sit can indicate that we are bored or interested and, like visual behaviour, gestures can be intimately connected with verbal communication. We can point in order to establish reference – *I'd like a pound of those*, *please* – and gesture and posture can also be involved in conversational 'turn taking'. Nor should we forget non-linguistic vocal communication, for everything we utter is not language. Coughs, sneezes, 'clicks of the tongue' and so on are communicative but are not language. Similarly, various features of voice quality and articulation can be a guide to how old a person is, whether he has a cold or has food in the mouth, or is smiling or scowling.

'Paralinguistic' features of this sort found in association with language need to be distinguished from language itself, but they can be fruitfully discussed in terms of the types of meaning mentioned in the preceding section. As far as cognitive meanings are concerned, paralinguistic communication is generally rather restricted. We can use gestures to draw attention to objects we want to refer to, we have a range of signs – some conventional and others *ad hoc* – for various objects and actions, and we can use gesture to indicate dimensions, to agree and disagree and so forth. However, the range of gestures available to most speakers would hardly permit the transfer of much cognitive information on their own, and certainly not the wide range of such meanings that we normally wish to convey. This does not mean that gesture is in principle incapable of expressing a range of cognitive meanings, and indeed, conventionalized into a proper system, as in the sign languages of the deaf, it can be as expressive as 'verbal' language: cf. Klima and Bellugi (1979).

Emotive meanings, by contrast, are often rather well conveyed by non-verbal means. Utterances can be modified by the manipulation of the pitch range, the speed of speech and such facial expressions as smiling, scowling and 'speaking through the teeth'. These can often convey depression, interest, excitement or boredom more effectively than language itself, and we are in general rather sensitive in such matters. Interpersonal meanings, too, are importantly conveyed by non-verbal means. We have already mentioned that the way people look at each other provides clues to their relationships, the level of attention they are paying to each other, and so on. Functional meanings and pragmatic inferences can also be conveyed by paralinguistic means, particularly through intonation. Textual meanings, too, are frequently conveyed by gesture, vocally and, perhaps most importantly, by the manipulation of eye contact and gaze. We have already mentioned the importance of these regulators of conversation, and it is not hard to think of other non-verbal signposting round the structure of speech.

Verbal language, the use of words, is, then, not the only means we have of conveying meanings. When language is used, it is typically accompanied by other, paralinguistic, communicative signals. The extent to which linguists interest themselves in such matters will depend on the aim of the investigations. Approaches which concentrate largely on the analysis of sentences and their cognitive meanings will tend largely to ignore paralinguistic phenomena. They will, however, be important for approaches which take account of language in use; for instance, anyone interested in a description of the way conversation is structured will obviously wish to pay attention to paralinguistic features of the kind we have just been discussing, and to consider just how these features interact with language. They will clearly be particularly interesting to those concerned with the study of language in use – the analysis of conversation, for example. We do not, however, have the space to concern ourselves with them in this book, since we shall be concentrating on the role of language itself.

It will be appreciated that concentrating on language itself, rather than on the total communicative process, inevitably involves a degree of abstraction. Furthermore, it immediately invites us to draw a further distinction: between 'language' and 'using language'. This distinction involves yet a further abstraction since it opens up the question of the extent to which we wish to consider language as a relatively concrete phenomenon or as a more or less self-contained abstract system. What is at issue can be illustrated by calling on de Saussure's well-known analogy between language and chess (de Saussure, 1916). He compares the abstract rules of chess – rules that determine how pieces can move, how the game is won, and so on – with the abstract rules of language, and the strategies used in chess with the rules governing the use of language. A particular game of chess will then be the product of both the rules of chess and the strategies used in that particular game, and might then be compared with a particular concrete instance of language use. Someone anxious to describe chess might wish to concentrate on any one of these, but it will be clear that a description of the rules of the game, a discussion of the strategies used in playing the game and an account of a particular game are all quite different kinds of things, and each is at a different level of abstraction.

As far as language is concerned, we can and do treat it as both an abstract and a concrete phenomenon. When we write, we write words and sentences. These can be regarded as concrete objects in the sense that we can observe them on the page, count them and so forth. Spoken language too has an obvious physical form. It can be recorded and subsequently played back, it can be analysed acoustically and can itself be transcribed into words and, with more difficulty, into sentences. A moment's thought, however, will show that both the 'word' and the 'sentence' can also be thought of as abstract units. In its orthographic form, a word can be realized in a multitude of different handwritings or printed in a variety of different styles and sizes of type. Similarly, repeated utterances of a word either by an individual or by many individuals will in an objective sense differ from each other. In both cases, however, we recognize that these are all in some sense the 'same' word. We operate, in fact, as though we have an abstract notion of word identity that makes all these instances of the 'same' word.

The abstract nature of the concept word is particularly clear if we consider 'words' in spoken language. The acoustic analysis of an utterance will reveal that typically there are no pauses between items that we may wish to identify as discrete words, and the transcription of the physical record into words requires the transcriber to know the language in question and to know that the continuous stream of speech realizes a string of items that can be regarded as words. Consider, for instance, how impossible it is to recognize word units in an unknown language. The orthography sometimes recognizes the fact that words are run together in speech by using forms like *d'you wanna*, but we recognize this as a 'contraction' typical of speech and will readily relate it to the string of words more usually represented as *do you want to*. We can, of course, also produce the words one by one in speech if we choose to do so. Doubtless this ability is to some degree influenced by the fact that we have an orthography which we can appeal to, but a comparable process is also apparently available to speakers of 'unwritten' languages, who will equally readily identify their language as consisting of word-sized units, and when the language is eventually 'reduced to writing', word units are accepted as quite natural.

The same is true of the sentence. A sentence can be written or printed or spoken, yet we will recognize all these as instances of the 'same' sentence. Furthermore we will recognize that different sentences – *The cat sat on the mat* and *The book lay on the table* – are instances of the 'same' abstract pattern. The ability to recognize these abstract patterns is important, and one to which we will return.

Descriptions of language are typically concerned with these more abstract units, and this fact leads us immediately to distinguish between 'form' and 'medium': 'form' relating to the abstract units we have been discussing, and 'medium' to the physical form in which these units appear. The 'same' unit at the level of form – some particular word, say – can be realized by a variety of media. An obvious distinction is between the spoken and the written forms of language, but there are other media too: sign language, morse code, semaphore, shorthand and so on. Distinguishing between form and medium in this way implies that language itself, the formation and manipulation of words, can be considered independently of the medium used to convey it.

Many linguists would wish to draw a distinction of this sort between form and medium precisely because it enables language to be treated as a system independent of the particular circumstances of its use. This position does not, of course, imply that the medium is not itself communicative. On the contrary, we have already seen that the medium is indeed communicative, and may in certain cases be a more efficient means of communication than language itself. Nor does it imply that the boundary between what one might wish to consider as belonging to the level of form and what to the level of medium is entirely clear-cut. What it does imply is that for methodological reasons a clear distinction should be drawn. It also asserts that the study of language is primarily concerned with the language system itself.

Other linguists, particularly those engaged in the textual or social study of language in use, might wish to adopt a less abstract view, particularly if they are concerned with language as part of the communicative process as a whole. Some such linguists consider the relationship between the structure and communicative function of language to be so intimate that the structure itself is to some degree determined by the functions it serves. In this view, form and medium would be seen as closely interrelated. It is not hard to come up with corroborative evidence. Language, one might argue, must have some substantial realization, and the relationship between language and the spoken medium is particularly intimate for obvious reasons. Historically, as far as we know, all languages were spoken before they were written and many, of course, are still unwritten. Our first encounters with language are through speech: we learn to speak before we learn to read and write. We use spoken language more often in our everyday life and in more diverse situations than we use written language. Facts like these suggest that the relationship between form and medium is intimate, and this is indeed the 'ordinary man's' view of the matter.

In this section we have been considering ways of communicating meanings, what part language has in this, and how it interacts with and yet differs from other systems of communication. We have seen that different approaches to the study of language can take different views on the relationship between language and other communicative systems. We have also suggested that using language involves an abstract knowledge of the nature of the units involved – words and sentences – and the ways in which they can be brought together to communicate meanings. In the next section we will explore the nature of this knowledge.

1.2 Language and knowledge of the world

Towards the end of the previous section it was suggested that using and understanding language calls on implicit knowledge about it. Other types of knowledge are also involved. In this section we shall be looking at the way in which knowledge about the world interacts with more specifically linguistic knowledge, knowledge about the language system.

We will consider the matter within the framework of a concrete example, so let us consider the kinds of knowledge that are involved in trying to understand the following brief extract from Iris Murdoch's novel *The Italian Girl*:

'I dreamt last night', said Otto, 'that there was a huge tiger in the house. It kept prowling from room to room and I kept trying to get to the telephone to ring for help. Then when I did get to the phone I found I couldn't dial properly because the dial was all made of marzipan –'

'Do you mind,' I said, 'I do want to catch the train. And there are still various things to be settled!'

As a first step we will try to distinguish those aspects of the text that rely for an interpretation on our 'knowledge of the world' from those that bear more specifically on our 'knowledge of the language'. We will then try to draw a distinction between knowing about language and knowing how to use it.

Our knowledge of the world is multifarious and varies from the most general to the most particular. At the most particular level we have our own individual stores of knowledge that make us individuals. At the most general level we share with other members of our culture expectations about the world and how people react to real and imaginary events and situations. We know, for example, something of the prototypical properties of objects: what kind of animal a 'tiger' is, where it lives and how it behaves; what sort of object a 'telephone' is, what it is made of and what it is used for and so on. We also have expectations about normal situations and know that dreams have a bizarre logic of their own where expectations of normality can be frustrated. In the text we have a typical dream situation – an unexpected and potentially frightening element, a tiger, is introduced into an apparently ordinary domestic situation. The tiger maintains its natural behaviour, it prowls around, presumably looking for prey: we would expect this in its natural environment but hardly in an English house. The speaker's reaction is equally natural, he tries to telephone for help. But as is the way in dreams, such obviously prudent behaviour is at first inexplicably frustrated, and when, equally inexplicably, he eventually manages to reach the phone, he is again frustrated because the dial is improbably made of marzipan. To understand the passage, then, we need some knowledge about the characteristic properties of objects and events, assumptions about normal situations and behaviour, and the expectation that in dreams normality and irrationality interact in peculiar ways.

We can hardly dispense with knowledge of this sort if we are to understand what is going on, and we should then enquire how it relates to language. To begin with, we will immediately recognize that however bizarre the situation, there is nothing peculiar about the language. This might not have been the case: just as we can construct bizarre situations, so we can construct equally bizarre uses of language, as we do in puns, riddles and jokes. Some writers are notorious for such linguistic manipulations. In this passage, however, the language is not being manipulated in an unusual way. The fact that we recognize this implies that we have expectations of the way words can be put together in English.

To start the discussion we will assume that two kinds of expectation are involved: one concerns the structure of the language itself, which we will take to mean rules for the formation of sentences, and the other concerns the way sentences are put together to form a text. Insofar as we recognize the passage as a coherent piece of text, our world knowledge has a not inconsiderable influence. The event described is a dream, but it is a coherent dream and the sequence of events in it to some extent regulates the order of the sentences used to describe it. If we jumbled the sentences up, then both the language and the event described would be incoherent. We will look at such matters in more detail in the next section. By contrast, knowledge of the world seems to have little to do with the rules for the construction of the sentences themselves. It is this that we shall be concerned with in this section. Here, even though the reader may not command the technical vocabulary necessary for a discussion about the language, he can certainly make judgements about it. Part of the purpose of this book is to provide an introduction to such a vocabulary, and in what follows we will be trying to externalize some of this implicit knowledge about the language.

As speakers of a language, we know a great deal about the linguistic properties of individual words. We know their grammatical properties. We recognize different classes of words (KEEP and TRY are verbs and TIGER and MARZIPAN are nouns)★

★ We will use capitals to indicate the 'dictionary entry' of a particular word: thus KEEP covers different forms like *keep*, *keeps*, *keeping*, *kept* etc.

because different word classes behave differently. They have, for instance, different 'morphological' properties: words from different classes are constructed differently. So verbs can occur in both 'present' and 'past tense' forms (*keep : kept*; *try : tried*) but nouns cannot (*tiger : *tigered*; *marzipan : *marzipanned*).* We also know that different word classes have different co-occurrence possibilities. Nouns can co-occur with articles, like *a* or *the* (*a tiger*, *the telephone*) but verbs cannot (*a kept, *the tried). Individual members of particular word classes also have different co-occurrence properties. KEEP can be immediately followed by another verb in the 'present participle', *-ing* form (*kept prowling*), but it cannot be directly followed by a verb in the past tense form (*it kept prowled) or in the 'infinitive' form (*it kept to prowl). TRY, too, can be followed by a second verb, but this time we need the infinitive form (*trying to get*) and neither the past tense (*trying got) nor the present participle (*trying getting) will do. Properties of this kind have nothing to do with knowledge of the world. Indeed it is notable that many of the strings marked with an asterisk are not nonsensical. *It kept to prowl, for instance, is not well-formed English, as any speaker of English knows, but it is perfectly interpretable, which suggests that the meaning itself is well formed. It is worth observing that such examples remind us of 'foreigner talk': the sort of speech produced by speakers who have not mastered the idiosyncratic rules for the correct formation of English verb forms and hence do not yet know the language perfectly. For each of the words in the passage we have grammatical knowledge of this sort.

Words also have semantic properties. Here, however, there is something of a problem since it is not obvious how we should distinguish clearly between the semantic properties of words, part of the language, and the properties of the things the words can be used to refer to, a matter of our knowledge of the world. We will nevertheless attempt to draw a broad distinction of this kind along fairly traditional lines. Consider for example the words MARZIPAN, TELEPHONE and DIAL. The

---

* A word preceded by an asterisk indicates an unacceptable or non-occurring form.

relationship between words and objects is arbitrary and conventional, and part of our linguistic knowledge is that we know what sorts of things the words can be used to refer to. What we know about the objects called marzipan, telephone and dial, both in general and in particular, will then be part of our knowledge of the world. We know, for instance, something about the typical construction and use of these objects, the detail varying with our general expertise but the broad outlines being shared: thus we know that a dial is part of a telephone, that both telephones and dials are usually made of plastic, that the dials of telephones have holes in them through which can be seen both letters and numbers, that a telephone is used for long-distance communication, that marzipan is edible and is sticky and that a telephone is not, and so forth. 'Real-world' properties of this sort are naturally reflected in the language, some more centrally than others, but a linguistic description cannot be expected to incorporate all such 'encyclopedic' knowledge or it will be a description of everything. Following a common approach, we will suppose that the more central properties may be regarded as semantic properties of the words themselves, and that these semantic properties will then be reflected in the ways the vocabulary is structured.

We do not have the space to consider the question of structure in the vocabulary in any detail, but a few examples will be relevant to our purpose. The commonest way in which this structure is described is in terms of the kinds of relationships words contract with each other: these relationships can then be thought of as semantic properties of the words concerned. One common way of distinguishing between these semantic properties and the properties of objects in the real world involves the following assumption: if the semantic properties are violated, the resultant sentences will be contradictory, tautologous or involve other semantic anomalies and these will be present in sentences in isolation. The anomaly will also persist if these sentences are used in particular contexts, but here they may have sensible interpretations since we sometimes use contradictions deliberately. For instance, the sentence *That cow is a bull* contains an obvious anomaly in isolation. In context it may convey an important meaning, but to understand the contextual meaning we also need to understand the contradiction. By contrast, real-world properties will rely for their interpretation on particular contexts of utterance.

Let us consider an example. One pervasive structural relationship between words is that of 'class inclusion', or 'hyponymy'. So for example TIGER, LION and DOG are members of the class ANIMAL, and FLY, WASP and MOSQUITO are members of the class INSECT. Hyponymy is a 'one-way' relationship and this is reflected in the fact that a sentence like *A tiger is an animal* is well formed, but *An animal is a tiger* is not. The latter example is ill formed in or out of context and its deviance derives from the fact that *is a* can be used to express the relationship of hyponymy, and since the relationship is one-way the nouns are not reversible around *is a*. Another relationship can be illustrated with reference to the text. Compare the two sentences *A telephone has a dial* and *A dial has a telephone*. The fact that a dial is part of a telephone, but not vice versa, is part of our knowledge about how telephones are constructed. We can, however, also regard the 'part of' relationship as a semantic property relating the word DIAL to the word TELEPHONE. As before, the ill-formedness of the asterisked sentence derives from a semantic incongruity inherent in the meanings of the words. The sentence can thus have no well-formed 'cognitive' interpretation and will not only be semantically incongruous as an isolated sentence but will remain so in any context, even a dream world. By contrast, whether an object is or is not edible does not seem to be a semantic property since this will depend on who or what is doing the eating and, in the case of humans, on cultural norms. It could be argued that what an object is made of is not a semantic property either, although it is clearly a property of objects in the real world. So, even out of context, the sentence *The dial was all made of marzipan* is comprehensible even though it is decidedly odd in terms of our usual expectations about telephones. And once it is set in the context of a dream it is readily comprehensible, and indeed relies for its effect precisely on the conflict between the situation described and our real-world expectations. The distinction is, however, not at all clear-cut.

As a different example, consider the word HUGE. HUGE is not used to refer to an objective real-world size. It is a 'scalar' adjective and one of an ordered series of scalar adjectives of size including TINY, SMALL, BIG, HUGE. HUGE places the object it is predicated of at the 'big' end of normal expectations about the size of an object of the relevant kind, and it does so by virtue of its place in the series and its relations with the other adjectives in the series. So a 'huge tiger' is big 'as tigers go', but will be smaller than a 'huge whale' and bigger than a 'huge insect'. HUGE, then, does not describe a real-world size. Furthermore its scalar nature is a semantic property deriving from the relationship between HUGE and other scalar adjectives like TINY. It has nothing intrinsically to do with objective measurement.

The discussion suggests that although the linguistic properties of words can reflect the real-world properties of the objects they can be used to refer to, the linguistic properties are established primarily in terms of the kinds of relationships that words contract between each other, and these are reflected even in sentences in isolation. The distinction is a useful one, although it is not entirely clear-cut. Such systematic semantic relationships are part of our linguistic knowledge about words.

Finally, even though the passage is written, we know a good deal about the sound, or phonological, properties of the individual words. We know for instance how to pronounce MARZIPAN or TELEPHONE and that both are stressed on the first syllable ('*marzipan*, rather than **mar'zipan*). We can use this knowledge in constructing a possible reading of the passage in our 'mind's ear'.

We will call such grammatical, semantic and phonological knowledge about individual words 'lexical knowledge'. It is, of course, the kind of information that has traditionally been included, though often not very systematically, in dictionaries and thesauruses.

Lexical knowledge is only part of what we know about our language. We also have 'grammatical' knowledge: we know how words can be put together to form phrases and sentences, and what are and are not possible constituent orders in these units. We know, for instance, that nouns co-occur with articles and adjectives to form units we will call 'noun phrases', and that the various word classes that compose noun phrases can only be combined in certain orders: we can have *a huge tiger*, but not *tiger a huge* or *tiger huge a*. We know that adjectives can be preceded by intensifying expressions like *very* or *quite* to form adjective phrases, as in (*a*) *very huge* (*tiger*), (*a*) *quite enormous* (*tiger*). We know that verbs can combine with auxiliary verbs (in English forms of the verbs BE, HAVE and DO), to form 'verb phrases': *is prowling*, *was made*, *do want*. We know that prepositions, OF, IN, FROM, TO, can combine with noun phrases to make prepositional phrases: *of – marzipan*, *in – the house* and so on. At another level we know that phrases can be combined in certain orders to make sentences: we find *the dial – was made – of marzipan*, rather than, say, *was made – the dial – of marzipan*. And we know that sentences can themselves be combined, and that this often involves a main and various subordinate constituents, the latter usually being marked as subordinate by different 'subordinating conjunctions': 'temporal clauses' with *when* or *after*, 'clauses of reason' with *because* or *since* and so forth.

Most of these facts about English sentence structure are peculiar to English and have little to do with 'objective' reality. This must be so since other languages order things differently. In French, adjectives typically follow rather than precede the noun, and in Gaelic the verb is usually the first constituent in a sentence.

We also know how to use our grammatical and lexical knowledge to interpret the meaning of sentences. We know for instance that word order usually indicates the grammatical relations of 'subject', 'object': the subject typically preceding the verb and the object following it. This knowledge is obviously important since it is vital to know the difference between *I am chasing a tiger* and *A tiger is chasing me*. One construction illustrated in the text quoted is worth considering in a little detail because it demonstrates very well the way in which grammatical and lexical knowledge interact to create meanings. It is also a structure which involves a curiously specific ability in sentence interpretation. In the sentence *I kept trying to get to the telephone to ring for help* we have a sequence of four verbs (*kept . . . trying . . . get . . . ring*) but only the first has an overt subject expression (*I kept . . .*). How, then, does it come about that we immediately recognize, quite unambiguously, that the 'understood' subject of each of the subjectless verbs is the same as that of the first in the sequence? The sentence means, as it were, '*I* kept *me* trying for *me* to get to the telephone for *me* to ring for help'. In order to see how this comes about we will need to consider the properties of each of the verbs separately and see how they can combine to produce this interpretation. KEEP can be followed by either a subjectless verb or a verb with a subject: we can have both *I kept trying* and *I kept him trying*. When the second verb is subjectless its 'understood' subject will be understood to be the same as that of KEEP: *I kept trying* ('*I* kept *myself* trying'), *He kept trying* ('*He* kept *himself* trying') etc. By contrast, when the verb following KEEP does have a subject, it will be understood as different from the subject of KEEP: *He kept him trying* can only refer to two distinct '*he*'s. Let us now consider TRY. This differs from KEEP in that it can only be followed by a subjectless verb: we do not find **I tried him to get . . .* The understood subject of the second verb must once again be construed as co-referential with the subject of TRY: *I tried to get* ('*I* tried for *myself* to get'), *He tried to get* ('*He* tried for *himself* to get') and so on. Combining KEEP and TRY in *I kept trying to get* will then yield the interpretation '*I* kept *myself* trying for *myself* to get'. GET follows the pattern of KEEP, as the reader is invited to verify. Now, combining KEEP, TRY and GET in *I kept trying to get to the telephone to ring . . .* will produce '*I* kept *myself* trying for *myself* to get to the telephone for *myself* to ring . . .'

The kinds of knowledge that are at issue in this example partly concern individual lexical items, and partly the structural properties of the language. It seems clear, however, that they are properties of the language and have nothing to do with 'knowledge of the world'. It is, for example, possible to agree unambiguously about the interpretation of sentences of this kind out of any context, and this suggests that the ability to understand these patterns of cross-reference is concerned entirely with linguistic knowledge.

Phonological knowledge about sentences must also be mentioned briefly. Although the passage is written, it involves the representation of speech and we can, if we please, imagine the cadences of speech in our mind's ear, indeed with good writers we are often intended to do precisely that. Were the words to be spoken, then they would have to be divided into units united by an intonation pattern, and each unit would have an intonationally prominent constituent. The first sentence in our text might, for instance, be read as / I DREAMT *last night* / *said OTTO* / *that there was a huge TIGER in the house* / (the slashes indicate the intonation units and the capitals the centres of intonational prominence). This is not the only possible segmentation, and other constituents can be chosen as the intonation centres, as the reader is invited to verify. Such potential variability is inevitable when we are dealing with a written text because the written form of the language cannot mark these features unambiguously, though punctuation is a guide to the units. Moreover, some syntactic features, like the use of DO in the final sentence, can indicate points of intonational prominence. It is however important to note that, while there is potential for alternative acceptable readings, there are also some segmentations that are clearly impossible, particularly where syntactic constituents and intonational units are wildly at odds as in * / I dreamt last night SAID / Otto THAT there / was A huge / tiger in THE house /. This fact suggests knowledge about where such breaks can occur.

In this section we have been arguing that the interpretation of a text involves both knowledge of the world and knowledge of the language, and that these are different kinds of knowledge and need to be distinguished. Knowing about language seems to be quite different from knowing about how people behave in dreams or that telephone dials are not normally made of marzipan. It seems to be a highly abstract kind of knowledge, dealing as it does with the meanings of sentence patterns or the relations contracted between words, both surely some distance from knowledge of the world. Indeed, as we have seen, the sorts of linguistic features we have been discussing are as easily demonstrable with sentences out of context and with no obvious referent in a real or imaginary world as they are with examples from a text.

We shall refer to such knowledge as involving our 'linguistic competence'. It is this that we shall be concerned with in the main part of this book, where we shall be investigating how such kinds of knowledge about our language can be formalized into a system of rules that attempts to capture the undoubted regularities that lie behind our linguistic behaviour.

An obvious question now arises as to whether we would wish to see this competence as being a unitary capacity, or whether, as the discussion has tended to suggest, it can be regarded as consisting of several relatively separable kinds of competence – grammatical competence, semantic competence and phonological competence. Linguistic descriptions do in fact tend to separate these kinds of knowledge into different 'components' and describe each in terms of somewhat different kinds of rules. The fact that different rule types are involved suggests that the components are indeed dealing with different kinds of phenomenon. Further support for this view comes from the fact that it is possible for a sentence to be ill formed in only one of these respects. So, a sentence might be grammatically well formed but phonologically ill formed (by the mispronunciation of a word or the imposition of an impossible intonation) or semantically ill formed (perhaps because it contains a contradiction: *My brother is an only child*). The reader is invited to ring the changes with other combinations of factors. While it may be true that the various components are relatively separable, and it is certainly a descriptive convenience to consider them to be, it would be absurd to suppose that the components are entirely self-contained, for they are not. We have already seen examples of the interrelationships, for instance the relationship between grammatical and semantic structure when discussing co-reference between nouns and 'understood' constituents, and between grammatical and phonological structure in the characteristic coincidence between grammatical and intonational units. Even more strikingly, we have seen that in the word all three components find common ground: we will need to return to this matter.

1.3 Using language

In the previous section we argued that it was necessary and possible to draw a distinction between 'knowledge of the world' and 'linguistic competence'. There is, however, yet another kind of knowledge that we will need to bring to bear in trying to interpret the text we looked at in the last section. This is knowledge about the appropriate use of language.

The notion of appropriate use covers a variety of different sorts of knowledge. To begin with, we recognize this passage as a coherent text rather than as a random collection of sentences. The fact that we recognize the content as being coherent is important. This is not a specifically linguistic ability, but coherence of content makes an important contribution to the coherence of text, and can hardly fail to be reflected in the language. The extent to which we structure our knowledge of the world and the way this is done is not one of our concerns, but it should be briefly mentioned. In the previous section we noted that we know a lot about the objects, like telephones and marzipan, that particular words refer to. We must also have a comparable knowledge about typical events – how, why and where people use the telephone or buy marzipan, and so on. This sort of generalized knowledge is important for comprehension since if a text were to be explicit about all such matters, it would be endless and endlessly boring. An author must rely on the reader to cooperate actively in understanding text.

The structure of text is also marked by linguistic features, part of whose function is specifically to tie the words together into a text: the 'textual' function of language mentioned in 1.1. In our example we find such devices. The pronouns are interpreted as cross-referring between sentences: *I* recurs in each sentence of the first speaker's contribution; *it* in the second sentence refers back to *tiger* in the first and so on. There are lexical ties between the sentences that exploit the semantic relations between words that were mentioned in the last section: so *telephone . . . phone . . . dial* (verb) . . . *dial* (noun). Subordinating and coordinating conjunctions mark the relationships between sentences: *then*, for example, indicates a temporal relationship between the second and third sentences. The distribution of linguistic features of this sort marks the difference between a random collection of sentences and a text. We expect the contents of a text to be coherent, and we expect the sentences that realize this content to reflect this.

It is possible to make generalizations about such processes, since just as there are rules of 'linguistic competence' so too there are rules of 'communicative competence'. Indeed, it is often the latter that people refer to when they talk about a person's 'competence' in language, linguistic competence being taken for granted. As an example of a generalization in this area, consider the way in which items are introduced into text and subsequently referred to. For instance, the first mention of a new object typically involves an indefinite expression; *a tiger* rather than *the tiger*, the latter suggesting that we have already met the beast. When it is immediately referred to a second time we find either a definite expression, *the tiger*, or a pronoun, *it*, and these will be understood to cross-refer. A repetition of the indefinite expression *a tiger* would be grammatically well formed but it would be likely to be misunderstood as introducing a second animal. Similarly, we do not expect to find the repetition of a proper name in successive sentences (*Otto . . . Otto . . .*), but rather second and subsequent mentions will be pronouns which will be understood to cross-refer (*Otto . . . he . . .*).

We can do more than simply recognize this as a coherent text. We can make a reasonable guess about what particular kind of text it is. We will surely recognize it as an extract from a novel or short story rather than an advertisement or a *Times* leader. Once again the subject matter is an important clue to this identification, but we also recognize a literary rather than a journalistic genre in the careful way the language is used: for example, the syntactic parallelism in the second sentence (*It kept prowling: I kept trying*) and the subtle way in which the writing is manipulated to suggest the rhythms of speech.

We can, furthermore, and largely on the basis of the language, infer that this is a contemporary and not a nineteenth-century novel, and that it involves 'middle-class' characters, probably from the south of England, who doubtless speak 'standard

English' with an 'RP' or 'BBC' accent. On the basis of the language we can also make inferences about the nature of the relationship between the speakers in both the long and the short term: the 'interpersonal' function of language mentioned in 1.1. The fact that the second speaker interrupts the first, and the way this is done, suggests that they are not casual acquaintances, and the intonation and other paralinguistic features implied by *Do you mind* and *I do want* suggest irritation.

Our ability to draw conclusions about the literary genre, the temporal and social setting, the type of accent involved, and even details of the personal relationships, suggests that we know how language can be used to communicate meanings of this kind. Judgements of this sort rely on a somewhat different kind of knowledge from the 'linguistic competence' discussed in the previous section, which we took to be abstract knowledge about the language system. What we are now talking about is knowing how to put such knowledge to work to convey particular meanings in particular contexts: we have already referred to it as 'communicative competence'.

To illustrate a difference between these two kinds of knowledge we will return to the question of the introduction of new objects into a text. We noted that first mention frequently involves an indefinite expression. Sometimes, however, we find a definite expression, as in *the house* in the first sentence of our text. Our linguistic competence will tell us that this is a well-formed noun phrase, and the use of the definite article *the*, in contrast to the indefinite article *a*, will signify that a particular identifiable house is at issue. We are likely to assume that the house in question is the speaker's own, but how do we know this since this is the first time it has been mentioned? The answer appears to be that the context supplies this inference. With familiar objects like cars, houses and cats the use of *the* on first mention will imply some car etc. known to speaker and hearer, frequently the speaker's own. If I say to my wife *I am going to put my coat in the car* she will conclude, unless there is contextual evidence to the contrary, that it is 'our' car that is at issue. If I said *I am going to put my coat in a car* she might well wonder whose! We may suppose that it is part of our grammatical competence to know that the definite article will pick out a specific entity, but it is our communicative competence that will tell us how to settle on one identification rather than another in context.

In the discussion we have distinguished between 'linguistic' and 'communicative' competence. It will probably be clear, however, that this distinction, like others we have come across, is not entirely straightforward. It is certainly controversial, for reasons we will return to in the next chapter. We can, however, take some comfort from the fact that it broadly corresponds to a very traditional distinction between 'grammar', the description of how sentences are constructed, and 'rhetoric', the study of how sentences are manipulated in texts. In order to use language, a speaker needs both a linguistic and a communicative competence. Readers who were taught a modern foreign language in school some twenty or more years ago were probably taught a lot about the structure of words and sentences, a pedagogical version of linguistic competence, but may not have been exposed to anything very systematic about their use in real situations, the pedagogical correlate of communicative competence. The consequence is that while they may have a perfect command of the structure of French irregular verbs, they may be quite unable to order a beer in a pavement café.

2 Models of Language

> To demonstrate the legitimacy of an abstraction, it must be
> shown in the first place that it leads to interesting results.
> Then one must indicate how it is integrated within a more
> general schema.
>
> (Noam Chomsky)

Writing a description of a language or any part of one is an
investigation into the knowledge a speaker has about his
language, and the way he uses the language to communicate.
This knowledge is instantiated in acts of communication, but
these acts are only evidence of the knowledge, and not the
knowledge itself. Nor is the knowledge itself open to ordinary
inspection since we cannot see into the minds of speakers. A
description therefore will involve a set of interrelated hypotheses
about the principles by which the language is structured, and the
strategies used in communication. In this chapter we shall be
looking at the kinds of evidence that are available for a
description, and how descriptions are organized and justified.

2.1 Data and descriptions

Traditional descriptions are often based on a corpus of citations
collected by the grammarian over a period of time, and extracts
from the corpus are used to justify individual analyses: see, for
example, the extensive and pertinent use of quotation by
Jespersen (1909–49), Kruisinga and Erades (1911), Scheurweghs
(1959) or Wisser (1963–73). The material is typically gathered
from written language. The tradition of corpus-based studies is
still very active today, and, not surprisingly, modern corpora

tend to be computer-based, and to include transcribed texts of spoken material in addition to examples culled from written sources: see, for example, Kucera and Francis (1967), Quirk (1968). Data of this kind is clearly important because it contains 'authentic' examples of language in use.

Corpora, however, do not provide the only kind of evidence, and most linguists will also admit other kinds. The psycholinguist will often want to use experimental data collected under laboratory conditions: see, for example, the experiments reported in Matthei and Roeper (1983). The sociolinguist may wish to use data from surveys, questionnaires and the like: cf. Labov (1972), Trudgill (1974b, 1978). We do not have the space to consider data of this kind here, instead we will briefly discuss some ways in which corpora can be augmented, or in the case of some linguists, supplanted by evidence derived from elicitation (where an 'informant' is used to provide reactions to particular controlled stimuli, or even to answer direct questions) and from introspection (where the linguist is his own inform-ant).

Data of this kind is used partly for practical reasons, but, more importantly, because it enables a description to be systematic and thorough. Consider such an apparently straightforward example as collecting and ordering the names of the days of the week. Randomly collected data, unless there is a great deal of it, is quite likely not to contain the names of all seven days. It is of course possible to collect specially slanted data dealing with some activity that goes on every day of the week, perhaps a timetable, but this begins to approach direct elicitation. In such cases linguists are usually happy simply to ask an 'informant' to name the days of the week: the response will not only yield an exhaustive list, but is also likely to reveal that the information is stored as an ordered list, and we will probably want to regard this as a relevant part of the informant's knowledge of his language.

Problems connected with obtaining vocabulary data are relatively easy to solve. The problems with grammatical data are more acute. Suppose, for example, we find in our data the following two examples: . . . *The Archduke commissioned Mozart to write* . . . and . . . *Mozart was commissioned by the*

Archduke to write . . . Suppose, too, we discover that the sentences paraphrase each other. We will then be interested to know whether all the verbs in our corpus occur in both 'active' and 'passive' sentences as in the example. A search through the corpus is most unlikely to provide the necessary evidence for every verb, and in these circumstances we will probably want to use an informant to test the verbs (and we will probably be wise to confirm the results with other informants). From the responses we will acquire lists of verbs which do and which do not relate in this way, and probably also some verbs about which the informants are not entirely sure. We will need such lists for a description, and once again we can see the fact that the informant can perform this task as evidence of a linguistic ability. Any description that aims to be comprehensive generally relies to a greater or lesser extent on elicited data, as anyone who has tried an investigation of this sort quickly finds out, even if the original intention was to rely exclusively on 'natural' data. It is interesting to note that even in the days when it was supposed to be a matter of linguistic orthodoxy to derive grammatical descriptions exclusively from corpora of data, the resultant grammars are in fact usually supplemented to a greater or lesser extent with elicited data.

If it is legitimate overtly to tap an informant's knowledge and intuitions about his language, then the question arises as to whether in describing his own language the linguist can be his own informant and elicit data from himself by introspection. If it is the underlying structural principles that he seeks to uncover, then the linguist, as a member of the speech community himself, is a competent informant, and there is the advantage that the informant is always available. Such 'armchair' linguistics is obviously not suitable for all kinds of description and, as we shall see, it has its pitfalls. Properly used, however, it has much to offer since it can be seen as providing direct access to our knowledge about the language.

There are some abilities that lend themselves particularly well to an investigation by the use of informants or by introspection. One concerns the use of ill-formed sentences as evidence. There are some types of string (a 'string' is any sequence of words, whether it is a complete sentence or only part of a sentence) that occur naturally in conversational data, such as sentence 'fragments' and 'anacolutha', sentences which start in one grammatical construction and change into another halfway through. In context these cannot be regarded as 'errors', and they throw important light on the psychological processes of sentence formation. Note, however, that when such examples are transcribed, speakers will typically recognize them as ill formed according to the rules of sentence formation, even though they may be quite appropriate in context. There are other kinds of ill formed strings which do not normally occur in any kind of natural data, and, if they did, would be instantly recognized as 'errors' and almost certainly corrected. In 1.2 we noted some structural examples like *tiger a huge* or *of marzipan was made the cake* and cases involving co-occurrence like *I tried him to get* or *I tried got*. Instances of this sort seem to offend particularly basic principles of sentence construction, and judgements of ill-formedness are quite unequivocal. Both kinds of ill-formed sentences can play an important part in a description, since the ability to recognize a string as ill formed itself implies knowledge about well- and ill-formedness. Furthermore, if a grammar describes what strings are possible, then it implicitly excludes impossible strings, and knowing what is impossible is usually an invaluable guide to the limits of what is possible.

Another area where introspection is useful is in the analysis of ambiguity. In isolation, a sentence such as *He saw the man with a telescope* is ambiguous as between the readings 'He saw the man by means of a telescope' and 'He saw the man who had a telescope', and speakers have little difficulty in perceiving such ambiguities. They are, however, rarely perceived as ambiguous in context since the context will generally force one interpretation while the other will not be perceived, or, if it is, will be discarded as irrelevant. A description of sentences and their meanings will need to be able to account for both interpretations, and to assign a distinct analysis to each. And a description of the use of language might want to explore why the ambiguity is not perceived in context, a rather different problem. Ambiguities of this kind have always been of interest to linguists because they seem to be an unavoidable characteristic of any language system, and consequently throw some light on the nature of the organizing principles of language. They are interesting also because the ability to provide distinct analyses for ambiguous sentences has long been seen as a testing ground for descriptions. Introspection, then, can provide valuable evidence, especially in respect of the language system itself.

We should, however, also recognize its limitations and pitfalls. Some of the pitfalls are obvious. Both introspection and elicitation need independent validation either from other informants or from actual data, since introspection can, often unwittingly, provide data to fit the analyst's preconceptions. Moreover, people's beliefs about their own capacities are often incorrect. To take a well-worn example, a speaker might believe that he consistently uses MAY for 'permission' and CAN for 'possibility' or 'ability' (*Can I leave the room? You can, but you may not!*). An examination of data will almost certainly demonstrate in this case that the purported intuition is either incorrect or stated too categorically. Another problem is 'forcing a paradigm'. In the systematic investigation of a particular pattern it is easy, through constant repetition, to establish a disposition to respond in a particular way, and this may incline an informant to overgeneralize. Such a thing might happen, for example, in investigating the active and passive forms mentioned earlier. Finally, a purportedly comprehensive description based entirely on introspection may have gaps simply because relevant examples fail to occur to the investigator. This is a particular danger these days when many investigators regard linguistics as a theoretical rather than a descriptive enterprise: see for example Chomsky (1982b), and, for an opposing point of view from one of Chomsky's former disciples, Gross (1979).

2.2 Idealization

In the previous section we saw that different descriptive aims will focus on different types of 'fact'. In a real sense, the nature of the investigation determines what data is relevant. Data may be independently interesting, but the linguist is generally only interested in it for the light it can throw on the underlying principles which generate it. An attempt to get at these general principles must involve generalization, and this in turn will involve ignoring certain aspects of whatever data we choose to examine. Data is thus rarely 'raw': it is usually 'idealized' to a greater or lesser extent to suit the purposes of description, and it is difficult to see that it would be possible to proceed in any other way. In this and the next section we will consider some ways in which descriptions relate to data, and the way different types of description demand different levels of idealization of the data.

We will start by considering approaches which seek to draw a very clear distinction between the language system and the use of language. In terms of the history of modern linguistic study, the first to insist on a clear distinction of this sort was de Saussure (1916). He drew a distinction between *langue* and *parole*. *Parole* refers to individual acts of speech, and *langue* to the abstract system which underlies and unifies them. De Saussure pointed out that individual spontaneous acts of speech are necessarily fugitive and tied to particular contexts of utterance. They may contain 'errors', like 'slips of the tongue', and will almost certainly contain hesitations, false starts, sentences broken off halfway through, and other familiar characteristics of informal speech. De Saussure claimed that data of this sort does not constitute an appropriate object of study since it is inherently idiosyncratic and influenced by too many extraneous factors, psychological, social and individual. It is not homogeneous enough to constitute the data for a systematic study of the language system, since the accidental features associated with speech production must be characteristic of the use of language, *parole*, and cannot be attributed to the system, *langue*, itself. In this view, the linguists will ignore such features, and seek to identify the system behind them. This system is the proper object of a linguistic study since, unlike *parole*, it is a 'well-defined object in the heterogeneous mass of speech facts'. It can be regarded as an object which is relatively stable, free from individual whimsy and exists, as it were, outside the individual who can neither create it for himself nor modify it arbitrarily. De Saussure treats this system as a 'social fact' on a par with other facts about social behaviour.

A distinction along similar lines is proposed in Chomsky's opposition between 'competence' and 'performance'. Competence, the language system, corresponds roughly to de Saussure's *langue*, and performance, the use of the system, to *parole*. Like de Saussure, Chomsky claims that the study of performance, the use of the system, can logically only follow the study of competence, the system itself. To return to de Saussure's chess analogy mentioned in the previous chapter: it makes no sense to study a particular game of chess without knowing both the rules of chess and the strategies for playing chess. Furthermore, the strategies cannot be studied without understanding the rules, since the rules constrain the strategies. Chomsky claims therefore that the first and central concern of linguistic theory should be the study of competence. To this end, Chomsky articulates the proposition that 'linguistic theory is concerned primarily with an ideal speaker-listener, in a completely homogeneous speech community, who knows his language perfectly and is unaffected by such grammatically irrelevant conditions as memory limitations, distractions, shifts of attention and interest, and errors (random or characteristic) in applying his knowledge of the language in actual performance' (Chomsky, 1965:3).

If we view speech data in this light, then data derived from this source will need to be somewhat 'tidied up' ('sanitized', some people have complained) before it will be acceptable evidence of the underlying system. Lyons (1972) suggests that the idealization involved can be thought of under three heads: 'regularization', 'decontextualization' and 'standardization'. We will consider each briefly.

Regularization involves disregarding those features we have

already noted as characteristic of speech production – slips of the tongue, hesitations, false starts, anacolutha and so on. These are 'performance errors'. To classify them as features of performance does not of course mean that they are uninteresting. On the contrary, insofar as they can be regarded as 'windows on the mind' they have considerable interest as evidence about the mechanisms of language production and processing. They are indeed the subject of a considerable amount of research.

Decontextualization can best be illustrated by example. Consider the following imaginary exchange:

A: Are you going out tonight? Are you going out tonight?

B: Yes, I am. Yes, I am going out tonight.

A: Where to? Where are you going to?

B: The cinema. I am going to the cinema.

The exchange on the left is supposed to represent the kind of thing that might occur in a 'real-life' conversation. In particular it contains several of the 'sentence fragments' typical of such exchanges. The exchange on the right is unreal as an example of an actual conversation, consisting as it does of the 'full' sentences that correspond to the fragments. The interpretation of any fragment is highly context-dependent as can be shown by considering any one of them. For example, B's final contribution, *The cinema*, can, in this context, be understood in terms of the full form on the right. In other contexts the remark might be understood in any number of ways: it might be a guide pointing out local landmarks (*[On the left you can see] the cinema*), or it could be the answer to any one of a huge number of questions, the particular interpretation being derived from the corresponding full sentence (*Which of these buildings are you going to buy?*:*[I am going to buy] the cinema* etc.). The interpretation of the fragments is dependent on context, and is parasitic on the interpretation of the full sentences. In contrast, the full sentences require no context for a comparable interpretation. If we regard the relationship between language and context as primarily a matter of language use, then it follows that a study of linguistic competence will disregard fragments and concentrate instead on the study of full decontextualized sentences. Decontextualization also has semantic consequences, since it involves drawing a distinction between the 'literal' meaning of the sentence and its 'pragmatic' meaning, which will include its intended function in context and any inferences that can be drawn in context. For instance, the literal meaning of the first sentence of the example conversation is literally a 'yes:no' question. In a particular context, however, all kinds of further implicatures can be drawn: if we suppose the conversation to be between a mother and her daughter, then the first sentence may well be more than a straightforward request for information; if it is a young man addressing a young woman then it could be an indirect invitation; and in either case other contextual inferences will be necessary for a 'full rich' interpretation.

Standardization will involve ignoring a number of ways in which language in use can vary. We will mention only three: dialect, individual idiosyncrasy and style. Dialects differ from each other in phonological and syntactic structure so it may seem a sensible restriction to concentrate on the description of a single form of language, at least in the first instance. As to individual idiosyncrasy, most of us have favoured and disfavoured words, we use catch phrases and we cultivate or avoid particular grammatical constructions. We are usually quite well aware of such idiosyncrasy, and some people, especially perhaps schoolteachers and politicians, consciously exploit it. Although the study of personality as revealed by speech may be interesting, it is surely no part of the study of the language system, and a competence grammar will ignore it. A competence grammar will take the same attitude to style, that is, variation in language appropriate to particular contexts. Conversation requires a less formal style than lecturing, as does letter writing in contrast to an academic paper. A strict view of competence will argue that such matters are, once again, concerns of the way language is used. In particular, it may be claimed, styles differ from each other in terms of the frequency of occurrence of particular constructions. The rules of a competence grammar will take no notice of such statistical variation because the rules of sentence formation do not, in principle, differentiate between a common and a rare construction.

The view of linguistic competence just presented covers the kinds of knowledge discussed in 1.2. Such a view has the advantage that in abstracting away from 'the heterogeneous mass of speech facts' it defines a language system that is, or can be made to appear, largely determinate and well defined. This can then be formalized into a coherent system of precise and explicit rules which have a predictive value that can be empirically tested, and the mathematical properties of which can be explored. It also has the advantage, if advantage it be, that it can be considered as a largely autonomous system.

Not surprisingly, the view of linguistic competence just presented has its critics. We noted in 1.3 that knowing how to construct or identify well-formed sentences in isolation is of little use to a user of language unless he also knows how to use them for communication. Just as the language system, linguistic competence, has rules, so too there are rules governing the use of language, communicative competence. The question is, how do the two interrelate, and can they be kept apart?

The notion of communicative competence is of interest to a number of disciplines other than linguistics, such as psychology, ethnography, sociology and artificial intelligence. Each of these disciplines has its own particular interests, and so it is hardly surprising that these different disciplines concentrate on different aspects of language use. We will look briefly at one: Dell Hymes's notion of an 'ethnography of speaking', a 'second descriptive science of language' concerned with 'the ways in which speakers associate particular modes of speaking, topics or message forms, with particular settings and activities' (Hymes, 1971a). This approach seeks to identify the different factors that can systematically influence the use of language.

An obvious factor, which we have already mentioned, is the *channel* used for communication. We all know that there are differences between written and spoken language, and other channels, telegraphy or semaphore flags perhaps, will impose other constraints on the use of language.

The *participants* in a 'speech event' and the nature of the relationship between them can condition the language used. An obvious example is the distinction between the 'formal' and 'familiar' pronouns found in French, German or Spanish. The pronouns are part of the language system, but their use is governed by situational factors like the perceived relationship between speaker and hearer, and the formality of the situation. In some communities of the Far East, Japan for example, 'honorific' language penetrates the language system even more deeply. More striking still is the situation reported in Dyirbal, an Australian 'aboriginal' language: 'each speaker has at his disposal two separate languages: a Dyalnguy, or "mother-in-law language", which is used in the presence of certain "taboo" relatives; and a Guwal, or everyday language, which is used in all other circumstances. Each dialect has a Guwal and a Dyalnguy' (Dixon, 1972:32). In the English-speaking community we are unused to such dramatic variation, but the relationships between participants nevertheless affects the way language is used. Consider, for example, 'naming' or 'greeting' behaviour, a well-known indicator of perceived or intended social relationships: one would hardly use the same address forms to the Queen and the milkman. We can also find behaviour that is not totally dissimilar to that mentioned above for Dyirbal when speakers control more than one dialect of English. Each dialect will have grammatical forms and vocabulary items foreign to the other, and circumstances and topics of conversation can cause speakers to prefer one or the other, or they may switch from one to the other during a conversation as topics change.

Setting and *topic* will similarly influence language behaviour. Even in these permissive days, much of the language of the pub is likely to be considered inappropriate in church, and topics appropriate to one setting may be inappropriate to the other. Some types of language event are indeed exclusively restricted to the one or the other environment: most forms of religious service would be inappropriate in a pub, and the traditional cry of *Time gentlemen please* has no appropriate function in a church.

The *purpose* of an interaction is also relevant. Sometimes, as in greeting and parting, the appropriate language is highly idiomatic and largely restricted to this particular purpose. In religious ceremonies or legal documents the highly stylized language, containing words and constructions not found in more informal uses of language, is often attributed to the fact that the language is focused on a particular purpose. Conversation, too, has different styles and levels of formality. We might distinguish 'interactional' conversation, whose primary purpose is the maintenance and establishment of social bonds, from 'transactional' conversation, which is directed towards a more pragmatic goal.

With respect to each of these factors, and indeed any others that may seem to be relevant, we will assume that it is possible to establish *norms* of usage which can be stated in statistical terms. For given participants in a particular setting on a particular topic and so on, there will be such and such a probability of the occurrence of some structure or vocabulary item in preference to another. It will clearly be a difficult task to work out the probabilities (and people do not generally do this even though they assume that it is possible) but what is clear is that we are no longer dealing with the 'categorical' rules of competence, but with 'variable' rules. Nevertheless, there seems to be no reason to doubt that we are indeed dealing with rule-governed behaviour, and that we can talk about rules with no less confidence than when we speak of rules governing any other type of social behaviour. If this were not so, then how would we recognize appropriate and inappropriate uses of language? Further, as in other areas of social behaviour, how would we recognize that rules of this kind can be deliberately violated for particular communicative ends? If the Duke of Edinburgh exhorts the British worker to *pull his finger out*, then the very use of this expression with its obscene overtones, used by that person, attributively and in public, has a deliberate communicative effect. We should note too that such norms of linguistic usage are regulated by further social norms relating to such matters as who is to speak, to whom, when, how much, what about and so on. A consideration of factors like these may lead one to ask whether the hypothesis of an 'ideal speaker-listener in a homogeneous speech community' is realistic.

One way of attempting to reconcile the clearly variable nature of instances of language use with the notion of a homogeneous linguistic competence is to propose two interacting sets of rules: a set of rules of competence, delineating possible structures, and a set of rules of communicative competence, perhaps formulated as frequency possibilities, regulating the use of these structures in situations. We are familiar with something of this sort in dictionaries which mark particular lexical items as 'colloquial' or 'formal', and the same principle has been applied to grammatical constructions by using 'variable rules': cf. Labov (1972), Hudson (1980). According to this notion, individual rules of grammar would be marked with indices showing the probability of their use in some particular type of discourse, the probability being derived from the kind of factors we have just been discussing.

In the chapters that immediately follow we will assume a division of descriptive labour which respects a competence: performance distinction of the sort we have been discussing. We must, however, note that there are other possible views on this matter. In particular, there are views which hold that it is, in principle, impossible to make the distinction that we have drawn between the 'system' and the 'use' of the system. Such a view would argue that the two are so inextricably intertwined, and the degree of idealization involved in attempting to separate them is so great, that to do so distorts language almost out of recognition.

We have already seen instances where the system and the use of the system interpenetrate. We noted that both formal and informal pronouns are part of the language system, although they may be mutually exclusive in context. We have also seen that some speakers control a variety of different forms of language which are not mutually exclusive. A particularly striking instance of this is found in communities like those of the West Indies where 'Creole' and 'standard English' exist side by side. In this situation speakers operate as though their language forms a 'continuum', varying from the most 'Creole-like' usages to the most 'standard-like'. At each end of the continuum there are forms that are so foreign to the other that two distinct language systems seem to be involved. Yet speakers can, as the situation demands, move freely from one system to the other, or mix them in a way that suggests one heterogeneous system, rather than two distinct systems and some kind of rules which blend them: see, for instance, Hymes (1971b).

Another kind of argument against the compartmentalized view of language presented above seeks to show that the functions language serves determine its very nature, so that it would be as foolish to ignore these functions in a description as it would be perverse to describe a motor car as a stationary object ignoring its purpose. Some examples will illustrate what is at issue. Consider first the distribution of words and phrases like *therefore*, *consequently* and *in the first place* whose function as we noted in 1.2 is predominantly textual. They are part of the language, yet it is difficult to envisage a coherent description of their meaning deriving from an examination of sentences in isolation. A different example involves the functional meaning of sentences in context. We have at various points already mentioned this. Here we note that these functional meanings can penetrate the language system. Consider the sentence *Can you hand me that pencil?* This can be understood as an enquiry about the hearer's ability (cf. *Are you able to hand me that pencil?*), and there are contexts, perhaps talking to an invalid, when this is precisely the meaning intended. More usually a sentence of this sort is understood as an indirect 'request for action'. We could argue, and many have, that the literal, competence, meaning of the sentence is the 'ability' sense, and that the functional meaning of 'request for action' is inferred from the context, and is hence a matter of performance. According to this view, a hearer might compute the intended meaning along the following lines: 'He is asking me if I am able to hand him the pencil, but he knows that I can reach the pencil, that I am able-bodied, and that there is nothing that would prevent my handing him the pencil, therefore he can hardly be making an enquiry about my ability since this is obvious. He must therefore have some other end in view. I see that he has no pencil, so he is probably asking me to hand him one.' This account is rather long-winded, but is perhaps not totally implausible as an indication of the kind of process by which speakers draw inferences of this kind in context. Consider, however, what happens if we put *please* into the sentence: *Can you please hand me that pencil?* The sentence now can only be interpreted as a request for action and it is difficult, either in or out of context, to interpret it as an enquiry about ability.

Examples of this kind, which can be multiplied, may lead one to suppose that form and function are indeed inextricably intertwined, and we need an integrated description. In later chapters we will return to some of these questions, and see how this kind of view can be incorporated into a description.

Before leaving this question, there is one further consideration that is worth mentioning: the psychological limitations of humans as language producers and processors. What is involved can be best illustrated by example. Suppose that a competence grammar is a device which will describe well-formed sentences such as, say, *John laughed* and *Mary danced*. It will need to allow such units to be coordinated, since *John laughed and Mary danced* is also a sentence, and for such units to be embedded, or inserted, into other units, as in *Harry said that John laughed*.

Unrestricted coordination will produce sentences of infinite length (S and S and S . . . as in *Jane laughed and Kate danced and Sarah sang and Moggy turned somersaults* . . . and so on). We may then enquire whether a limit should be put to the process since such strings do not naturally occur, if for no other reason than that we are eventually mortal. In a competence grammar the answer is usually 'no'. There appear to be no comprehension problems, and there seems to be no sensible way of determining where a limit should be set. It would, for example, be quite possible to put *and* between every sentence in this book and turn it into one enormous sentence: the result might be stylistically offensive, but should present no additional comprehension problem. Furthermore, we are familiar with other systems, like the numeral system, that have a potentially infinite output from a finite set of rules.

Embedding is a more difficult case, which we will illustrate with a well-known example involving the formation of 'relative clauses' (these are sentence-like structures usually beginning with *who*, *which* or *that* which are used to modify nouns as in *the dog that worried the rat* or *the rat that ate the malt*). Relative clauses can be acceptably iterated in some circumstances but not in others. An acceptable iteration is illustrated by *This is the dog that worried the rat that ate the malt that lay in the house that Jack built*. *That Jack built* is a relative clause 'modifying' *the house*, *that lay in the house that Jack built* is a modifier of *the malt* and so on. In these circumstances we can have a series, perhaps infinite, of relative clauses and no comprehension problem is involved. Now consider another type of relative clause formation exemplified in the sentence *the birds* (*that*) *the woman fed died*. *That the woman fed* is a relative clause modifying *the birds*, and the whole string, *the birds that the woman fed*, operates as the subject of *died*. As the brackets are intended to show, *that* can be omitted without affecting syntactic well-formedness. When *that* is omitted, the sentence consists of two noun phrases, *the birds* and *the woman*, followed by two verbs, *fed* and *died*. In order to understand the sentence we need to impose some structure that will clarify the 'nested' dependencies between the various nouns and verbs. Suppose now that we modify *the woman* with another relative clause of the same structure, say *the woman* (*that*) *the man loved*. The result is now, omitting the *that*s, *the birds the woman the man loved fed died*. This is already difficult to interpret because it is hard to keep track of which noun phrase belongs to which verb. Further iteration will soon produce a sentence which is impossible to process.

The difference between the two types of relative clause embedding is that the first case, *the dog that worried the rat that . . .*, is an example of 'right' embedding, the relative clauses all occur at the right-hand end of the sentence, and the second case, *the birds the woman fed died*, is an example of 'centre' embedding, one relative clause occurs within another which is, as it were, wrapped round it. Right embedding presents no problems because we can interpret complete meanings for each constituent as it comes along. On the other hand, centre embedding is difficult to process because we overload the memory waiting for the right verb for the right noun phrase. The question is, should a grammar take account of these psychological limitations and put some restriction on centre embedding? A strict view of competence would say 'no'. Once again, the restriction seems to relate to statistical frequency of occurrence, which we have noted is to be ignored, and anyway it will be recalled that our ideal speaker-listener is 'unaffected by such grammatically irrelevant conditions as memory limitations'. It is not surprising that this view is not universally accepted either: people interested in a 'psychologically real' grammar may want to accommodate such limitations in their description.

2.3 Models

We have suggested that the real interest in the study of language lies not in instances of language behaviour, but in the ability to produce such behaviour. We have also noted that this ability is not in itself directly observable, so that we will need to form hypotheses about its nature. One way of articulating such hypotheses is to build a model which replicates the observed behaviour as closely as possible. We then suppose that the more accurately the model replicates the behaviour, the more likely is the structure of the model to mirror the unobservable ability.

Models can be understood at a variety of levels of abstraction. We are all familiar with literal models. The designer of a lifeboat will obviously be concerned that the boat should be stable. He will therefore be interested to investigate what wave conditions will make it capsize. In seeking this information he will be likely to want to test a model of the boat in a wave tank, itself, of course, a model of the behaviour of the sea. If the model under test is a model of an existing boat, then the designer will hope that the behaviour of the model will replicate the behaviour of the original, and if it doesn't then he will seek to improve either the model boat, or the model of the sea represented by the wave tank or both. Models of this kind can also be used to test hypotheses about lifeboat construction: will larger or differently distributed buoyancy tanks, or a bigger or differently shaped keel increase the boat's stability? It is clearly more prudent to investigate such matters on a model rather than actually to build boats and wait until time and extreme conditions at sea prove their stability. Models of this sort can also be used to help 'explain' phenomena. Suppose an actual lifeboat has capsized, but it is unclear why. If the model also capsizes in a replica of the conditions prevailing when the original foundered, this will provide useful data and hypotheses for those seeking an explanation of how the disaster happened. In other words, the model can be used in a number of different ways: as a tool to investigate the behaviour of a real object, as a means of testing hypotheses about the probable behaviour of putative objects, and as a tool for the explanation of phenomena.

We are equally familiar with abstract models. Indeed, boat designers will do much of the initial planning on a drawing board, and these days may well investigate various hypotheses about boat design using computer models. A more abstract example, and one which is much talked about these days, is the Treasury model of the 'economy'. This involves a set of hypotheses about how the economy 'works' and what factors might affect it – the rate of inflation, the level of wage settlements, industrial productivity and so on. A model of this kind, formulated in mathematical terms and mounted in a computer, can then be used for the same kind of purposes as the model lifeboat. It can be used to investigate the nature of the economy, can test hypotheses about what will happen if some factor is changed, and can be used as a tool in seeking explanations about the working of the economy. The model's predictions are also likely to influence policy on, amongst other things, the level of taxes we pay.

In the case of our lifeboat example, a real model is used because it would be dangerous and expensive to test the real thing. There can be said, however, to be a 'real thing' on which the model is based. In the example of the economy the situation is less clear. Although various 'facts', like the rate of inflation or the level of unemployment, may seem to be real enough, they are in reality themselves based on hypotheses which govern the collection of data. The notion of an 'economy' is a set of such hypotheses, the exact nature of which is the subject of fierce, almost theological, debate. In circumstances of this sort, where the object under investigation is a set of hypotheses, model building is the only way of proceeding since there is no 'real' object to model. Language falls into this latter category since, as we have seen, the nature of the object to be modelled and the sorts of factors that affect it are not self-evident, but are the product of hypotheses.

Models of language can range from the formal to the informal, but all linguistic descriptions rely implicitly or explicitly on some model. They can also be formalized or stated in informal terms. Nowadays there is particular interest in formal models because they require the investigator to be particularly explicit about the nature of the initial assumptions in terms of which the model is built, and they force him to be precise in formulating the operations that the model performs and the factors that affect performance. Explicitness of this kind is particularly important when dealing with one of our own abilities. If we are seeking to model the ability to produce sentences, and, *inter alia*, to distinguish between well- and ill-formed sentences, it is important that the model we produce should not implicitly call on the operator's ability to do just this. The model should, in fact, be able to 'work' independently of the judgement and ability of a human operator, and this requires great explicitness and attention to detail.

Exactly how a model is to be set up, what components and subcomponents it will have, and how they are related to each other, the nature of possible rules in each component, and so on, will obviously be matters at the discretion of the model builder, who will need to argue for the particular choices made. For this reason much of linguistics is a structure of arguments. This gives a particular importance to the initial assumptions about the nature of language which determine the structure of the model since the model will determine the type of hypotheses that can be entertained within it, the nature of the arguments that are used to justify it, and, as we saw in 2.1, can even determine the selection of data used to justify it.

The discussion in 2.2 above suggests the general architecture of a possible model, and one that will be implicit in much of the discussion in the next few chapters. According to this view of language, there will be two major components corresponding to linguistic and communicative competence. In what immediately follows we shall be primarily concerned with linguistic competence. The linguistic competence component will have three sub-components, syntactic, semantic and phonological. Each of these will have access to the lexicon, where words are collected and marked for their syntactic, semantic and phonological properties: we will be exploring this in Chapter 3. The model will also define types of possible rules for each component. For example, the syntactic component will have a set of rules, the nature of which we will examine in Chapters 4 and 5, defining well-formed sentence structures. It will also have access to the lexicon so that words can be fitted into the syntactic patterns it defines. The semantic and phonological components will be structured along the same general lines.

Models of language can serve the same variety of functions from description to explanation as our examples at the beginning of the section. Any description will involve classification which will be based on some criteria which the investigator must choose and justify. At its simplest, a classificatory model of this kind can be seen as a way of organizing data, and this in itself is useful. But given that the criteria must be justified, they cannot simply be descriptive conveniences since they will embody what the investigator sees as 'significant generalizations' about the data being classified, and hence about the structure of the language. Such simple taxonomic models can also have a predictive function, since the first tentative classification will need to be verified against further data, and will indeed be a useful guide in a systematic search for data to confirm or disconfirm the hypotheses which underlie the classificatory system. As new data comes in, so the hypotheses underlying the descriptive scheme will be modified to take it into account, and the revised model will then itself be the springboard for further investigations. Even at this level, it will be clear that the study of language can usefully be conducted in terms of an explicit model. As the model grows and becomes more complex, it typically also gets more abstract, and this is usually accompanied by an increasing interest in the 'explanatory' power of the model, the nature of the explanations depending on the preconceptions behind the model and its structure. We will not attempt to illustrate this here, since the process will, it is hoped, become clear as the book progresses.

In the next two chapters we shall consider the structure of

words and sentences, and how they can be accounted for in descriptive models. In the course of doing this, we will first be dealing with rather simple descriptive models. Later on we will become more concerned with some of the explanatory claims, and will be in a better position to assess them.

3 Words

Polonius: What do you read, my Lord?
Hamlet: Words, words, words.

(*Hamlet*, II.2)

In this chapter and the next two we will examine two of the basic units in any description of language: words and sentences. We will begin by talking about words, partly because they offer a microcosm of some of the descriptive problems of sentences, and partly because, after a period of some neglect, their analysis has once again become a subject of interest and controversy.

To people brought up in a literate society the notion of the word as a unit seems somehow obvious. It is quite clear, however, that the word is not the smallest unit a linguistic description needs to come to terms with. Consider, for example, the notion that a word corresponds to some 'unit of meaning'. At first blush this seems not unreasonable since items like *book*, *boy*, *car*, *house* and so on are indeed used to refer to items that seem to have at least a psychological reality as 'unitary concepts' and hence perhaps as 'units of meaning'. However, it is not difficult to demonstrate that the concept of a 'unit of meaning' is not easy to pin down and does not stand up to critical scrutiny. For example, we have only to turn these nouns into the corresponding plural forms, *boys*, *books* etc., and immediately we appear to have two relatively distinct 'elements of meaning', one associated with the stem *boy* and the other with the 'plural marker' *-s*. The whole complex is nevertheless identified as a single word. We could meet this problem in a fairly traditional way by supposing that in cases like this we have two different kinds of meaning: 'lexical' meaning associated with the stem *boy*, and 'grammatical' meaning associated with the plural marker -*s*. The definition of a 'unit of meaning' would then depend on 'lexical' rather than on 'grammatical' meaning. Traditional practice, both in the making of dictionaries and in the compilation of grammars, is indeed based on principles of this sort: we expect to find a lexical entry for *boy* but not a separate entry for *boys*, or indeed for the plural marker -*s*. By contrast we expect to find rules for the formation of plural forms in the 'grammar' rather than in the dictionary.

However, even supposing that we can distinguish between 'lexical' and 'grammatical' meaning, and we will return to this matter, this will not resolve all problems about the notion 'unit of meaning'. We will find, on the one hand, many words which as words are not themselves divisible, but whose meaning can apparently be resolved into smaller 'units of meaning', and on the other hand words that are divisible into smaller units, but whose meaning is not resolvable into smaller units that correspond one-to-one with the word segments. An example of the first case is a word like *boy*. This is not further segmentable into smaller units. However if we look *boy* up in a dictionary, we will find a definition of the kind 'young adult male'. This suggests that although the word *boy* itself is not divisible, the concept 'boy' is indeed resolvable into smaller units of meaning. These smaller units – let us refer to them as 'components of meaning' – can be justified on the grounds that they can be identified in other words and can be assembled with other 'components' to yield items like *girl* 'young human female', *child* 'young human', *bull* 'adult bovine male' and so forth. Like *boy*, none of the words cited can itself be segmented in any way that would correspond to any of the postulated 'components'. Nor is this the end of the problem since it is not clear whether it is possible to draw a distinction between 'components' and 'units' of meaning and if so how, since both 'components' and 'units' can be realized in various ways and in various combinations. In certain cases, like *boy* or *child*, they combine in such a way that the resultant word cannot be segmented to correspond with the components. In other cases the components can be combined such that the resultant word can be segmented, even though the whole is still recognized as a complete word unit; examples are *tigress*, *waitress* etc. In yet other cases each component corresponds to a separate word; examples are *bull elephant*, *dog fox*, *fox cub* and so forth.

The converse case can be illustrated by a word like *typewriter*. This can be readily segmented into the units *type-writ-er*, each of which is perhaps relatable to a 'unit of meaning': the first two segments obviously and the third into a meaning of the sort 'device for doing . . .' as in *roller*, *segmenter* etc. However, the item as a whole is regarded as a single word and, insofar as the notion 'unit of meaning' can be made sense of, as a unitary, even if complex, 'unit of meaning' and not as a sequence of discrete units. One justification for treating it as a unit is that the meaning of the whole cannot satisfactorily be resolved into the meaning of the parts: the *Collins English Dictionary* defines *typewriter* as 'a keyboard machine for writing mechanically in characters resembling print'. This definition contains 'components of meaning' not directly relatable to any of the constituent parts of the word, the element 'keyboard' for instance. In cases like this the dictionary will recognize words like *typewriter* as appropriate lexical entries, and speakers clearly recognize them as single words.

The discussion suggests that even though we may wish to continue to recognize the word as a unit of description, words are not unanalysable. They are neither the smallest physical unit nor the smallest semantic unit that can be identified. We should therefore enquire further into the internal structure of words, and particularly into the status of the smaller units into which words can be analysed. The discussion will focus primarily on the nature of the formal units into which words can be analysed. It will be convenient to have a name for these smaller units. We will call them 'morphs' and say that an unsegmentable word, like *boy*, consists of a single morph, and that the words *boy-s* and *type-writ-er* can be resolved into, respectively, two and three morphs.

The operative principle in making analyses of this kind is our ability to compare word forms and identify recurrent stretches as in some sense 'the same'. In prototypical cases the recurrent stretches will have some identity of both form and meaning. So, for example, a comparison between pairs of words like *boy*:*boys*; *girl*:*girls* invites the analysis that they are related by the affixation of -*s*, and that this affix is associated with a meaning 'more-than-oneness'. Similarly, comparing sets of words like *red*:*reddens*; *thick*:*thickens*; or *ripe*:*ripens* provokes the hypothesis that the -*en* affix has the function of changing an adjective (like *red*) into a verb (like *redden*) and is associated with a meaning 'become adj'.

In both cases speakers will use analyses of this kind as a basis for the generation of new forms. We are prepared to pluralize new nouns by the affixation of -*s*: so when a satellite is named a *sputnik* (borrowed from Russian), then it is natural that 'more than one' should be *sputniks*. Children, indeed, will overgeneralize, misanalysing words like *cheese* or *booze* and asking for *some chee* or what *a boo* is. Similarly, we would be unlikely to be astonished to encounter a new verb formed by the affixation of -*en* to an adjective – a form like *pinken* is readily comprehensible and even though most dictionaries do not list it, it will come as no surprise to find it in the *Oxford English Dictionary*.

There are in fact some important differences between the two types of example just illustrated, and we should investigate them further. To begin, we should notice that in ordinary language *word* is used ambiguously, reflecting the fact that we noticed in Chapter 1, that we can conceptualize language as both an abstract and a concrete phenomenon. It will be helpful to distinguish between the various senses involved. The first sense we will distinguish is the use of *word* to refer to the sort of units which compose the sentences you are reading; in this sense *word* is used to refer to a relatively concrete concept, as when we 'count the words' in a telegram. When we need to be quite explicit about this sense we will talk about 'word forms' and continue the practice followed silently thus far of quoting word forms in italics. Given our definition of morph as the smallest substantial unit, we can say that word forms are composed of morphs.

A second use of *word* is to refer to the sort of units we expect to find listed in a dictionary or lexicon. From this point of view both of the word forms *word* and *words* are instances of the same lexical word WORD. When we need to be explicit about this sense we will talk of 'lexical words' or 'lexemes' and will quote lexical words in the text in capitals. This use too is familiar to ordinary usage since it is what we generally intend when we think of a word as a 'unit of meaning', as when we ask someone to 'look up a word' in a dictionary or tell us 'the word that means such and such'. In this use we generally dispense with grammatical meanings, expecting to find a dictionary entry for WALK, but not separate entries for the regular grammatical forms of WALK – *walks*, *walking*, *walked* etc. A count of the lexical words in a text will almost invariably yield a smaller total than a count of word forms, since the various inflectional forms of words would all be counted under the single lexical item. The notion of 'lexical word' clearly involves an abstraction, and as such it will not make sense to think of lexical words as being 'composed' of morphs in the way that word forms can be thought of as being composed of morphs. Instead we will say that lexical words may be 'realized' in word forms by morphs or strings of morphs: the structure of lexical words will be the subject of the next section.

The third use of the term 'word' that we will distinguish is 'grammatical word'. This can be illustrated by considering word forms like *boys*, *men* and *geese*. We will immediately identify these as the 'plural' forms of the lexical words BOY, MAN and GOOSE. For the purposes of a grammatical description it is usually convenient to distinguish between the lexical stem in a word and any marker of plurality. In this spirit we could represent the relevant grammatical structure of the examples as {BOY pl}, {MAN pl} and {GOOSE pl}. Representations of this sort will be called 'grammatical words' since they overtly set out the internal grammatical structure of words. The elements which compose grammatical words are called 'morphemes' (strings of morphemes will be represented, as in the examples, enclosed in curly brackets). As we shall see, representations like {BOY pl} are convenient for grammatical description because they enable us to manipulate 'lexical' and 'grammatical' morphemes independently. This use of 'word' is as abstract as the last and, as with lexical words, it will not make sense to talk of grammatical words being 'composed' of morphs. As before, we will talk of the relationship between the abstract grammatical word and the concrete word form as one of realization: grammatical words are 'realized' in word forms, by morphs or strings of morphs.

We will be discussing the structure of lexemes and grammatical words and their relationship to word forms more fully in the sections to come, but it is worth mentioning here some of the advantages of postulating an abstract structure for words and of dissociating such abstract representations from their substantial realizations. To begin with, it is not always the case that there are as many morphemes in grammatical words as there are segments in the corresponding substantial realization. There are obviously occasions when the abstract and the substantial elements can be related in a 'one-to-one' fashion – an example would be {BOY pl} and *boy-s*. But there will also be occasions when there is a 'many-to-one' relationship between morphemes and their substantial realization – an example would be {GOOSE pl} and *geese*. From the point of view of a grammatical description it will be convenient to analyse the two word forms *boys* and *geese* in a parallel fashion, as {BOY pl} and {GOOSE pl}, since in both cases we want to recognize two grammatical elements, a lexical stem and a morpheme of number. However from the point of view of word forms and their internal structure nothing but confusion can arise if we try treating the demonstrably unsegmentable *goose* in a parallel fashion to the obviously segmentable *boys*. The analyses {GOOSE pl} and {BOY pl} are at a different, and more abstract, level from the analysis of the word forms *goose* and *boy-s*. In other words one of the advantages of postulating an abstract unit like the morpheme is that it frees grammatical description from the complications of irregular morphology.

This approach also removes another potentially distracting complication. Not infrequently the same phonological or orthographic segment sequence represents two quite distinct grammatical morphemes. An instance in English involves the {pl} and {gen(itive)} morphemes. Orthographically the forms are partially distinct – we find *dogs* for the simple plural, *dog's* for the genitive singular and *dogs'* for the genitive plural. Phonologically, however, the forms are not distinguished, so /dɒgz/ could realize either {sing gen} or {pl} or {pl gen}. Clearly {pl} and {gen} must be distinguished in the grammar since they have different grammatical properties and different distributions. Establishing the morphemes {pl} and {gen} allows the grammar to do its job more efficiently and the word formation processes to be stated most economically. In 1.1 we distinguished between 'form' and 'medium', and here we see an advantage of drawing this distinction. Distinct grammatical words at the level of form can receive the same substantial realization at the level of the medium. Indeed, the same grammatical word can be realized differently in different media, as in the case of genitive and plural mentioned above. If it were otherwise, we would find ourselves in the absurd position of proposing different grammatical analyses for the 'same' word when it is written and when it is spoken.

Yet another reason for postulating an abstract analysis is that it is often useful in the grammar to postulate an order for morphemes that is different from that of the corresponding morphs that realize these morphemes in word forms. So, for example, *worse*, *prettier* and *more beautiful* are the 'compared' forms of the corresponding adjectives *bad*, *pretty* and *beautiful*, yet the relation between morphemes and morphs is quite different in each case. From the point of view of the grammar it will be convenient to represent all three by a string {Adj comp} – or {comp Adj} for that matter – the details of morphological structure being left to the morphological part of the description.

Finally, we shall see that it is frequently convenient and illuminating for the grammar to be able to manipulate a unit smaller in size than the word. For instance, strings like *this man*, *these men*, *that man*, *those men* exhibit 'concord' or 'agreement' in number between the determiner (*this*, *these* etc.) and the head noun (*man*, *men*). Both must agree in number since strings like *these man and *this men are ill formed. There are different ways of accounting for these facts, but they all rely on an element like the morpheme: we might, for instance, represent the strings by morpheme sequences like {THAT+pl MAN+pl} and stipulate that the morphemes of number must agree; or we might postulate a 'basic' form of the string as {THAT MAN+pl}, where only the noun is marked for number, and have a rule to copy the number morpheme from the noun to its modifying determiner. Whichever way is chosen, it is clearly convenient to have a unit like the morpheme to perform such manipulations.

Having drawn these distinctions the next step is to see how we can describe the 'grammar of the word', an area of study traditionally called 'morphology'. Traditionally morphology has involved the study of two different but related types of word formation process corresponding to the distinction we have drawn between grammatical and lexical words. One set of word formation processes, 'lexical', or 'derivational', morphology, is concerned with the analysis and construction of lexical words; the other, 'inflectional morphology', involves the ways in which lexical stems, which may be simple, or derived through lexical processes, can combine with grammatical markers to form grammatical words. For instance, the rules of lexical morphology will permit us to combine TYPE and WRITE together with the formative *-er* to form the new lexical item TYPEWRITER. The rules of inflectional morphology will then permit us to combine this lexical item with the plural marker {pl} to derive the grammatical word {TYPEWRITER pl}, which will be realized as the word form *typewriters*. For many purposes it is useful to draw a distinction of this kind, and in the next two sections we will examine each kind in turn. It is not, however, an entirely clear-cut distinction, and we will return to re-examine it at the end of section 3.2.

3.1 The structure of lexical words

'Lexical', or 'derivational', morphology is concerned with the ways in which our existing stock of lexical items can be analysed, and the processes by which new ones are formed. In this section we will first look at some general characteristics of word formation, and then see how different models of word formation accommodate them. To begin, let us suppose, as dictionaries always have, that the lexicon is a list of all the lexemes in the language, each being assigned to some particular form class or part of speech. So a simple unanalysable item like READ will be classified as a V(erb), GOOD as an Adj(ective), GIRL as a N(oun) and so forth. Quite obviously, not all lexemes are unanalysable, and alongside these simple forms we will find complex forms like READABLE, an Adj, GOODNESS, an N, and GIRLISH, another Adj. It seems reasonable to suppose that the latter are related in some systematic way to the former.

We noted above that words are analysed by comparing sets of similar items, and isolating segments that have a similar form and meaning. According to this principle we can analyse the examples as *read-able*, *good-ness* and *girl-ish*. In each case we can associate the form and meaning of the lexical root with the corresponding simple word, and we can make generalizations about the meaning of the suffix. We will represent these analyses in formulae of the following kind:

1   $_{\text{Adj}}(\text{V}+\textit{-able})$

    'capable of being Ved'
    e.g. *drink-able*, *read-able* etc.

2   $_{\text{N}}(\text{Adj}+\textit{-ness})$

    'with the attribute of being Adj'
    e.g. *good-ness*; *thick-ness*; *happi-ness*

3   $_{\text{Adj}}(\text{N}+\textit{-ish})$

    'having the manner or qualities of or attributed to N'
    e.g. *girl-ish*; *slav-ish*; *prud-ish*

Now what exactly is the point of these formulae? Are they to be understood as sets of instructions for creating items? Or do they show us how to divide up already existing items? Or are they meant to do both of these things? As expressed, it is the latter that is at issue. As templates for word formation they can be read as 'take a verb base and suffix to it the lexical formative *-able* to yield an adjective with the semantic interpretation shown'. So, in accordance with the rule, a verb like *like* will yield the adjective *likeable*. As formulae for analysis they can be understood as: 'an adjective ending in *-able* can be analysed as the corresponding verb stem and a lexical formative *-able*, with the semantics noted'. So *analysable* is *analyse*, a verb, and *-able*. Information of this kind has sometimes been included in grammars under the separate heading 'Word Formation', but most contemporary descriptions consider rules of this kind to be part of the lexicon, since then the existing word stock together with rules for the analysis of existing words and the formation of new ones will be in the same place.

The formulae are deliberately ambiguous as between analysis and generation, because both are living and productive parts of our linguistic ability. We can coin new words to meet new situations, and we can analyse existing words, either as a first step towards word creation, or simply for verbal games. They are also intended to capture the fact that even though words may have an analysis we do not necessarily have to call on it whenever we use common words like those in the examples. An item like *readable*, although it can be analysed if we wish, might well be stored in our 'mental lexicons' as a unit and called on as a unit. The fact that it is analysable does not entail our having to construct it every time we use it.

Although the formulae accommodate both analysis and generation, it will be convenient in the discussion to focus on one approach, and we will initially regard them as formation rules. Rules 1 to 3 involve the affixation of a 'lexical formative' (*-able*, *-ness* etc.) as a suffix to a 'lexical base'. There are of course also rules involving prefixation, like:

4 $\text{Adj}^{(un\text{-}+\text{Adj})}$

'negative of Adj'
e.g. *un-clean*, *un-helpful*

The lexical base used in word formation is frequently identical to the free form, as it is in these examples, but this is not always the case. For example, in a rule like:

5 $_{\text{N}}(\text{Adj}+\text{-}th)$

'having the quality of Adj'
e.g. *long : length*; *strong : strength*

the free form *long* differs from the 'derivational base' *leng-*, which is not itself found as a free form. We will say that LONG is realized by two 'allomorphs', variant forms of the 'same' item distributionally restricted to particular environments, and return to see how a description can handle the matter.

Lexical formatives are a class of items whose function is to assist in the formation of new lexical items. English has large numbers of these, as any dictionary of affixes and suffixes will testify. In the contemporary language, one area in which they are particularly productive is in the formation of new technical terms in medicine and science, as those who read their medicine bottles will know. They too are often subject to allomorphy. For example, the 'negative prefix' recorded as *un-* in rule 4 has a variety of allomorphs: *in-decent*, *im-perfect*, *il-legal*, *ir-relevant* etc. We have supposed that lexemes are abstract items, though they need to be represented by some concrete form and we have used capitals for this purpose. Lexical formatives can be considered in the same way, but they too will need to be represented by some form. In rule 4 we have chosen *un-* as the representative of the whole class of allomorphs of this formative.

The processes we have discussed do not by any means exhaust our word-forming capacities, and we should also touch briefly on other, and, in English, no less productive word-forming processes. One such is 'conversion', which involves the simple transfer of an item from one lexical class to another. English is particularly open to this kind of operation, and many examples are long-established: *They manned the ship*; *They shipped the man*. Another common process is 'compounding', which involves taking two potentially free forms and simply juxtaposing them. Many kinds of combination are possible, for instance:

$_N(N\,N)$ e.g. *windmill*, *paperknife*, *inkwell* etc.

$_N(N\,V)$ e.g. *backchat*, *waterski*, *colourwash* etc.

$_N(Adj\,N)$ e.g. *blackbird*, *whitethroat*, *redskin* etc.

We have already seen that established words like those quoted have properties that indicate that they should be treated as unitary lexical items, and their spelling shows that they traditionally have been. Compounding is extremely productive in English, as a few minutes' study of any newspaper will reveal. It is not, however, always clear where the process of compounding ends and regular noun phrase constructions begin, because there is a continuum between the very intimate association between elements that characterizes a compound word, and the looser association of elements characteristic of a noun phrase. Consider, as an example, an expression like *nuclear power station*. The reader is invited to decide for himself whether one, two or three word units are to be identified here: the fact that it is written as three words need not be conclusive.

Before seeing how a description might cope with word formation, we should mention some general characteristics of lexical rules. First note that many of the rules involve taking an item from one word class and deriving an item in a different class. A consequence of the change of class is that once an item has been recategorized it will, as it were, completely forget its original class membership and neither it, nor any part of it, will undergo any of the grammatical processes that were appropriate to the original class. For instance, rule 1 takes a V(erb) and yields an Adj(ective): so *read→readable*. As an adjective, the new form can participate in processes appropriate to adjectives, but it has lost the capacity to participate in the morphology appropriate to a verb. As a verb we find *read:reading:read*, and as an adjective *readable:more readable* etc., but mixed forms like **readingable* are impossible.

The process is iterative in that the output of one rule can be the input to another and items can change their part of speech affiliation several times in the course of their derivation: *read* (Verb)→*readable* (Adj)→*readability* (Noun). This can lead to quite complex structure within individual words, illustrated in Figure 3:1. Although words have this kind of internal structure from a derivational point of view, the structure is quite irrelevant to the grammar which will be concerned only with the superordinate, or topmost, node. This suggests that rules of this sort are indeed rules of the lexicon and should be kept apart from grammatical rules.

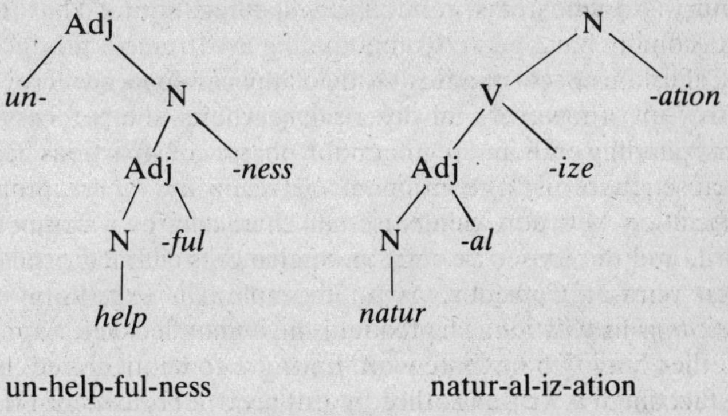
Adj
un-
N
Adj
-ness
N
-ful
help
un-help-ful-ness
N
V
-ation
Adj
-ize
N
-al
natur
natur-al-iz-ation

Figure 3:1

A further feature of lexical rules is that they differ markedly from case to case in their 'productivity' and 'applicability'. 'Productivity' means the freedom with which a rule can be used to form new items. Some, like rule 1, are highly productive, and alongside the well-attested *readable* and *enjoyable*, which we will expect to find in a dictionary, we will, in conversation, readily coin and understand new words like *unplasterable* or *peelable*. By contrast, a rule like 4 is hardly used productively in modern English: we have a few items like *warmth* and *length* but we do not readily coin forms to this pattern, though forms like *shorth* are sometimes found in the speech of children before they are bound by the conventional vocabulary.

'Applicability' refers to the fact that derivational rules are usually restricted in terms of the lexical items to which they can be applied. So, for instance, rule 4 applies to *long* and *strong* to derive *length* and *strength*, and rule 3 to *thick* and *weak* to derive *thickness* and *weakness*. But the converse is not possible. There are usually a number of formative processes operating on one word class to derive another, and when this is the case it is common to find that the applicability of the individual derivational operations is restricted to particular lexical items.

This being so, applicability seems to be largely a 'lexical' matter, and the bounds of applicability will be determined within the lexicon.

The concepts of productivity and applicability lead to the heart of a set of interlocking descriptive problems for derivational morphology. There is no doubt that we behave as though derivational rules are part of our capacity to use language creatively, for how otherwise could we coin new words to fill what we perceive to be communicative gaps with the confidence that our interlocutor will understand? Sometimes such neologisms will get accepted into the common usage, especially if they have the prestige of having been introduced by an established writer. At other times they are fugitive and do not persist even in our own individual lexicons. The fact that we operate in this way suggests that this ability should be reflected in the grammar. There are, however, difficulties for a thoroughgoing 'productive' approach, since it is unclear how far it should be carried. One might indeed wish to argue that different individuals have different abilities in this area. Part of the problem for a productive approach is the fact that the English lexicon is far from homogeneous, our word stock being of mixed ancestry. If, as a full-blooded productive approach requires, we assume that words like *readable* are produced by rule whenever they are used, then we may well enquire how we should deal with a word like *legible*, which was borrowed as a whole from Latin through French, as can be verified in an etymological dictionary. It too can be analysed, as *leg-ible*, and it would be perfectly possible to postulate an 'abstract' verb *leg-*, annotated to prevent its use as a free form itself, and derive *legible* by rule 1, but this does not seem a very sensible solution, though there are in fact linguists who have proposed just such a derivation for words of this kind. On the other hand if *legible* is a single unanalysed entry, then perhaps *readable* should be too. But do we then miss an important generalization?

This seems an appropriate point to consider a different approach to the formulae. Suppose that instead of being templates for generation they encapsulate generalizations about analysis, some of which may subsequently become established as templates for formation. Rule 1 will now express the generalization that adjectives in *-able* are potentially analysable into a suffix, with the general meaning shown, affixed to a verb stem. With this view of the matter it is no surprise to be offered an analysis of *legible*, even though there turns out to be no independent verb *leg*. We might not even be surprised if one day *leg* did indeed turn up, since 'backformation' is in fact a regular provider of words to the language. It produces, *pace* P. G. Wodehouse, the admittedly facetious *buttle* (what butlers do) and *vic* (what vicars do), but also forms like *aggress* from *aggression* or, as the reader can verify from a dictionary, *act* from *action*. The basis for processes of this sort is analogy. In the case of rule 1 the analogy is so common that it has become established as a productive pattern, but analyses can as easily be *ad hoc*, and this is surely the basis for many neologisms. As an obvious example, consider the process that must have been at work on *hamburger* to permit *beefburger*, *cheeseburger* and so on. *Hamburger* was borrowed as a whole from German, where the *-er* suffix can mean 'of or coming from', just as it can in English in *Berliner*, *Londoner* etc. In German a *hamburger* is a 'kind of steak served in the fashion of Hamburg'. The German analysis, *hamburg-er*, is, however, quite clearly irrelevant to English, where the word has been reanalysed as *ham-burger*. By analogy with forms like *ham sandwich*, a 'sandwich made with ham', we perhaps assume that a *burger* is 'a cake made of . . .' From here it is a short step to *potato-burger*, *fish-burger* and so on. There are endless examples of this kind, where our analytic ingenuity leads to the formation of a new word for some particular communicative purpose. The popular newspapers are full of them: some of the more colourful examples, mostly from this source, quoted in Adams (1973) are *broadcast~telecast~beercast* (broadcasting by brewers); *bulldozer~calfdozer* (a little bulldozer); *nightmare~beermare* (a night disturbed by over-indulgence in beer); *Utopia~Pornotopia* (Soho) and so on. And one has only to think of Joyce's *Finnegan's Wake*.

Nor need our interest in word structure always be turned to the creation of new words. Sometimes we appear only to be interested in analysis for its own sake, and once again we use the same analogical process. Our interest might be aesthetic, as is often the case with 'onomatopoeia' or 'phonaesthetics'. For example, there are analyses of words like *flame*, *flare* and *flicker* which postulate an element *fl-* with the meaning 'swift moving'. This is a relatively conservative example, since in this area analyses can get as subtle as the analyst cares, and some analysts can be very subtle. Another area for word analysis, among both professionals and amateurs, is etymology. The professional's interest tends to be scholarly and its results can be found in the larger dictionaries; the amateur's interest gives rise to such notorious folk etymologies as the supposition that a *sextet* should not perform in public in polite society and that a *fakir* is some kind of charlatan. This kind of analysis frequently suggests elements that cannot be recombined with other formatives to form new words. English yields a host of examples, some of which, like the *cran-* of *cranberry* (compare *strawberry*, *loganberry* and so forth), have generated a literature all of their own.

We have looked at some of the general characteristics of word formation rules and considered some examples. We have also looked at the question of whether such rules should be regarded as templates for the formation of new items or as guides to the analysis of existing items, or perhaps as both. We should now consider how a description is to cope with this field. The main problem is: how many distinct lexical entries do we need? And what sorts of generalizations about word formation do we expect to capture? We have already mentioned that the traditional approach of lexicographers is to treat all attested words, whether basic or derived, on a par and give each a separate lexical entry, perhaps of the sort:

Long: Adj /lɒŋ/   Having relatively great extent in space and time.

Leng-th: N /lɛŋθ/   The linear extent or measurement of something from end to end, usually being the longest dimension.

The entries specify the pronunciation, state the relevant part of speech and give a semantic definition. A derivational relationship is not explicitly stated, though it may be inferred from the semantic definition and the analysis in the second entry.

Many contemporary accounts would prefer to envisage a lexicon which overtly relates words where it can. For instance, adopting a derivational approach, we might find a single entry of the form:

Long: Adj /lɒŋ/   Having relatively great extent in space or time.

N (by rule 5: derivational base /lɛŋ-/)   Usually the longest dimension from end to end.

In this statement, both the form and part of the meaning of the noun are derived by rule, though the semantic definition also includes additional semantic information that is specific to *length*: it refers to the 'longest dimension'. Within an approach of this sort we will want to derive *readable* in a parallel fashion. We will, however, presumably not want a thoroughgoing derivational approach for all items, and will be willing to accept a 'mixed' lexicon, where an item like *legible* is entered as a unit, the potential analysis being performed if necessary by reference to the rule that will derive *readable*.

A model formalizing these kinds of generalizations will contain (i) a specification of lexical items together with information about their semantics and, where appropriate, their derivational bases; (ii) a specification of lexical formatives and their meanings and allomorphs; (iii) a set of rule schemata for the generation of regular forms and the analogical analysis of idiosyncratic items. Furthermore we must suppose a general ability to create new analogical analyses, and expect some of these new analyses to develop into rule schemata themselves.

Even this 'mixed' approach is not without problems, since we have not settled on the limits of the productivity of the schemata we have proposed. To demonstrate how far this can go, consider the relationship between the pairs *elate : elation*, *gyrate : gyration*, *act : action* and so on. Here stems ending in /-t/ change this to /-ʃ/ (the sound often represented by *sh* as in *ship*) when *-ion* is suffixed. We could relate such pairs by a phonological rule like:

/t/→/ʃ/ when followed by *-ion*

and perhaps we should have such a rule since it seems to capture a relevant generalization about word structure. Now consider another similar case: *electric : electricity*, *elastic : elasticity* and so on. These suggest a rule:

/k/→/s/ when followed by -*ity*

But how valid is this generalization, and how widespread is it? Phonological generalizations of this sort were pursued with great vigour in the early 1970s, but have in the last few years fallen from favour, partly because it is only too easy to carry them to ludicrous extremes. We might, for instance, relate *foot* and *pedal* by rules changing /f/ to /p/ and /t/ to /d/ and so on. The words are in fact historically related by just such processes, but the sound changes involved are surely no longer a productive part of our word-forming abilities.

In this section we have seen that it is advantageous to include rules for the formation of lexical items in the lexicon. It is not, however, clear how many such rules we need. In the 1970s it was generally the fashion to have relatively few entries, and a large number of extra rules to generate new items and to account for lexical relations. These days the pendulum has largely swung in the other way and the suggestion is that we need fewer rules and more lexical entries: we shall be returning to this issue in 6.2a.

Let us now go on to consider the other aspect of the internal structure of words – inflectional morphology.

3.2 The structure of grammatical words

'Inflectional' morphology is concerned with those aspects of word structure that relate to variations in word form associated with such 'grammatical' categories as {number} – the alternation between {singular} and {plural}, {tense} – the alternation between {past} and {non-past}, and so on. Inflectional morphology can thus be considered as that part of the grammatical description of sentences that is concerned with the way grammatical words are formed, and how they are realized in word forms. In comparison with a language like Latin or German, English exhibits rather little inflectional morphology, which is perhaps why English is sometimes said to have little 'grammar', the notion of 'grammar' being incorrectly associated with inflectional morphology alone. For our immediate purposes this limited morphology has the advantage that it is possible to demonstrate the problems that arise using straightforward examples from only two grammatical categories in English – tense and number. The reader should be warned in advance that some of what follows will inevitably be rather technical since we shall begin to look at formal models of language in this section.

Let us begin by proposing a grammatical description for the various words in the sentence:

The cats killed the mice.

We would agree that *cats* is the plural form of CAT (since there is the alternation *cat:cats*) and *mice* the plural of MOUSE (the alternation *mouse:mice* paralleling that of *cat:cats*). The word *cat-s* is analysable as involving the affixation of *-s* to the base form of the noun, the regular plural formation in English. *Mice*, on the other hand, is not similarly analysable since the plural formation here involves 'vowel change' rather than affixation, an irregular formation in English. Both are, however, indubitably plural formations, and a grammatical description will want to treat them in a parallel fashion. Following the notation we used on pages 59–60 we will represent them as {CAT pl} and {MOUSE pl}.

Turning to the other constituents in the sentence, *killed* is readily segmentable as *kill-ed* and since this represents the past form of KILL we will give it the grammatical analysis {KILL past}. Just as some nouns, like MOUSE, have irregular plural formations, so some verbs have irregular past tense formations: so paralleling the regular, and analysable, *kill:killed* we have the irregular, and unanalysable, *eat:ate*; *think:thought* etc. As before, even though the word forms are unsegmentable, they realize the same grammatical structure as the corresponding segmentable forms, and so we will represent them in a parallel fashion as {EAT past} and {THINK past}. *The* is an invariant form and for the present we will suppose that it has no further analysis. The grammatical description of our sentence is then:

THE CAT+pl KILL+past THE MOUSE+pl.

We have referred to the various elements of the analysis as 'morphemes' and offered some reasons why it is useful to recognize such units in a grammar. We saw that morphemes are abstract entities postulated for the purpose of grammatical analysis, and thus by definition the smallest units with which the grammar will be concerned. They are established by analytic procedures which need not necessarily be constrained by the facts of word structure (though the analyst would be unwise to depart too far from word structure, since this offers a welcome restraint on wild analyses). For example we might well want a grammatical analysis to describe the singular forms corresponding to the two nouns above as {CAT sing} and {MOUSE sing}, even though there are no segments in the word forms that realize these grammatical descriptors.

The example illustrates two different types of morpheme: lexical and grammatical. Lexical morphemes include items like {CAT}, {MOUSE} and {KILL}, which derive from the lexicon. In the previous section we noted that they are assigned to 'lexical categories' or 'parts of speech', noun, verb and so forth. Grammatical morphemes include {pl} or {past}, and they too can be assigned to categories, in this case the 'grammatical categories' of {number} and {tense}. We will suppose for the present that these categories derive from the grammar. Given this view, it will be the business of the lexicon and lexical morphology to account for the internal structure, if any, of lexemes, and the business of the grammar to account for the distribution of morphemes, both lexical and grammatical, and their association into grammatical words. The internal structure of lexical morphemes will thus be of no concern to the grammar as such. Indeed, for the purposes of a grammatical description, all nouns are equal whether they are simple or derived: so the nouns in the example could be replaced by complex lexemes

The farmers killed the ducklings

and the analysis will be exactly parallel to that of our original sentence:

THE FARMER+pl KILL+past THE DUCKLING+pl.

We saw in 3.1 that although both *farm-er* and *duck-ling* have internal structure, information about this will be a distraction the grammar can do without. It will not wish to know, for example, that *farmer* is an 'agent nominal' deriving from the verb FARM since it will not want to associate any kind of verb morphology with the segment *farm* – a form like **farmeder* being obviously deviant.

We should now consider how grammatical words are constructed. One type of model treats all morphemes in an exactly parallel fashion as 'units'. In such a model we might find rule statements of the sort shown in Figure 3:2.

1 N(oun): NS+Num(ber)   [NS = N(oun) S(tem)]

2 Num: $\begin{cases} \text{Sing(ular)} \\ \text{Pl(ural)} \end{cases}$

3 V(erb): VS+Tense   [VS = V(erb) S(tem)]

4 Tense: $\begin{cases} \text{Past} \\ \text{Non-past} \end{cases}$

Figure 3:2

The conventions are: a constituent to the left of the colon is to have the constituent structure shown to the right of it; items bracketed together by curly brackets are alternatives. Given a further convention that associates lexemes of the appropriate category to 'NS' and 'VS', the rules will define analyses of the form shown in Figure 3:3.

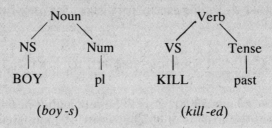

Figure 3:3

An approach of this sort lies behind an 'item and arrangement' model of word structure. The 'items' are the morphemes, whether lexical or grammatical, and the 'arrangements' are the patterns determined for the items by the grammar. In those parts of English morphology where the morphs, *-s* and *-ed*, correspond in a one-to-one manner with the corresponding morphemes, {pl} and {past}, this seems an appropriate and attractive model of description. When applied to other areas of the language, however, it is often rather clumsy: this is particularly the case with the 'irregular' plural and past tense forms. For example, it seems sensible that all syntactically parallel forms, whether segmentable or not, should receive a parallel analysis: so on the analogy of the analysis in Figure 3:3, forms like *mice* and *ate* will be analysed as in Figure 3:4.

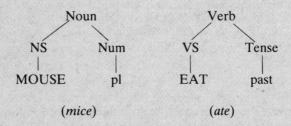

(*mice*)   (*ate*)

Figure 3:4

An item and arrangement model for words like these presents

difficulties, since a word like *mice* has no obvious analysis into morphs. If we require a one-to-one correspondence between morphemes and morphs, then, since there are more morphemes than there are morphs, we will be forced into curious analyses. We might, for example, suppose that *ate* is that form of the verb EAT that occurs before the past tense morpheme, and that the past tense morpheme has a zero realization after items like *ate* – i.e. that the analysis of *ate* is {ate+∅}. A more appropriate solution to this matter is to apply a 'process' model of analysis. In this case, there is no objection to a number of morphemes corresponding to a single morph: we will see examples of rules of this kind later in the section.

To illustrate how a description might use models of this kind to define words, and to see how morphology and grammar relate to each other, consider the derivation of noun phrases like *this boy* and *these boys* where the Det(erminers), *this* and *these*, must agree with the noun in number. One way of handling this matter is to suppose that number is primarily a category of the noun, in other words developed from rules like 1 and 2 in the grammar shown in Figure 3:2, and that a morpheme of number is copied from the noun to the determiner. The rules 1 and 2 will need to be supplemented by a rule defining the structure of the noun phrase, and we will assume this to be of the form

5   NP: Det+N

These three rules will now define NPs like those in Figure 3:5:

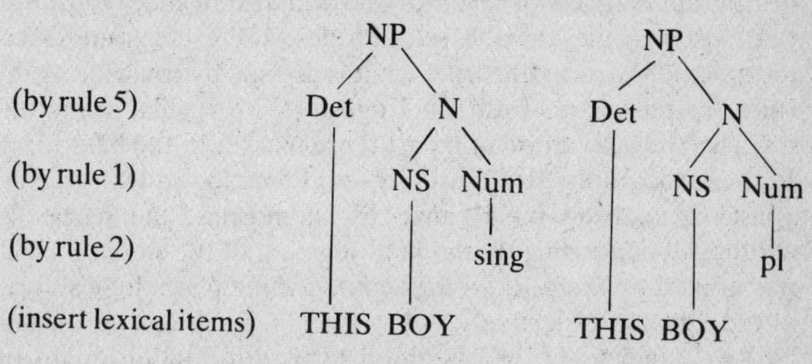

Figure 3:5

If we now propose a rule which will copy a morpheme of number from the noun on to its modifying determiner, this rule will alter the structures of Figure 3:5 into those of Figure 3:6:

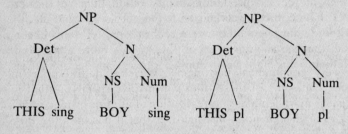

Figure 3:6

The grammatical rules will, of course, need to be complemented by a set of 'realization' rules which will relate morpheme strings to word forms or segments of word forms. That is, abstract morphemes need to be put together into concrete phonological representations: {BOY pl} must become *boys*, {MOUSE pl} must become *mice* and so on. These rules are usually gathered into a separate subcomponent of description called, appropriately enough, a 'morphophonemic' component.

The morphophonemic component will need to have access to the lexicon for information about the phonological or orthographic forms of lexemes and will also need a realization rule, or in some cases a set of rules, for each grammatical morpheme. We will illustrate what is at issue by considering the rules for past tense forms in English. With regular verbs this involves the suffixation of a past tense marker to the base form. In the orthography this is usually *-ed*. Phonologically, however, {past} is realized by a range of allomorphs, the particular allomorph depending on the final segment of the stem to which it is affixed: in *hugged*, *kissed* and *patted* the phonological form of the affix is, respectively, /-d/, /-t/ and /-ɪd/, as can be verified by pronouncing the words aloud. This information might be made available in some such form as the following:

{past}: /-ɪd/   following verbs ending in /t/ or /d/

        /-t/   following verbs ending in voiceless con-
                sonants other than /t/ – i.e. /p/, /k/, /s/ etc.

        /-d/   following verbs ending in vowels or
                voiced consonants other than /d/ – i.e.
                vowels and /b/, /z/ etc.

The morphophonemic component will need a rule of this kind for every grammatical morpheme. We should also note in passing that some of these rules will involve specifying that a particular morpheme has no realization at all. For instance, the mark of a singular noun in English is that it has no affix: this implies rules like

    {sing}: ∅   [where '∅' means a 'zero' realization]

Let us now consider the irregular forms. The morphology of irregular past tense forms in English is complex, and the forms can be, and have been, analysed in many different ways. The simplest solution to the problem, which is also a very traditional one, is to put all such irregularity in the lexicon, so we could envisage entries like:

    MEET, V, /mit/; {MEET+past}→/mɛt/

    STICK, V, /stɪk/; {STICK+past}→/stʌk/

The rule for inserting lexical stems will now need to be sensitive to the context in which stems are inserted, since /stɪk/ must only be inserted when STICK is followed by {past}, and the general rule for {past} must be prevented from applying when an irregular form has been supplied from the lexicon, or we will generate *stucked as a past tense form. While this solution may be the simplest way of dealing with the matter, it has the disadvantage of treating all 'vowel change' past tense forms as idiosyncratic, whereas in fact there is partial regularity. If we wish to capture this regularity we can devise rules like

{past}: /i/→/ɛ/ when VS = {MEET, KEEP . . .}
/ɪ/→/ʌ/ when VS = {STICK, STING . . .}

In a 'process' morphology of this sort the lexicon will insert the same 'base' form on all occasions and the vowel change will be performed by a rule in the morphophonemic component. How far one would wish to carry this type of analysis is, as in the parallel case of the rules for lexical morphology, up to the analyst.

Even this limited discussion will show that 'irregular' morphology poses a problem for an item and arrangement model, since there is no direct correspondence between morpheme and morph. The item and arrangement model is in fact most suitable where words can be analysed so that the word segments, morphs, correspond in a one-to-one fashion with morphemes. Languages with this property, like Turkish and Swahili, are said to be 'agglutinating'. The item and arrangement model is less satisfactory when words cannot be easily segmented, or when there is a many-to-one relationship between morphemes and morphs.

A model of this kind is not the only possible way of handling word formation. Another way is to consider only lexical morphemes to be 'units' and treat grammatical morphemes as 'features' which can be attached to lexical morphemes. In this model our rules will need to be recast, perhaps as in Figure 3:7:

Noun: NS, $\begin{cases} [\text{sing}] \\ [\text{pl}] \end{cases}$

Verb: VS, $\begin{cases} [\text{past}] \\ [\text{non-past}] \end{cases}$

Figure 3:7

The convention here is that an item on the left of the colon is developed as the item on the right together with whatever features are specified, alternatives, as before, being in curly brackets. Together with a further convention that 'higher level' features can 'trickle down' on to lexemes, these rules will define analyses like those of Figure 3:8:

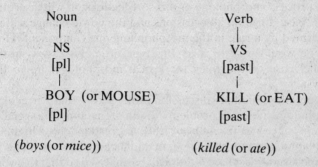

Figure 3:8

Rules of this kind can be made the basis of a 'word and paradigm' model of morphology. This model cannot be well exemplified from English because English has rather restricted morphology, so we will briefly illustrate it with a Latin example. Latin nouns have a complicated morphology, and word forms are not readily segmentable so that the parts of a word uniquely correspond to particular morphemes. To begin with, both singular and plural nouns can be realized in a number of different 'case' forms, the cases realizing various grammatical functions, like 'subject' and 'object'. To complicate matters further, the case markers differ in form depending on the noun stem to which they are attached. The traditional solution to this problem is to assign nouns to different 'declensions', such that the items in each declension inflect to a common pattern. A representative example of each declension is then chosen as a model or 'paradigm' for word formation. Figure 3:9 shows a tiny part of the total system, illustrating only some of the singular forms of four nouns.

Let us suppose that the morphemes of number, {sing} and {pl}, and case, {nom}, {acc} etc. derive from the grammar, and that individual nouns are marked in the lexicon for their declension, as well as various other features that may be

		First declension	'A'	'B'	'C'
			ANNUS	PUER	BELLUM
		PUELLA	'year'	'boy'	'war'
		'girl'			
Sing	Nom	puella	annus	puer	bellum
	Acc	puellam	annum	puerum	bellum
	Gen	puellae	anni	pueri	belli
	etc.	...	...	...	...

('A', 'B' and 'C' indicate different paradigms within the second declension. The case labels are Nom(inative), Acc(usative) and Gen(itive).)

Figure 3:9

grammatically relevant, such as their gender. This implies lexical entries like:

PUELLA: N,1, fem(inine) 'girl'
PUER: N, 2B, masc(uline) 'boy'
AGRICOLA: N,1, masc 'farmer'
DOMINUS: N, 2A, masc 'master'

and so on. From the lexical entries and the paradigm we will know that the {gen, sing} of AGRICOLA is *agricolae* and the {acc, sing} of DOMINUS is *dominum*.

To show how this model might work, consider in outline the derivation of a sentence like *Puer puellam amat* 'The boy loves the girl'. We will suppose that the grammar will specify a sentence structure of the general form

(1)   N   N   V

The nouns may be {sing} or {pl}; in this example {sing} is chosen for each noun. The grammar will further tell us that the subject noun will be in the {nom} case, and the object noun in the {acc} case. The grammar will also tell us about choices open to the verb: we shall not be concerned with verb forms and merely stipulate that the verb will be {indic(ative)} and {pres(ent tense)}. This information can be represented like this:

(2) N   N   V
     [nom, sing]   [acc, sing]   [indic, pres]

The grammar will also tell us that verbs must agree in number with their subject and this information too will need to be added:

(3) N   N   V
     [nom, sing]   [acc, sing]   [indic, pres, 3sing]

If we now insert the various lexical items, adding their lexical features to the appropriate feature bundles, we get:

(4) PUER   PUELLA   AMARE
     [N, 2B, masc,   [N, 1, fem,   [V, 1,
      nom, sing]   acc, sing]   [indic, pres, 3sing]

Reference to the paradigms will yield our sentence *Puer puellam amat*.

The example is straightforward, but it will illustrate the point at issue clearly enough. In an item and arrangement model of the kind we first discussed, a word like *puer* will represent a morpheme string {PUER+sing+nom} yet the word cannot be segmented so that there is any correspondence between morpheme and morph. In such a model the morphophonemic rules will need to be very complex to achieve a proper description and there will be numerous rules declaring that particular morphemes have a zero realization. In a word and paradigm model the lexeme together with its associated features will be realized as a unit. A model of this kind seems to be particularly suited to highly inflecting languages like Latin or Classical Greek.

The discussion now raises several interesting problems. One is whether it will be appropriate to attempt to use a single morphological model for all languages, or whether different language types are best served by different morphological models. Opinions differ on this question. Some linguists would prefer to see a uniform model, others believe that a variety of models can co-exist, different models being suitable for different languages. For agglutinating languages, where there is a one-to-one relationship between morphemes and morphs, the item and arrangement model seems revealing since it enables the linguist to capture the generalization that words are composed of strings of separable morphs each of which can be related to a grammatical element. For inflecting languages, on the other hand, where there is a many-to-one relationship between morphemes and words or word segments, the word and paradigm model may be more appropriate since this enables a word as a whole to relate to a whole bundle of lexical and grammatical features. However this difference is resolved, it is clear that there are many common features since both rely on a unit like the morpheme, treating it either as a unit, in the item and arrangement model, or as a feature, in the word and paradigm model. They differ in that the grammars they are associated with will have different formal properties depending on whether we are distributing items or features, and it is possible to do some things with features which cannot be so easily done with items and vice versa.

A second interesting question concerns the distinction we have kept hitherto between lexical (or derivational) and grammatical (or inflectional) morphology. We have assumed that the former is a matter for the lexicon, and the latter is the concern of the grammar. The distinction clearly also implies that some elements of meaning derive from the lexicon, and others from the grammar. We should question this distinction.

To illustrate what is at issue, let us take our Latin example a little further. Consider the sentence *Puer puellam bellam amat* 'The boy loves the beautiful girl'. This differs from our previous sentence only by the addition of the adjective BELLUS 'beautiful' modifying the noun PUELLA 'girl'. We need not concern ourselves in detail with the morphology of Latin adjectives, and it will be sufficient to say that they agree in number, gender and case with the noun they modify. So here, *bellam* is the {fem, acc, sing} form of BELLUS to concord with the {fem, acc, sing} *puellam*. If BELLUS had been modifying PUER 'boy', to yield a meaning 'The beautiful boy loves the girl', then it would have taken the appropriate {masc, nom, sing} form, *bellus*, to agree with the {masc, nom, sing} PUER.

Suppose now that we insert an adjective into the string shown in example (4) above to yield the string shown in (5).

(5) PUER   PUELLA   BELLUS   AMARE
     [N, 2B, masc, [1, fem,   [1, indic,
     nom, sing]   acc, sing]   pres, 3sing]

We will now need additional rules to copy features of number, gender and case from the noun on to its modifying adjective to yield:

(6) PUER   PUELLA   BELLUS   AMARE
     [N, 2B, masc, [1, fem,   [fem,   [1, indic,
     nom, sing]   acc, sing] acc, sing] pres, 3sing]

This after consultation with the relevant paradigms, will yield the desired *Puer puellam bellam amat*.

We can now approach a number of issues concerning the distinction between grammar and lexicon. Our position so far has been that lexical meanings are the meanings associated with lexemes like PUER, PUELLA and BELLUS. These derive from the lexicon. Grammatical meanings are the meanings associated with case and number morphemes which indicate, among other things, the functions of the various nouns in the sentence. These derive from the grammar. In these terms it will be no part of the lexical meaning of PUER 'boy' whether it occurs in the nominative, to indicate subject, or the accusative, to indicate object. Clearly there is a difference in meaning between *Puer puellam amat* 'The boy loves the girl' and *Puella puerum amat* 'The girl loves the boy' which depends on which noun is subject and which object, but this does not seem to have anything to do with the meaning of PUER or PUELLA as such, and we would not expect their lexical entries to include information of this kind.

In these terms a string like *Puer puella amat* is anomalous because we cannot tell, because of the lack of case markings, who loves whom. This, however, seems to have little to do with the meanings of PUER and PUELLA themselves. We will consider strings of this sort to be grammatically ill formed. Conversely, while the string *Puella librum amat* 'The girl loves the book' is well formed from all points of view, a string like *Liber puellam amat* is nonsense. In this case the unacceptability stems not from the wrong case assignment, since this sentence follows all the rules of the grammar, but from the difficulty of making sense of 'The book loves the girl'. This string is, then, semantically anomalous.

The distinction at issue is relatively clear and along rather traditional lines, but closer examination of our examples reveals that all is not quite so straightforward as it seems. Consider, for instance, the ascribed assignments of number and gender. We have hitherto supposed that the choice between singular and plural is not inherent in the noun, and hence a lexical matter, but is rather a choice to be made in the grammar. By contrast we have treated gender in the noun as a lexical matter, since gender is an invariant, and often arbitrary, feature of individual lexemes themselves.

So far so good, but now consider gender in adjectives. Adjectives do not have gender assignments in the lexicon because, as we have seen, they derive their gender by means of the rule copying the feature from the noun they modify. Gender is, then, treated in one way in one rule and in another way in another rule. Is this reasonable? Or should we perhaps seek a more unified approach?

Before answering the question we will return briefly to the category of number. This time an example from English will make the point. There are a few nouns in English which are inherently plural – SCISSORS, SUDS, CATTLE, PEOPLE and so on. Items like this will simply need to be marked in the lexicon as inherently plural. There are other nouns which are typically only found in the singular. These are that subclass of nouns that are usually referred to as 'mass' or 'uncountable' nouns. They are nouns like WINE, WATER and INK which are used to refer to agglomerates of some substance that literally cannot be 'counted' as items. Such nouns do not usually occur in the plural, *I like inks*, and cannot be counted, *one ink*, *two waters* and so on. One way of accounting for this categorization is to suppose that all nouns are characterized in the lexicon in terms of a feature, say [+/-count], and that only [+count] nouns can occur in plural environments. Number has now entered the lexicon.

But this is not the end of the story since it is, in fact, possible to find 'mass' nouns in the plural, but that when they do occur in the plural they acquire a particular meaning. So *We are serving two wines this evening* is interpreted to mean 'two kinds of wine'. The choice of number has affected the meaning.

If we wish to maintain the distinction between lexical and grammatical morphology, we could always propose a derivational rule which can change the value of the feature [+/-count]. Alternatively we might suppose that the distinction which we have so rigidly drawn thus far is not in fact worth maintaining and revise our description so that all morphology is dealt with in a single unified component. In the chapters which immediately follow we will take the first approach, returning later to question this matter further.

In this chapter we have been looking at words and have seen that an apparently straightforward concept is in fact rather more complicated than appears at first sight. One reason why it is useful to think about word structure is that it raises a number of issues which concern the description of a language which will recur in other situations. In particular we found that it is possible to erect a number of different models of description, and we found that the apparently clear-cut distinction between 'grammar' and 'lexicon' is not at all clear-cut when we look at it carefully. The same problems, in a slightly different form, will crop up again when we come to consider the description of sentences – the topic of the next chapter.

4 Sentences

The Extensions of Speech are quite indefinite, as may be
seen if we compare the Eneid to an Epigram of *Martial*. But
the *longest Extension* with which the Grammar has to do is
the Extension here considered, that is to say a SENTENCE.
The greater Extensions (such as Syllogisms, Paragraphs,
Sections and complete Works) belong not to Grammar but
to Arts of a higher order, not to mention that all of them
are but Sentences repeated.

(James Harris)

Having discussed the structure of words we must now turn to the
ways in which words are put together into sentences, for
sentences are not simply strings of words, but structured strings
of words. This must be so, since if there were no structure, how
could we possibly understand a sentence like

'He had breathed on me, bafflingly (for no banquet would
serve, because of the known redolence of onions, onions)
onions.' (Anthony Burgess)

In this admittedly extreme example the elaborate punctuation is
a guide to unravelling the gross structure, and hence the
meaning. But punctuation can never do all the work, and where
there are no such signals, as is the case most of the time, an
analysis will need to be postulated and argued for.

In this and the next three chapters we will be concerned with
two different, though complementary, approaches to the study
of sentence structure. Here, and in Chapters 5 and 6, we will look
at sentences primarily in *structural* terms: in other words, we
shall be examining the rules for the construction of the various

'building blocks' out of which sentences are formed, the way in which words are assembled into phrases, and how phrases are put together into sentences. In Chapter 7 we will turn to examine the *functional* relationships which these 'building blocks' contract with each other: in other words, we will be concentrating on the semantic role of the various sentence constituents rather than the rules for their construction. The two approaches, as we will see, come from rather different views about the basic units of grammatical description, and hence lead to different kinds of grammars.

4.1 Constituent analysis

In this section we will consider the structural analysis of sentences and the kinds of arguments that are used to support analyses of this kind. In the next section we will see how these general observations can be brought together into a particular type of grammar. Let us start by looking at an example. The sentence *The cat sat on the mat* might be assigned the analysis shown in Figure 4:1. Analyses of this type are known as 'constituent structure' or 'immediate constituent' analyses. The

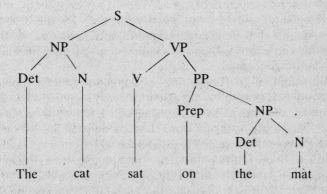

Figure 4:1

analysis divides the sentence into a number of chunks, each of which is then subdivided until we reach the smallest constituents with which the analysis is concerned. Each chunk, or subdivision within a chunk, is a *constituent*. The analysis explicitly sets out what the analyst has considered to be constituents and hence implicitly denies that any other strings, perhaps *cat sat* or *sat on the*, are proper parts of the sentence. For obvious reasons, the process of grouping constituents together is known as 'bracketing'.

For reasons of simplicity the smallest units with which we will concern ourselves in this chapter will be words. It will, however, doubtless be clear that a description of the sort illustrated in Figure 4:1 can be readily extended to include a description of the structure of words. Indeed the first type of morphological model discussed in 3.2 lends itself naturally to this kind of analysis, and many constituent structure grammars incorporate such a morphology. The reason for this will be clear: the kind of analysis which that model proposes for words is exactly the same as the kind of analysis proposed above for sentences, and consequently the kinds of rule systems involved will be a natural extension of the kinds of rule systems we will propose in the next section for constituent structure grammars. Furthermore, if the morpheme is the minimal unit of grammatical analysis we ought to extend the description of the syntax down into a description of the internal structure of words. We will, however, for the sake of simplicity, and because we have already discussed some morphological issues, largely ignore word structure in this chapter and words will be the smallest constituents with which we shall be concerned.

In addition to bracketing constituents together, each constituent is assigned to a syntactic category – a process known, again for obvious reasons, as 'labelling'. Each word has been labelled as a member of a word class: *cat* and *mat* are N(ouns), *on* a Prep(osition), *sat* a V(erb) and *the* a Det(erminer). When words have been brought together into phrases these too have been given labels: N(oun) P(hrase), P(repositional) P(hrase) and V(erb) P(hrase). The structure as a whole is assigned to the category S(entence).

There are several ways in which this information can be displayed. All show exactly the same information, though some are easier to read than others. Figure 4:1 displays the information as a 'tree diagram', or 'phrase marker'. Another common representation is as a 'labelled and bracketed' string, a type of representation we used in 3.1 in discussing the structure of lexical items:

$$S(_{NP}(_{Det}(the)_N(cat))_{VP}(_V(sat)_{PP}(_{Prep}(on)_{NP}(_{Det}(the)_N(mat)))))$$

In this example, for reasons of space, only the opening brackets have been labelled with the category name: hence the five brackets at the end of the string represent, respectively, the constituent boundaries of N (*mat*), NP (*the mat*), PP (*on the mat*), VP (*sat on the mat*) and the sentence as a whole. Representations of this sort are sometimes difficult to read because of the amount of detail involved, so they often are simplified to show only the gross structure necessary for some particular stage in an argument. For some purposes it might be convenient to show the gross structure of our sentence as perhaps:

$$S(_{NP}(the\ cat)_{VP}(_V(sat)_{PP}(on\ the\ mat)))$$

This outline representation does not, of course, imply that the unanalysed constituents have no internal structure, but merely that it is not relevant to whatever point is being made.

It will be convenient to have some technical vocabulary to enable us to talk about configurations in the analyses. The vocabulary will apply to both the labelled and bracketed string, and to the tree diagram, but will probably be easier to follow with respect to the tree. The diagram shows the structure of the sentence as a whole developing from an *initial (category) symbol* S, for S(entence), and the tree is said to be *rooted in S*. The structure from S then *branches* into two constituents – a N(oun) P(hrase) and a V(erb) P(hrase). A point at which branching occurs is a *node*: thus we can talk about the 'NP node', 'VP node' etc. Nodes which branch further are *non-terminal* (in Figure 4:1, S, NP, VP, PP) and nodes which do not branch any more are *terminal*. Since we are ignoring morphological structure in this chapter we will treat the lexical category nodes Det, N, V etc. as terminal. If we wished to include morphology in a description of this kind, and this, as we have already remarked, is straight-forward with an item and arrangement model, then morphemes would be terminals. When a branching structure is developed from any node, that node *dominates* the nodes which branch from it, and when some node dominates another node with no other nodes intervening, then the first node *immediately dominates* the second. These relationships between nodes are often described in 'family tree' terminology – the dominating category being the *mother* and the dominated categories the *daughters*; daughters of the same mother will obviously be *sisters*, and we can then go on to identify the *left sister*, *right sister* and so on. In the tree in Figure 4:1, S dominates all the other nodes (since they can all be traced back to the root S) but it only immediately dominates one NP and the VP. This description has focused on *dominance relations*. It could however equally well have been formulated in terms of constituency relations: the *immediate constituents* of S are NP and VP and so on. The section title, 'Constituent analysis', derives from this latter terminology.

A constituent analysis cannot begin without some principles which determine what can and what cannot constitute a proper analysis. It will be no surprise to learn that, although all linguistic descriptions involve labelling and bracketing, and although many of the more general principles outlined below are common to all approaches, there is, since the principles are framed in very general terms, latitude for considerable variation in the way they are applied. Furthermore, some theories of constituent structure will permit analytical configurations that others will disallow: we will come to some examples of this at the end of the section. The theory of constituent structure outlined in this section is compatible with that associated with the constituent structure component of a 'standard theory' transformational grammar because we will be looking at this approach in the next chapter. In later chapters we will look at some other models.

The analysis shown in Figure 4:1 rests on a number of

assumptions that should be made overt. An obvious assumption is that analyses will capture what the analyst considers to be relevant generalizations about the structure of the language. The ultimate aim is to describe the language as a whole, and the sentence before us is just one of a multitude of sentences that might have been chosen, so any analysis we assign to this particular sentence must be consistent with analyses we will wish to give to other sentences. There will, for example, be sentences which differ from this sentence only in the selection of lexical items – like, say, *The dog lay under the bed*, *The bat hung on that rafter*, *The man leant against the wall* and so on. We will want these to have exactly the same analysis as that given in Figure 4:1. There will be others that differ minimally in that one of the constituents we have recognized will be replaced by a smaller one like *It sat on the mat* or *The cat sat there*, or by a larger one like *The ginger cat sat on the mat* or *The cat sat on the mat near the window*. We will expect the analysis to capture these partial similarities and differences.

An obvious way to capture these similarities is to assume that items or strings of items that are mutually substitutable and can occur in the same set of environments are assigned to the same category. This principle will apply at all levels of analysis. So we will group {ON, NEAR, UNDER} into a class, called Prep(ositions), on the grounds that they are mutually substitutable (*on/under/near – the bed*) and occur with a noun phrase in a prepositional phrase (*on – the bed/ that branch/ the table*). By the same logic {CAT, DOG, GIRL, MAT, BRANCH} will be grouped together into a class of N(ouns) on the grounds that they are mutually substitutable, and co-occur within the NP with a class of Det(erminers), {THE, A, THIS, THAT . . .}. In this way we will establish a number of 'lexical categories' or 'parts of speech', Prep(osition), N(oun), V(erb) etc., and every lexical item will be assigned to a lexical category. The same procedure will yield a set of 'phrasal categories', noun phrase, verb phrase etc., which will consist of strings of lexical or phrasal categories or both.

This leads to another assumption behind the postulated analyses. Corresponding to each of the major lexical categories N(oun), V(erb), Prep(osition) and so on, is a phrasal category

NP (Noun Phrase), VP (Verb Phrase), PP (Prepositional Phrase) and so on. These phrasal categories are constructed so that a particular phrasal category will dominate the corresponding lexical category, perhaps along with other material: so NP will dominate { . . . N . . .}, VP, { . . . V . . .} etc. It will be clear that if lexical items are assigned to lexical categories, and if there is this special relationship between lexical and phrasal categories, we will in this way explicitly define the range of possible phrasal categories: there will be as many phrasal categories as there are major lexical categories.

An immediate consequence of this assumption about the relationship between lexical items and lexical and phrasal categories is that all analyses will necessarily be *hierarchical* in structure. Lexical categories will be grouped into phrasal categories which will themselves be grouped into yet other phrasal categories and so on. The assumption that the structures to be found in languages are hierarchical has a variety of consequences, some of which will be explored in the next section.

This leads to another observation: the nodes in the tree of Figure 4:1 are all labelled with the names of 'categories', like noun, or noun phrase, for which we have offered distributional definitions in terms of their mutual substitutability and their potential for co-occurrence with other categories. None of the labels involves the names of grammatical 'functions', like 'subject' or 'object'. The decision to exclude functional information of this sort from the analyses does not mean that it is irrelevant, but it does mean that it has been decided that structural information is primary, and functional information is of secondary importance. If we need such information, we will have to find a way of deriving it from the trees. For some functions this is straightforward: for example, we can identify the 'subject' as the NP which is dominated by S, and the 'object' as the NP dominated by VP. The relative weight to be given to structure and function is one on which linguists disagree quite considerably, and it is a matter to which we will return in Chapter 7.

Within the framework of these general assumptions, let us now develop our analysis a little further. To do so we must return to our first assumption, that categorization is principally determined by distributional similarities and differences. These similarities and differences can involve either the internal structure of constituents, or their permissible positions, or *distribution*, within the sentence, or both.

Let us start by considering internal structure. In the case of lexical categories, similarity of internal structure can only involve morphological similarity – and we have seen that English is not exactly rich in this respect. Most nouns can inflect for plural (*cat:cats*), verbs typically occur in the present and past tense forms and in the appropriate participial forms (*walk*, *walks*, *walked*, *walking*), and sometimes there are derivational clues to class membership (a word in *-ness* is usually a noun, and one in *-able* normally an adjective, as we saw in 3.1).

As far as phrasal categories are concerned, their internal structure will normally be defined in terms of those other categories, either phrasal or lexical, that go together to form the category concerned. So, for example, the phrasal category of NP contains, as a minimum, an N, which may co-occur with other specified phrasal or lexical categories, as in the following:

> NP: N, e.g.: *boys*, *dogs*, *vermin*, *people*
> PN, e.g.: *John*, *Mary*, *Harry*
> Det N, e.g.: *the – boy*, *those – dogs*
> Det Adj N, e.g.: *the – big – boy*, *those – little – girls*
> Det N PP, e.g.: *the – girl – with pigtails*, *the – cat – with a fluffy tail*

or any appropriate combination of these, say,

> NP: Det Adj N PP, e.g.: *the – little – girl – with pigtails*

The structure of the phrasal category has been specified in terms of other categories, lexical and phrasal, rather than in terms of individual words, because this leads to a greater economy of description. Instead of specifying every possible sequence of words that could count as an NP, we need only specify what sequences of categories will count as an NP, the membership of that category being determined elsewhere. An additional advantage is that we will be able to describe the distribution of NPs without being concerned with the identity of particular lexical items, an important consideration as we shall see.

On similar lines we can establish a category of VP – it will consist minimally of a verb, which may optionally co-occur with other constituents. So, for example, any of the following will occur as VPs in English:

> VP: V PP, e.g.: *sat – on the mat*; *lay – on the table*
> V NP, e.g.: *ate – the bread*; *killed – the cat*
> V Adj, e.g.: *seemed – clever*; *was – big*; *became – fat*
> V NP NP, e.g.: *gave – the boy – a bar of chocolate*;
>   *sent – his mother – a Christmas present*
> V, e.g.: *died, laughed, smiled*

By the same procedure we can establish the internal structure of other phrasal categories in English. The P(repositional) P(hrase) will have as constituents a Prep(osition), usually followed by an NP:

> PP: Prep NP, e.g.: *on – the mat, near – the door*
> Prep, e.g.: *down* (cf. *he fell – down*), *up* (cf. *he came – up*)

Our example sentence does not contain an Adj(ective) but the principles we have introduced will allow us to establish an A(djective) P(hrase) which will consist minimally of an Adj(ective) optionally preceded by an Int(ensifier):

> AP: Adj, e.g.: *big, small, happy* etc.
> Int Adj, e.g.: *very – happy, extremely – big*

So much, then, for the internal structure of categories. We should now consider their distribution within sentences. The general principle here is that different instances of the same category, whatever their internal structure, should be mutually substitutable in the same environments. This can be illustrated by considering the distribution of some of the NP types outlined above. NPs like *the cat*; *John*; *the girl with pigtails* etc. are substitutable in a wide variety of environments, as, for example, those shown in Figure 4:2.

$S^{(\underline{\quad} \text{ V PP})}$ $\left\{\begin{array}{l}\text{the cat} \\ \text{John} \\ \text{the girl with pigtails}\end{array}\right\}$ sat on the mat

$S^{(\text{NP V} \underline{\quad})}$ Mary stroked $\left\{\begin{array}{l}\text{the cat} \\ \text{John} \\ \text{the girl with pigtails}\end{array}\right\}$

$PP^{(\text{Prep} \underline{\quad})}$ on $\left\{\begin{array}{l}\text{the cat} \\ \text{John} \\ \text{the girl with pigtails}\end{array}\right\}$

Figure 4:2

This potential for substitution is reflected in a number of other ways. One is the use of 'proforms' and '*wh*' interrogative words. Most of the major categories are associated with one or more proforms. For NPs, the proforms are the traditional pronouns: the NPs in the examples above could be substituted by *he*, *she* or *it* as appropriate. For PPs, the proform is often *there*: *The cat sat on the mat/ there*. For VPs it is usually *do* (*so*), often also associated with inversion: *John stroked the cat and so did Bill* (sc. *stroke the cat*). Each major category is also associated with particular *wh* words used for questioning the constituent as a whole, *who* or *what* for NPs, *where* for PPs and so forth:

Qu: Who (or what) sat on the mat?   Ans: John/ the cat etc.
Qu: What (or who) did the cat sit on?   Ans: The mat/John etc.
Qu: Where did the cat sit?   Ans: On the mat/under the bed etc.

Another reflection of this categorization is the fact that, in general, only like constituents can be coordinated. So at a lexical level, nouns will conjoin with nouns (*men and women*); prepositions with prepositions (*up and down*) and so on. Cross-category coordination is usually infelicitous, so a noun will not readily conjoin with a preposition, **man and up*. In the same vein, like phrasal categories will conjoin: so NPs will conjoin with NPs or VPs with VPs, but NPs and VPs will not mix: we can have *the men and the women* (NP and NP); *laughed and jumped for joy* (VP and VP); but a conjunction like **the men and jumped for joy* (NP and VP) is not possible.

These general principles are fairly widely acceptable to a variety of kinds of model, and examples of the kind we have been discussing may give us some confidence in the methodology proposed and confidence that the generalizations that it produces have some validity. It certainly seems to be the case that a structural account of these matters will take us some distance, and there is some experimental evidence to suggest that speakers do indeed have some intuitive perception of the kinds of analyses proposed.

The discussion does, however, raise a number of questions – do the procedures yield unique analyses? If they do not, is there some way of evaluating analyses? Is there a 'right' analysis? The answer to the first question is 'no', and to the others, that it depends on what kinds of generalization about language structure the analysis is designed to capture. To illustrate this, consider the constituency proposed at the sentence level. We have analysed simple sentences to have a 'bipartite' structure, NP VP, with subsequent differentiation of the VP. The principles would, however, also allow us to dispose of the VP category altogether and postulate instead a variety of different sentence types:

S: NP V PP
    NP V NP
    NP V AP

and so on. This will yield an analysis for the sentence we began with as in Figure 4:3 (which ignores structure in the NP and PP, which we will assume not to change):

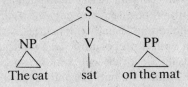

Figure 4:3

Is this analysis 'better' than the last? The question can only be answered if we know what sort of generalization we want the grammar to capture. Most analyses that concentrate on categorial rather than functional structure, as we are now doing, adopt the VP analysis since this enables the grammar to capture various distributional generalizations that will escape the tripartite analysis: that all sentences consist of an NP and something else, that VPs can be conjoined, that there is a special VP proform and so on. On the other hand an analysis that considers the verb as the central sentence level constituent, and is particularly interested in the functional relationships between the verb and the various constituents it co-occurs with, will tend to favour the tripartite analysis.

We should now consider some types of structure for which there are competing analyses. In these cases, some particular model may, for reasons internal to the model, declare certain types of structural configuration unacceptable. We will look briefly at two such cases, one involving *discontinuous* and the other *understood* constituents.

Discontinuous constituents can be illustrated by comparing *lick up* in the two sentences: *The cat licked up the milk* and *The cat licked the milk up*. Using the distributional arguments we have relied on so far, we will probably want to treat the two words of *lick up* as a syntactic constituent, particularly as it also forms a semantic unit of the sort we would expect to find in a single lexical entry. The first sentence, an analysis of which is offered in Figure 4:4, presents no particular problem.

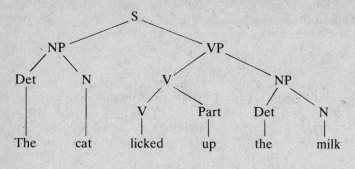

Figure 4:4

LICK UP is analysed as a verb, which itself consists of a V(erb) and a Part(icle). What now of the second sentence, where *lick . . . up* is discontinuous, its two parts separated by the object NP? If we wish the analysis still explicitly to recognize it as a constituent, then we will want a representation like that of Figure 4:5.

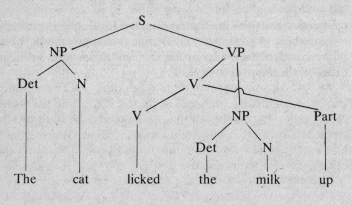

Figure 4:5

The analysis has 'crossing' branches. In some models of constituent structure such analyses are permissible, but in the model we are developing they are disallowed for reasons that will become clear in the next section. An alternative analysis which does not involve crossing branches is shown in Figure 4:6,

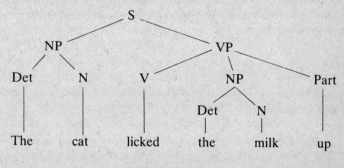

Figure 4:6

but now *lick* and *up* are not explicitly related, and if we still wish to relate them we will need to devise some additional machinery to do so.

Understood constituents were mentioned in 1.2. Here we will illustrate the problem with a different, and simpler, example. A sentence like *The cat sat on the mat and the dog sat by the fire* might be analysed as in Figure 4:7.

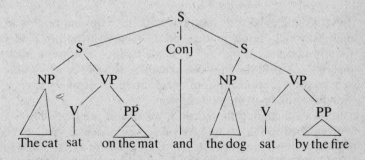

Figure 4:7

What then of the comparable *The cat sat on the mat and the dog by the fire*? Here *sat* is 'understood' as the verb of the second conjunct, and furthermore no other verb can be understood – the example could not be construed as, say, *The cat sat on the mat and the dog slept by the fire*. An analysis which makes this clear is shown in Figure 4:8.

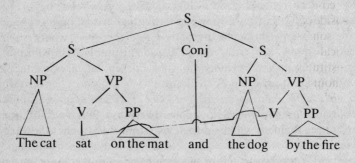

Figure 4:8

Here the single word *sat* has two 'mothers'. Once more, this an analysis which some models permit, but which our model disallows because it imposes a 'single mother' condition on all analyses. As with the previous example, we will see why this is so in the next section and consider additional machinery to cope with this problem in the next chapter.

Before concluding this section, we should briefly mention a problem associated with lexical co-occurrence. We have proposed that items like {CAT, DOG, BOY, GIRL, MAT, BONE} should all be grouped into the same category N. How reasonable is this? The answer depends on what sort of generalization it is that the categorization is designed to capture. At the level of morphological form the generalization is reasonable enough: as nouns they all have the same morphological potential in that they can occur in both the singular and plural forms. The generalization also holds good at a gross syntactic level to describe their distribution within the NP, they all co-occur with the same range of determiners etc. Furthermore in NPs they all have the same general distribution within sentences as subject, object, object of preposition etc. So as a morphological and syntactic generalization the classification is reasonable. The trouble comes when we leave a consideration of co-occurrence between lexical categories and begin to consider co-occurrence between individual lexical items. There are some environments, perhaps *I like the* ——, where such lexical items are truly mutually substitutable. But mutual substitutability is certainly not possible in all circumstances without creating semantic incongruity – *The bone gave the dog a girl*, *The mat sat on the cat* etc.! The problem is usually described as involving 'selection restrictions'. We could say, for instance, again at a fairly gross level of generality, that the verb GIVE requires, or 'selects', an animate, and normally human, 'subject' expression (the 'giver'), an animate, and again characteristically human, 'indirect object' expression (the 'recipient') and a typically inanimate 'direct object' expression (the 'gift') – so in these terms *The girl gave the dog a bone* is well formed, but *A bone gave the girl the dog* is not. The nature of the incongruity seems clear enough – the problem is how and where to account for it. In particular, is ill-formedness of this type to be considered as 'ungrammatical', and hence to be excluded by a grammatical description, or is it to be accommodated in some other way, perhaps as a semantic incongruity to be accounted for by a semantic description?

If we want to say that sentences like this are 'ungrammatical', then we will need to exclude them using the techniques of grammatical description – (sub-)categorization, co-occurrence and so on. This will mean establishing grammatical subclasses of nouns categorized as 'animate', 'inanimate' and so forth and then stating the co-occurrence restrictions of verbs using these classes. It is possible in principle to see what is at issue, but working it out in practice is another matter. We will, to begin with, need to establish separate subclasses of noun for every verb selection restriction: this will lead to a multitude of sub-, subsub-, subsubsub- etc. classes of noun. For instance the subclass of nouns that would be identified as possible subject expressions for the verb KNIT would include just those nouns used to refer to objects that can 'knit'. The problem is difficult enough if we concentrate only on 'literal' meaning, but consider the problems that arise if we want to include an account of 'metaphorical' meaning. Macbeth's *sleep that knits up the ravelled sleeve of care* would in these terms be 'ungrammatical' since undoubtedly we would not want to let a verb like KNIT select a noun such as SLEEP as its subject! But this seems an inappropriate way to handle metaphor.

The problem takes us back to the problem of the relationship between language and knowledge of the world that we addressed in 1.2. We concluded there that a grammar can hardly be expected to account for world knowledge. It also relates to our decision earlier in this section to consider lexical classes rather than individual lexical items to be the terminal nodes in the grammatical description. The solution for the grammar seems to be to say that KNIT is a verb and hence needs an NP subject, but to leave the selection of the actual noun to a total semantic description. In other words, sentences of this sort do not offend 'grammatical' propriety. The sequences of classes at both the phrasal and the lexical levels are among those stipulated as possible, and if we were to make a tree analysis of such sentences they would be well formed down to the level of lexical items. The impropriety involves the selection of particular lexical items.

This is a rather traditional solution to the problem, implying that a grammar as such is responsible for statements about the distribution of lexical items only insofar as they are members of lexical classes recognized by the grammar. The grammar is not responsible for describing the total distribution of individual members of lexical classes, since this also involves semantic considerations that are idiosyncratic to particular lexical items and no part of the grammar proper. This of course means that a competence grammar cannot account for a total description of the relations between form and meaning. An additional advantage of this approach is that new lexical items can then easily be accommodated, since all we need to know of any such item is its lexical class, other distributional properties will follow. This division of labour, or something like it, can perhaps help explain how it is we have at least a partial understanding of 'nonsense' verse like Carroll's 'Jabberwocky', and is surely involved in our understanding of metaphor.

In this section we have been looking at some of the general principles involved in sorting out the constituent structure of simple sentences. We have also looked at some potential problems – discontinuous and understood constituents. We will now go on to look at a model of grammar which can capture the kinds of generalization we have been making.

4.2 Constituent structure grammars

In the preceding section we discussed some of the general principles in terms of which constituent structure might be assigned to sentences. In this section we will consider one way of writing a grammar that will capture these generalizations. The grammar of a language can be thought of as a set of statements defining the construction or analysis of the sentences of the language. It will determine which strings of words are and which are not among the well-formed sentences of the language, and specify what are and what are not possible analyses for these sentences.

The analyses in the preceding section are immediate constituent analyses, so a grammar to account for analyses of this type will be a constituent structure grammar. There are a number of ways in which such grammars can be formalized into a set of explicit rules. The one we will choose is that first popularized by Chomsky and used with various modifications in subsequent versions of transformational grammar. It is known as a 'phrase structure grammar'.

PS grammars are generally expressed using rule statements of the following sort:

$$X \rightarrow Y Z \quad \text{e.g. NP} \rightarrow \text{Det N}$$

X, Y and Z are to be interpreted as the names of categories, NP, VP, N and so on, and the arrow, →, as 'has the constituents' or 'can be expanded as'. So the rule above will have the reading – 'a member of the category X has as constituents a member of the category Y followed by a member of the category Z'. In the example, a N(oun) P(hrase) has the constituents a Det(erminer) followed by a N(oun). Rules of this sort are well suited to describe the kind of tree diagrams discussed in the preceding section, since they define configurations of the kind shown in Figure 4:9,

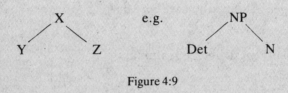

Figure 4:9

which is precisely the kind of structure we have been discussing. A number of restrictions are placed on phrase structure rules in order to ensure that there is no possible confusion in constructing analyses. Some of these will reflect the constraints on possible analyses we mentioned in the previous section. A single rule must expand only a single category. The left-hand side of a rule will thus contain only a single category symbol. The right-hand side of the rule will, of course, contain as many constituents as the analysis requires. A second restriction is that items introduced on the right-hand side of the rule are considered to be ordered; in our example an NP consists of a determiner and a noun in that order. A third restriction is that no rule should change the categorial status of a constituent, nor any sequence of rules lead to such a change: we want to exclude a rule that seeks to change, say, an NP into a VP or a noun into a verb. Derivational rules in the lexicon will handle changes of the latter kind. A final restriction is that rules of this kind should not lead to deletions – if these were permitted then we should find analyses with 'dangling' and uninterpretable categories. The rationale for these restrictions is that they should make the process of assigning analyses to sentences clear and explicit.

It will be clear that if we accept these restrictions on rule types, then the resultant grammar cannot possibly construct analyses that involve crossing branches or that violate the single mother condition: it was in anticipation of this that we disallowed such configurations in 4.1.

Let us now apply this formalism to a partial description of English. In the last section we supposed that the basic structure of all English sentences consists of an NP followed by a VP. This can be captured by the rule:

(1)   S → NP VP

to be understood as 'A S(entence) is 'to be expanded as' or 'has the constituents' an NP followed by a VP'. We now need rules to expand the categories introduced by this rule. A set of rules for the VP which will account for the VP types introduced in the last section will be:

(2a)   VP → V NP PP   (*put – the cat – on the carpet*)
(2b)   VP → V NP NP   (*gave – the cat – a piece of fish*)
(2c)   VP → V PP   (*sat – on the mat*)
(2d)   VP → V NP   (*killed – a mouse*)
(2e)   VP → V AP   (*seemed – clever*)
(2f)   VP → V   (*died*)

These rules can be condensed by the kind of abbreviations we introduced in Chapter 3. Alternative choices will be in curly brackets:

$$VP \rightarrow V\ NP \begin{Bmatrix} PP \\ \\ NP \end{Bmatrix}$$

combines 2a and 2b. Optional items will be in round brackets:

VP → V (NP) (PP)

combines 2a, 2c, 2d and 2f. Using these conventions together we get:

$$(2) \quad VP \rightarrow V \left(\left\{ \begin{matrix} AP \\ (NP) \left\{ \begin{matrix} NP \\ PP \end{matrix} \right\} \end{matrix} \right\} \right)$$

The reader is invited to check that the rule will in fact introduce the set of VPs it claims to! Using the same conventions, the rule:

$$(3) \quad NP \rightarrow \left\{ \begin{matrix} PN \\ (Det)(AP) N (PP) \end{matrix} \right\} \quad \begin{matrix} \text{e.g. } \textit{Felix} \\ \\ (\textit{the}) (\textit{big}) \textit{cat} (\textit{with} \\ \textit{ginger fur}) \end{matrix}$$

will account for the NP types from the last section. PP and AP constructions can be introduced by the rules:

(4)   PP → Prep NP   e.g. *with – ginger fur*
(5)   AP → (Int) Adj   *very – ginger*

These rules will develope structure down to lexical category nodes, N, V and so on, which we are treating as the terminal nodes of the grammar because we have agreed to ignore the internal structure of words. They are terminal nodes because the grammar itself contains no rules which expand them.

We now need to introduce lexical items. For this we will assume a lexicon with entries like this:

CAT, N	IN, Prep	THE, Det	EAT, V, — NP
MAT, N	ON, Prep	A, Det	READ, V, — NP
BOY, N	BIG, Adj	VERY, Int	GIVE, V, — NP NP
FISH, N	SMALL, Adj	SIT, V, — PP	PUT, V, — NP PP
TABLE, N	BOOK, N	LIE, V, — PP	DIE, V, — #

In the entries N, V etc. indicate noun, verb etc. A 'selection frame' like — NP shows that EAT can only occur in a VP which has been developed into these categories. The entry for DIE, — # shows that this 'intransitive' verb is not followed by an object NP. If a verb can be inserted into more than one such environment, then its lexical entry will obviously need to contain a selection frame for each environment. In a fuller lexicon we would also need selection frames for nouns and adjectives, but we will ignore these here. We now need a rule to insert lexical items:

(6) Attach a lexical item to each lexical category node on condition that the categorization of the lexical item matches the category of the lexical node concerned, and that the environment specified in the lexical entry matches that in the tree.

Given this rule, we can lexicalize the trees of Figures 4:10a and 4:10b to produce the strings relating to the sentences recorded below each tree, all of which have the same immediate constituent analysis.

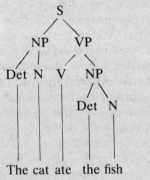

The cat ate the fish

The boy read a book

Figure 4:10a

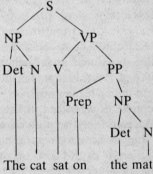

The cat sat on the mat

The dog lay under the table

Figure 4:10b

At the beginning of this section we said that grammars are

statements of how words can be put together to form sentences. They are thus, in principle, neutral as between the creation or 'generation' of sentences and their analysis or 'parsing'. We should be able to use the grammar as the basis of a 'parser', a device which will decide of some particular string of words whether it is or is not a sentence of the language, and if it is a sentence what its analysis is. Equally we should be able to use the grammar as the basis of a sentence generator which will construct sentences together with their structural descriptions. In either case the grammar will need to be interpreted by an additional set of rules which will actually do the parsing or generating. This would be the case if, for instance, we wanted to use the grammar as the basis for a computer parser or a sentence generator. This 'neutral' approach to the rules may remind the reader of a similarly neutral approach to the word analysis/generation rules of 3.1.

Yet another way of looking at such rules is to regard them as a set of 'well-formedness conditions' on possible trees. Under this view the grammar can be called upon to determine of any given analysis whether it is or is not well formed in terms of that grammar. So, for example, if the grammar we have been developing were presented with an analysis with crossing branches or a tripartite analysis of the sentence, then it would declare it to be ill formed. As we noted in the last section, this does not mean that such analyses are in any absolute sense 'wrong', merely that they do not conform to this grammar. The notion of a right analysis is relative to a particular grammar and relates, as we noted in the previous section, to what kinds of generalization the grammar seeks to capture.

Let us now look at some of the properties of the analyses grammars of this sort assign. An important property is that all the analyses generated by the grammar will be hierarchical in nature. This implicitly embodies the claim that the structure of language is necessarily hierarchical. Another property is that they offer appropriate alternative analyses for a common class of ambiguous sentences. Indeed, since grammars of this kind cannot help but generate alternative analyses for particular sorts of sentence, this implicitly embodies the claim that certain types of linguistic structures are necessarily ambiguous, and hence that structural ambiguity is a necessary feature of language. To illustrate this point consider the following set of phrase structure rules:

(1)   S→NP VP
(2)   VP→V NP (AdvP)
(3)   AdvP→ $\begin{cases} \text{PP} \\ \text{Adv} \end{cases}$

(The VP rule accepts the possibility of an optional 'adverbial modifier' in the form of either a prepositional phrase or an adverb: for example, *He stirred the jam – with a spoon/ slowly.*)

(4)   NP → (Det) N (PP)
(5)   PP → Prep NP

(This will generate NPs with PP modifiers like *the – man – in the moon.*)

   Between them these rules will generate sentences like the following (only partial analyses are shown):

$$_S(_{NP}(\text{he})_{VP}(_V(\text{stirred})_{NP}(\text{the jam})_{AdvP/PP}(\text{with a spoon})))$$

where the PP is an adverbial modifier deriving from rule 2, and

$$_S(_{NP}(\text{he})_{VP}(_V(\text{likes}))_{NP}(\text{the – man – in the moon}))$$

where the PP is a constituent of the NP deriving from rule 4. Given that the two analyses are well formed, as they are, it will be clear that the grammar will inevitably generate an enormous number of strings to which either analysis might be assigned, in other words they are ambiguous. For example, the sentence *He saw the man with a telescope* will be assigned two analyses along the lines of the two patterns above:

$$_S(_{NP}(\text{he})_{VP}(_V(\text{saw})_{NP}(\text{the man})_{AdvP/PP}(\text{with a telescope})))$$

which has the adverbial reading, paraphrasable as *He used a telescope to see the man*, and

$$S(_{NP}(he)_{VP}(_{V}(saw)_{NP}(the-man-with a telescope)))$$

which has the NP modifier reading paraphrasable as *He saw the man who had a telescope*.

That two analyses are indeed involved can be demonstrated by showing that the sentences answer different questions. *Who did he see?* is addressed to the NP object of *see* and would be appropriately answered by *The man* for the first analysis of the sentence, and by *The man with the telescope* for the second. By contrast the question *How did he see the man?*, which is addressed to the adverb, is appropriately answered by *With a telescope* if it is addressed to the first analysis, but is unanswerable if addressed to the second, which has no adverb.

This leads to an interesting question. If *He saw the man with a telescope* has two analyses, do the other example sentences also have two analyses, and if not why not? The answer must surely be that if we simply look at the syntactic categories involved, the sentences will indeed have to be given two analyses, however vanishingly improbable on semantic grounds the 'other' analysis might be. For example, although it is perhaps unlikely that anyone would interpret *He shot the rabbit with an arrow* as 'He shot the rabbit who was holding an arrow', the analysis is perfectly possible structurally, and the sentence could doubtless be contextualized, perhaps in a fairy story of some kind! We will need then to suppose, as in the matter of 'selection restrictions' discussed in 4.1, that this will be resolved by a semantic interpretation which will rule out the incomprehensible analysis. In this area, as in others, a competence grammar cannot be the sole determiner of the relation between meaning and form.

Another consequence of formulating the rules as we have done is that they naturally lead to the embedding of one structure within another. This can be illustrated by an NP like:

The book on the table by the window

The intended interpretation can be paraphrased by: *the book which is on the table which is by the window*, which implies an analysis:

$$\text{NP}^{\text{(the book}}{}_{\text{PP}}\text{(on}{}_{\text{NP}}\text{(the table(}{}_{\text{PP}}\text{(by}{}_{\text{NP}}\text{(the window))))))}$$

The NP *the window* is embedded in the PP *by the window* which is in turn embedded in the superordinate NP *the table by the window* and so on. The rules:

NP → Det N PP
PP → Prep NP

cannot help but generate such embedded structures if the first rule is permitted to reapply as it must to the output of the second:

NP
Det N PP (by the NP rule)
Det N Prep NP (PP expanded by PP rule)
Det N Prep Det N PP (NP expanded by NP rule)
Det N Prep Det N Prep NP (PP expanded by PP rule)

and so on. Rules which have this property are known as *recursive* rules. One complete pass through the rules, in this case one application of the NP rule followed by one application of the PP rule, is one complete 'cycle' of the rules. Recursive rules will permit repeated cycling, and repeated cycling through even a pair of rules like the ones we have here can produce long and complex NPs. The reader will recall the discussion in 2.2 about the embedding of relative clauses in *the dog that chased the rat that ate the malt . . .* Recursion permits a grammar with a finite number of rules to generate an infinite number of strings.

Constituent structure grammars of the type described seem to offer a simple and elegant way of capturing the sorts of generalization we want to make about the basic structure of individual sentences. We must however raise the question of whether a phrase structure grammar of this type is capable of describing the full variety of syntactic structures found in a language and of capturing all the generalizations we want to make about them. There are a number of interrelated questions here, two of which we will consider in this chapter. One concerns the formal properties of grammars of this kind (are there structures which rules of this kind literally cannot generate?), the other concerns the types of generalizations we want the rules to capture (do the rules prohibit us from making certain kinds of desirable generalization?). There are other questions that can be raised about the adequacy of constituent structure grammars of this kind, but we will leave them until Chapter 6.

We can relate these issues to the question of understood and discontinuous constituents raised in the previous section. Consider first discontinuous constituents of the kind exemplified by LICK UP in *The cat licked the milk up*. A phrase structure grammar with the restrictions we have placed on it is inherently unable to relate *lick* and *up* in this sentence, and indeed all discontinuities are a problem for the rules as formulated. A particularly serious problem of the same kind involves features of agreement like that between subject and object in English: *the book is* . . . and *the books are* . . . This has not emerged as a problem in this section because we have deliberately avoided it by ignoring the internal structure of words. The problem is this: if we have an item and arrangement morphology, as is usually the case in grammars of this kind, and if we wish to use phrase structure rules to account for the distribution of morphemes, then there are considerable difficulties in ensuring that the appropriate morphemes co-occur. In our brief discussion of agreement in 3.2 we assumed that this would be handled by copying morphemes from one node to another. But this solution to the problem is not available to a phrase structure grammar of the kind we have been looking at because the rule involved does not conform to any permissible rule type. A phrase structure grammar which accommodates an item and arrangement morphology will need to generate all morphemes 'in place', and then truly ghastly problems arise of ensuring that a morpheme in one part of the sentence is replicated by an identical morpheme in another. The grammar gets very complicated indeed. More damaging still, if the grammar permits infinite recursion in the NP, as we have suggested for examples like *the book on the table by the window* . . ., then subject and verb may be infinitely far apart. But if this is the case then a grammar of this kind will be literally unable to handle this feature in a finite set of rules.

The problem with understood constituents involves, as we have seen, the identity of the understood item, and this, as we have also seen, is quite intractable within a grammar of this sort. There is also another problem: what is the category of the constituent which dominates the understood item? In our original example, *The cat sat on the mat and the dog on the rug*, the constituent structure of the conjunct *the dog on the rug* is presumably {NP PP}. But what sort of constituent is this? If it is a 'sentence', then it is a funny sort of sentence with a funny sort of distribution: it cannot stand independently and it can only be a conjunct in this particular kind of construction. If, on the other hand, it is not a sentence, what is it? This is an important question since we have supposed that only constituents of the same category can be coordinated.

Yet another, more general, question involves the relatedness of constructions and where this is to be captured, if it is. Consider the pair of sentences

1.   The cat has scratched the dog
2.   Has the cat scratched the dog?

A phrase structure grammar of the type we have developed will generate the two sentences as quite distinct sentence types. It cannot explicitly relate them within the grammar. Nor is the interrogative, 2, the only kind of sentence we may want to relate to the declarative 1. There are others like

3.   The dog has been scratched by the cat
4.   The cat hasn't been scratched by the dog
5.   It is the cat that has been scratched by the dog
6.   What the cat has done to the dog is scratch it

and so on. A phrase structure grammar will generate all these sentence types independently, and cannot relate them in the grammar. The fact that large numbers of rules are involved is not in itself a problem, unless economy of description is an important consideration and except insofar as it makes writing grammars more difficult. The important thing is that if we want to relate sentences explicitly in the grammar, a phrase structure grammar of this kind cannot do it.

The reader will doubtless think that many of the difficulties mentioned are a direct consequence of the way we have chosen to formulate the rules and the restrictions we have placed on them. He is of course quite right, and in the discussion we have been careful to make the qualification that the problems are problems of the grammar as formulated. A description will clearly have to be more complicated. The question then will be, where shall we locate the additional complication? One way is to have a different and more elaborate theory of phrase structure grammar, and we will see the implications of this in Chapter 6. Another way is to adopt a different perspective on syntactic structure, considering functional rather than categorial structure to be primary. We will look at this approach in Chapter 7. Yet another way is to keep the phrase structure rules relatively simple and augment them with an additional set of rules which will deal precisely with the kinds of problem raised. This is the path followed by transformational grammars, and in the next chapter we will see how this is done.

5 Relations between Sentences

Were it not for the idea of transformation, structures would lose all explanatory import, since they would collapse into static forms.

(Jean Piaget)

In this chapter we will be concerned with the general question of how sentences are structurally and semantically related to each other and with some of the problems of discontinuity and understood constituents that were raised in the preceding chapter.

There are many aspects to the question of sentence relatedness. One concerns our perception that an 'active, declarative' sentence like *The cat has killed the mouse* is related both structurally and semantically to the 'passive, declarative' *The mouse has been killed by the cat*, to the 'active, interrogative' *Has the cat killed the mouse?* and so on. Another concerns the perception that there is a comparable systematic relationship between these independent simple sentences and various embedded structures like *I know that the cat has killed the mouse* and *I wonder whether the cat has killed the mouse*. The embedded structures *that the cat has killed the mouse* and *whether the cat has killed the mouse* seem to be related to the independent sentence *The cat has killed the mouse*, yet they are clearly not themselves capable of standing independently and can only serve as the 'complements' of verbs like KNOW and WONDER.

While these relationships may be widely recognized, there is little agreement on how to handle them in a description, and different models account for the 'same' phenomena in different ways. In this chapter we will explore the descriptive problems involved through an informal version of a 'transformational' grammar. In 5.1 we will look at relationships between simple sentences, and consider discontinuities and understood constituents. In 5.2 we will take a look at some embedded structures beginning with some straightforward examples and then concentrate on some of the analytical problems raised by interrogative sentences. This structure is chosen partly because it raises interesting problems in its own right, and partly because we can use it to illustrate how and why models of transformational grammar have changed from the standard theory of the mid 1960s and early 1970s to the models in vogue today. Finally, in 5.3 we will consider the general architecture of 'standard theory' transformational grammars and why they have stimulated so much interest.

5.1 Syntactic transformations

We have already observed that the sentence:

1. The cat killed the mouse
      (affir(mative); act(ive); declar(ative))

is an 'affirmative, active, declarative' sentence. Each of these descriptors is established by comparing the sentence to others to which it is perceived to be related, and each of them can be associated with particular syntactic and semantic characteristics. The paired descriptors, affirmative:negative, active:passive, declarative:interrogative, can be varied one by one to produce related sentences:

2. The mouse has been killed by the cat
      (affir; pass(ive); declar)
3. The cat hasn't killed the mouse
      (neg(ative); act; declar)
4. Has the cat killed the mouse?
      (affir; act; interrog(ative))
5. Which cat has killed the mouse?
      (affir; act; wh interrog)

    6.   Which mouse has the cat killed?
         (affir; act; wh interrog)

The differences can also be compounded, as in:

    7.   Which mouse has been killed by the cat?
         (affir; pass; wh interrog)

The reader is left to explore other combinations for himself.

As totalities, it is clear that the sentences do not 'mean the same thing': 1, for example, might be used to report an event, 3 to deny it, 4 to question it, and so forth. These semantic characterizations are implicit in the descriptors, assuming, for the sake of simplicity, a direct relationship between 'declarative' and 'making statements', 'interrogative' and 'asking questions' and so on. We will return to question the directness of this relationship in Chapter 8. While the sentences do not as totalities have the 'same' meaning, they are clearly semantically related, in that 'who is doing what and to whom' remains constant from sentence to sentence. This is reflected in the fact that the lexical items and some of their grammatical functions remain constant, even though their relative order may change from sentence to sentence. In the first sentence the 'agent', *the cat*, precedes the 'patient', *the mouse*. In the second sentence the physical order of the two NPs is reversed but *the cat* is still 'agent' and *the mouse* remains 'patient'.

To capture this semantic relatedness we will use a simplified form of logical notation, of a sort that has recently become quite widely used by transformational grammarians. Two things need, however, to be said about such representations. The first is that in the early days of transformational grammar, although a good deal was said about semantic representations, very little actually appeared in print which showed what they might look like: the kind of representation used here therefore somewhat anticipates matters. The second point is that it should be realized that a representation of this kind is of a strictly limited nature: it is indeed usually referred to as a representation of 'logical form'. A 'full, rich' semantic interpretation would, of course, also include information about many other features of meaning including those derived from 'performance'. Models of the kind we are now considering, however, exclude such considerations, as we have already noted.

Given these reservations, we can say that the sentences all express the same basic 'proposition' which we will represent as:

KILL(CAT, MOUSE)

Following the traditional supposition that active and passive sentences express the same 'proposition', and differ only in 'emphasis', which the representation does not attempt to reflect, the formula will represent the meaning of both 1 and 2. Sentence 3 will receive the representation:

NOT (P)
|
KILL(CAT, MOUSE)

Negation is interpreted as an 'operator' on a proposition, 'P', which is the same as that of the corresponding affirmative. This again corresponds to a traditional view of the matter, and note the rather pompous paraphrase *It is not the case that . . .* which follows this representation rather exactly. We will represent the 'interrogative', 4, as:

QU (P)
|
KILL(CAT, MOUSE)

where 'QU' is regarded as another operator, on a par with negation – and note again the pompous paraphrase *Is it the case that . . . ?* Finally we will represent *wh* questions with two operators:

wh CAT QU (P)
|
KILL(CAT, MOUSE)

For a variety of reasons this last is not an entirely happy representation, but it will serve our immediate purposes. Note the paraphrase *Of which cat is it the case that . . . ?* These representations are intended to capture the intuition that 'who is doing what and to whom' remains constant by assuming that the semantic representation of each sentence expresses the same 'basic' proposition – KILL(CAT, MOUSE). Any differences in meaning will then be attributable to the way this basic proposition is embedded under one or more of the operators – NOT, QU and *wh* N. We will return in due course to see how these representations can be associated with particular sentences.

Let us now turn to the structural relatedness of the sentences. As we remarked at the beginning of the chapter, we will look at this in transformational terms, and suppose that the structure underlying the active affirmative declarative sentence, *The cat has killed the mouse*, realizes the most 'basic' structure from both a semantic and a syntactic point of view. We will refer to such basic structures as the 'deep' or 'underlying' structure. This structure will be the base from which the active declarative sentence can be derived using only the most basic transformations (like 'number agreement' between subject and main verb, which will not concern us here) and from which the other structures will be derived by various syntactic manipulations. The general philosophy of this approach is rather traditional, and will be familiar to many readers through a favourite exercise in some foreign-language teaching materials: 'turn the following into the corresponding negative/passive/ question sentences'. Manipulations of this kind are 'transformations'.

We will need a set of rules to define this basic underlying structure, and these can be formulated as a phrase structure grammar of the kind described in the previous chapter. For our example sentence we will assume that these rules will define the structure shown in the relevant detail in Figure 5:1. One or two additional details should be noted immediately. In the structure underlying the interrogative sentences the rules will generate the relevant *wh* NP 'in place'. This means that the base structure underlying 6 will be of the form *the cat has killed which mouse*, and of 5 *which cat has killed the mouse*. The *wh* NP will then be moved to the front of its sentence by transformation. This analysis implies that we will treat *which* as a 'determiner', in this case an 'interrogative determiner', exactly parallel to the 'definite determiner' *the*. This is a justifiable analysis since there are circumstances where a sentence like *The cat has killed which mouse* do indeed occur. Appropriate further modification to the PS rules, which will not concern us here, would enable us to account for the interrogative words *who*, *what* and so on.

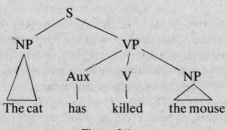

Figure 5:1

A transformational grammar treats the question of sentence relatedness as primarily a matter of syntax, so we will now need a set of syntactic transformations to derive the other sentences from the basic structure of Figure 5:1. These rules will be formulated entirely in structural terms and in a more formal account would be formulated in two parts, a 'structural index' which identifies the class of structures to which the rule applies and a statement of 'structural change' which specifies how the structure is to be modified. The permissible structural changes will involve the movement or deletion of constituents already in the structure or the addition of additional constituents. Our rules will be presented in a more informal fashion, and readers interested in a more formal presentation are directed in the notes to the expository literature. A derivation in these terms will express syntactic relationships very directly, since all the sentences will be derived from a single underlying structure by the operation of the various transformations:

Passive: Given a structure of the form NP – Aux(iliary) – V – NP, move the object NP to the front of the sentence so that it becomes the subject; take the former subject, adjoin *by* to form a PP and move this to the end of the sentence; add the 'passive auxiliary', an appropriate form of BE, to the verb group so that it immediately precedes the main verb, which must now itself appear in the 'passive participle' form.

> e.g. *John is kissing Mary : Mary is being kissed by John*
> *John kissed Mary : Mary was kissed by John*

Negative: Given a structure with one or more auxiliary verbs, affix *-n't* to the first auxiliary. If there is no auxiliary verb insert an appropriate form of the 'supportive' auxiliary DO and affix *-n't* to it.

> e.g. *John is kissing Mary : John isn't kissing Mary*
> *John kissed Mary : John didn't kiss Mary*

Subj(ect) Aux(iliary) inversion (interrogative): Invert the first auxiliary and the subject NP. If there is no auxiliary, supply an appropriate form of DO and invert it and the subject NP.

> e.g. *John is kissing Mary : Is John kissing Mary?*
> *John kissed Mary : Did John kiss Mary?*

wh movement: Move an NP containing a *wh* word to the front of its sentence.

> e.g. *John is kissing which girl : Which girl is John kissing?*

Three brief comments are in order. First, as formulated, all the rules are 'optional' in the sense that all, none, or any subset of the rules may apply: this must be so or we would always generate 'passive, negative, *wh* interrogative' sentences, which would be absurd. In a larger set of rules, which we will not examine, some rules would be optional and others obligatory.

Secondly, as formulated, the rules are exceptionless. In fact there are usually exceptions to particular rules. With these rules, a straightforward example is the passive transformation, since there are some verbs which do not occur in passive sentences: *John resembles Mary*: **Mary is resembled by John*: *This cake weighs ten pounds*: **Ten pounds are weighed by this cake*. In cases of this sort, since there are only a small number of individual verbs that behave like this, the restriction can be considered to be 'lexical', and a verb that will not go through the passive transformation will be marked for this idiosyncrasy in its lexical entry. The lexical entry for RESEMBLE, for instance, could be annotated with a 'feature' [− passive], and transformational rules will need to be sensitive to such features.

Thirdly, the rules, as formulated, need to be applied in the order given. We can illustrate this by looking at the interaction between passive and negative. If the rules were applied in the order negative passive we can generate ungrammatical sentences: applying negative to *John kissed Mary* we get *John didn't kiss Mary* (since there is no auxiliary verb to attach *-n't* to, an appropriate form of DO is supplied) and applying passive to this we get **Mary didn't was kissed by John*.

In order to connect the syntactic structures to the semantic representations we offered earlier in the section, we will once again call on lexical representations. Let us suppose that verbs have lexical entries like

    KILL V,——NP
          NP1(agent)——NP2(patient)
          'KILL' (NP1 NP2)

The first line specifies KILL as a transitive verb, a notation we met in the last chapter. The second line shows the functional relations that the subject and object NPs bear to the verb: relationships of this kind will be discussed in Chapter 7, and this notation will need to be taken on trust for the moment. The last line specifies the 'logical' representation we are interested in here; 'KILL' represents the meaning of KILL, and the representation of the arguments of KILL shows that they are to be understood as being ordered. NP1, the 'logical' subject, precedes NP2, the 'logical' object: the identity of these NPs being derived from the second line. Given access to such an entry, it will be possible for the semantic component to derive the semantic representation we require for the basic sentence. For the time being we will suppose that semantic representations for the derived sentences can then be constructed by noting what transformations, if any, have applied to the basic structure and modifying the semantic representation with the appropriate operator. Passive will have no effect, since we have determined that passive sentences have the same logical representation as their semantic counterparts. If negative or interrogative apply we will embed the basic representation under the appropriate operator. If the basic representation contains a *wh* word we will also extract this as an operator.

The discussion has assumed a particular way of relating the sentences. This takes the 'active declarative' as basic to both the syntactic derivation and to the semantic representation. The discussion has also assumed that sentence relatedness is to be handled primarily in syntactic terms by the use of syntactic transformations. Syntactic relatedness stems from the fact that the different sentence types all derive from the same underlying structure to which various transformations apply. Semantic relatedness derives from the fact that all the sentences relate to a common proposition which is modified by various operators. It is, of course, no accident that the operators correspond to the transformations, a fact also recognized in the traditional descriptors we started with. 'Negative', 'interrogative' and so forth face two ways, they are either the names of sentence types or they describe their semantic characteristics. These semantic and structural descriptions may also go some way towards accounting for our intuition that active declarative sentences are in some sense the simplest and most basic type of sentence. In terms of the description we have been developing they are indeed both syntactically and semantically the least complex structures.

We will now turn briefly to the topic of 'discontinuous' and 'understood' constituents. A transformational approach will cope with the problems of discontinuity by generating the relevant constituents as a unit in underlying structure and then separating them by transformation. The example we looked at in 4.1 involved the two sentences

1. The cat licked up the milk
2. The cat licked the milk up

If we consider 1 as representing the underlying structure we can propose a rule of 'particle movement' which will hop the particle *up* over the NP object. An advantage even flows from this treatment. The rule can be considered as 'optional' when the NP object contains a lexical noun as in the examples. When the NP object is a pronoun, however, the rule must be considered 'obligatory'. This will ensure that we derive the required:

3. The cat licked it up

but block the unwanted:

4. *The cat licked up it

The rule not only gets the data 'right', but also captures a variety of generalizations: that the sentences are paraphrases, that *lick up* is, at some level, a unitary constituent and that *up* may, in certain circumstances, be separated from *lick*.

The model copes with 'understood' constituents by assuming that the basic structure will contain a 'real' constituent which is deleted if it is identical with some other constituent in the sentence. The example we used in 4.1. was *The cat sat on the mat and the dog by the fire*. If we assume that the deep structure corresponds to the sentence *The cat sat on the mat and the dog sat by the fire* and that the second mention of *sat* is deleted under identity with the first, then once again we simultaneously account for a number of features of the syntax and semantics of the sentence: we have an account of why we understand the sentence as 'missing' a constituent and where this missing constituent is understood to be situated, we have an appropriate categorization for the 'fragment' which will satisfy ·our requirement for the coordination only of like categories, and we have an account of the identity of the understood element, since the sentence can only be construed as . . . *the dog SAT by the fire*, not as . . . *the dog SNORED/SLEPT/WAS SICK etc. by the fire*.

Finally a brief mention of various morphological issues and in particular problems like 'long-distance' agreement. This can be handled by postulating a rule which copies the relevant morpheme from the controller of the agreement on to the controlled item. So if singular subjects require singular verbs and plural subjects plural verbs, we can generate a morpheme {sing} in the subject and copy it on to the verb. The grammar we have proposed can identify subject and main verb through categorial configurations: subject is the NP dominated by S (and it will not matter what further structure is developed under this NP node) and the main verb in question will be the V dominated by the VP that is dominated by the same S. Given these identifications, it will be possible to formulate a transformational rule that can cope with this kind of problem. This solution can indeed be thought of as a formalization of an old insight: that agreement involves copying the relevant category from the controller of the agreement on to the controlled.

5.2 Embedded sentences

In this section we will look at the way a transformational account of the kind that we outlined in 5.1 can be elaborated to deal with embedded sentences. The syntax of embedded sentences is often complex and the reader will not be surprised if some of this complexity is reflected in the discussion. It will, however, be helpful to make a foray into this area of syntax partly because it will offer a limited insight into the kind of complexity that a linguist is faced with in attempting to account for our linguistic abilities and partly because it will offer a taste of what an elaborated standard theory transformational grammar looks and feels like, how it approaches the task of description and what sorts of 'explanation' it may hope to offer. It will also enable us to look at some of the 'technical' problems that assail the writer of a formal grammar. These are both important considerations. Explanations are obviously important. But an appropriate solution to technical problems is also important because we want our system of rules to be able to generate the data under discussion, and, in doing so, encapsulate the kinds of explanations and generalizations about the language that we consider to be important. Sometimes the machinery developed to deal with some particular problem can be insightfully applied to another problem without substantial modification. Equally frequently, however, a new descriptive problem requires a new technical solution, and this new solution may have repercussions on other parts of the model which in the end may entail the restructuring of the model as a whole. This is an important issue, since one of the reasons why transformational grammar has been through constant change ever since its inception is precisely because the technical machinery has had to be modified and revised to deal with new descriptive and explanatory problems.

We will begin with a fairly straightforward example of sentence embedding. The sentence *John said that Harry needs a holiday* can be analysed, with some minor simplifications, as in Figure 5:2:

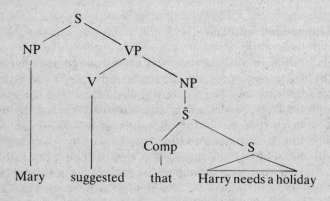

Figure 5:2

In talking about such structures it will be useful to distinguish between the 'main' or 'matrix' sentence *Mary suggested NP* and the 'subordinate' or 'constituent' sentence *that Harry needs a holiday*.

The constituent sentence is categorized as an NP because constituents of this type behave in many respects like other NPs. In the example, the constituent operates like the object of the verb SUGGEST. It can, for example, be substituted by a simple NP (*Mary suggested the answer*), both types of object can be passivized (*That Harry needs a holiday was suggested by Mary*, *The answer was suggested by Mary*) and both answer the question *What did Mary suggest?* In other sentences constituents of this might function as the subject of a sentence, as in *That Harry needs a holiday is indisputable*.

The constituent sentence is also shown as dominated by a node labelled S̄, which we will refer to as 'Sbar'. In 4.2 we noted that lexical categories like N and V are distributed in phrasal categories like NP and VP, and Sbar can be regarded as having an equivalent status with respect to S. The constituents of Sbar are, as the figure shows, Comp and S. S is the sentence node we are already familiar with. Comp is a node designed to accommodate 'comp(lementizers)' like *that* whose function is to indicate that the constituent to follow is an embedded sentence functioning as the 'complement' of SUGGEST and to indicate what kind of complement is involved: in this case a 'declarative' sentence. It should be clear that with a small modification to permit NP to be expanded as Sbar, Sbar to be expanded as {Comp S} and Comp as *that* our system of rules will be able to produce structures of the type shown in Figure 5:2. The rules will also generate recursive structures like *John said that Harry thinks that*...

In the previous paragraph we observed that in the example sentence, the embedded S is identical in form to an independent declarative sentence. This means that it must have a subject (in this case *Harry*) and that the verb (in this case *needs*) must be 'finite', or in other words it must be 'tensed' and agree in number with the subject. A wide variety of verbs occur in structures containing a *that* complementizer followed by a finite sentence. For SUGGEST we might substitute other verbs used to report assertions like SAY, CLAIM, DECLARE or REPORT, or verbs used to report 'mental attitudes' like BELIEVE, HOPE or EXPECT. Their lexical entries will need to reflect this, so the entry for SUGGEST will need to include:

> SUGGEST V, —— NP[*that* S]
> NP1(agent) —— NP2(declarative proposition)
> 'SUGGEST' (NP1 P)

The annotation '—— NP[*that* S]' is intended to indicate that the verb will co-occur with a finite declarative complement sentence, i.e. an embedded sentence with a *that* complementizer.

Given such an entry, we will be able to construct a semantic representation for our sentence along the lines:

> SAY (JOHN, P)
> |
>   NEED (HARRY, HOLIDAY)

SAY is shown with two 'arguments', the person who 'does the saying' and the proposition 'said': it will be clear that this representation follows the corresponding syntactic structure rather closely.

The sentence we have just been considering involves a reported 'assertion'. 'Questions' can also be reported. So if 'John' asks, 'Does Harry need a holiday?' this might be reported as *John asked whether Harry needs a holiday*, and we might reasonably analyse this sentence along similar lines to the last. The syntactic analysis will follow Figure 5:2 with *whether* instead of *that* as a complementizer, since if *that* is the complementizer for embedded finite declaratives, then *whether* can be regarded as the complementizer for embedded finite interrogatives. Comp, of course, will now need to be expanded as either *that* or *whether*. A lexical entry for ASK will, then, need to include:

> ASK V, —— NP[*whether* S]
> NP1(agent) —— NP2(interrogative proposition)
> 'ASK' (NP1 P)

This will then allow us to construct the semantic representation:

ASK (JOHN, P)
|
QU (NEED (HARRY, HOLIDAY))

where the embedded proposition is the same as that for the corresponding declarative except for the QU operator which marks the embedded predication as a question.

We have seen that embedded declaratives have the same syntactic structure as the corresponding independent sentences. Embedded interrogatives, however, show an important difference in comparison with their independent counterparts: the inversion characteristic of the independent sentence is not found in its embedded counterpart. Thus, corresponding to the independent interrogative *Does Harry need a holiday?*, the embedded interrogative is *John asked whether Harry needs a holiday*, with no inversion, rather than *John asked whether does Harry need a holiday*, which is not acceptable in Standard English. It seems that the inversion transformation will need to be restricted to the 'root' S and cannot be allowed to operate on constituent sentences. Here is another example of the kind of restrictions that need to be placed on the operation of transformational rules. The example we looked at before involved a 'lexical' restriction (RESEMBLE does not occur in passive constructions); this time the restriction is not driven by lexical exceptions, but applies to a whole class of structures, and it will need to be 'structurally' or 'configurationally' defined. However, in spite of this syntactic restriction we will still need to be able to identify the embedded constituent as interrogative because of the semantic interpretation, and the presence of *whether* will allow us to do this.

A further useful feature of identifying complements as we are now proposing, is that we can use *whether* or *that* in lexical entries as a way of distinguishing between those verbs that co-occur only with declarative complements, like CLAIM, those that co-occur only with interrogative complements, like ENQUIRE, and those that can co-occur with either, like KNOW.

We should now turn to embedded *wh* interrogatives like *I wondered which book John would choose*. We will suppose that this derives from a deep structure of the form shown in Figure 5:3.

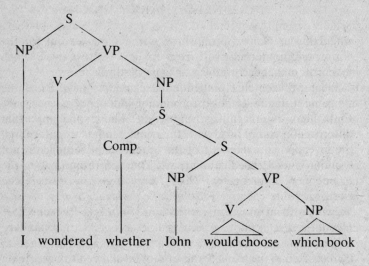

Figure 5:3

As before, the *wh* NP is generated 'in place', and it will be noted that the internal structure of the embedded S is identical to that which we would propose for the corresponding independent interrogative *Which book would John choose?*

The embedded interrogative resembles the corresponding independent sentence in some respects and differs from it in others. The main point of difference is that, as with other subordinate interrogatives, no inversion is found: **I wondered which book would John choose* being unacceptable in Standard English. The point of similarity is that the *wh* phrase is once again brought to the front of its S constituent, and it is proposed that *wh* movement has the effect of moving the *wh* word into the complement node displacing *whether*. Why should we do this? There are several arguments for this procedure, some syntactic and others semantic. The syntactic arguments are partly technical and partly descriptive. A technical argument is that movement into the Comp node will define precisely what 'moving to the front of its S constituent' means, since Comp provides a readily identifiable site for the *wh* NP to go to, a consideration that will become important in Chapter 6. A partially descriptive argument derives from the observation that sentences like **I wondered whether which book John would choose* are ungrammatical. If we suppose that when *wh* movement moves the *wh* NP into Comp it displaces *whether* (or that a later rule deletes *whether* in these circumstances, because of a general condition that comp cannot contain more than one item), then we seem to have some kind of an 'explanation' for this curious syntactic fact. Another justification is that if, as we suggested above, Comp is the site of items which indicate the function of the embedded clause, then the presence of a *wh* phrase in Comp marks what follows as an embedded interrogative.

This proposal now raises a more general question: if embedded sentences develop from an Sbar node, could we perhaps envisage a parallel analysis for simple sentences? In fact standard theory grammars do just this. They postulate that instead of the initial S we have assumed so far we should have an initial Sbar, developing into Comp and S, Comp still developing into *that* or *whether*. *That* in the comp node will lead to the development of a declarative sentence and *whether* to an interrogative. What justification can there be for such an analysis? As before, two kinds of argument can be presented, some looking to syntax and others to semantics.

The syntactic arguments have, as so often, to do with co-occurrence. There are a few items that can occur in interrogative sentences but not in declarative sentences (*Does he ever eat?* but not **He ever eats*) and vice versa (*Probably he is a doctor* but not **Probably is he a doctor?*). The item in Comp offers a useful way of controlling the insertion of words like *ever* or *probably* into sentences. The interrogative Comp has a further syntactic justification. In discussing embedded *wh* interrogative sentences we suggested that the *wh* word should move into the Comp node and displace *whether*. Suppose this were to happen to the main sentence too. An immediate advantage will be that we will then have a unified account of all *wh* movement: the *wh* word will always move into the Comp node.

A further use for *whether* in the Comp node is that it will clearly mark all structures which are eventually to become interrogative. In the superordinate Comp node, *whether* can be used, as it were, as a 'trigger' for the inversion transformation: any main sentence with *whether* in its Comp node will automatically go through the inversion transformation if it can. This modification, then, has some advantages. It will come as no surprise, however, to discover that there are compensatory complications. One of these is the fact that there are no independent sentences beginning *that* or *whether*. We could now either postulate some machinery to delete the complement from the topmost sentence after it has done its work, or perhaps take a more 'abstract' view of these postulated complementizers: we could, for example, treat them as abstract 'features', [+wh] and [−wh], say, which receive substantial form in certain circumstances (typically when they are in embedded structures), and have no phonological realization in others (in main sentences, for example).

We now come to the semantic justification. Under this new proposal, all interrogative sentences, whether main or constituent, will contain in their deep structures the complementizer *whether*. Now, since all interrogative sentences will need to receive the semantic interpretation appropriate to a question, we can use this item in the construction of the appropriate semantic interpretation: any sentence with *whether* in the deep structure Comp node will receive an appropriate interpretation as a question. The great advantage of this is that the semantic component will now no longer need to 'keep track' of whether the inversion transformation has or has not applied.

This proposal will obviously lead us to enquire whether this treatment cannot be generalized to other transformations. It seems that it can. For example, if we alter our base rule for the expansion of S to include an optional negative element,

$$S \rightarrow (neg) \, NP \, VP$$

then the presence of neg can serve both as a trigger for the negative transformation and as a guide to the semantic representation.

The importance of this development will be clear, and it leads to the pivotal position of the deep structure in relation to both surface form and semantic interpretation. The deep structure now contains all the information that will determine surface form, since it will contain elements that will trigger off transformations (which will not operate unless they are triggered). It also contains all the information necessary for a semantic interpretation, since these same elements are partly there for this purpose. The role of the transformations is now to interpret deep structures into surface structures. They will have no effect on the meaning which will be determined entirely by the deep structure. The consequences for this position, that transformations do not change meaning, are far-reaching, as we will see in the next chapter.

5.3 'Standard theory' transformational grammars

In this section we will summarize the main features of the model we have been developing thus far: a simplified and eclectic form of a 'standard theory' transformational grammar. Much of the influence of the transformational approach stems from models of this kind, or reactions to models of this kind, and they are still widely used as the basis for undergraduate syntax courses. It will therefore be sensible to have some idea of their general architecture. We can then use the model as a base from which to survey where transformational grammar has moved to today and why, and also to see why other models of description broke away from it.

The model proposes that a description should consist of three 'components' and a lexicon related as in Figure 5:4. The reader will recognize that these components correspond to the division of descriptive labour we identified in 1.2, and this is no accident. The directionality of the arrows linking the three components indicates that the syntactic component is considered to be the 'core' of the system. The lexicon is linked by dotted lines to each component to indicate that each will have its own reasons to consult it. In bare outline, structures generated by the syntactic component are sent to the semantic component for a semantic

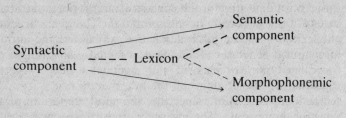

Figure 5:4

representation and to the morphophonemic component for a phonological representation. In this way the system as a whole relates forms to meanings.

A brief word is in order on each component. Since the syntactic component is the core of the system we will start there. This component will have an internal structure of the sort shown in Figure 5:5.

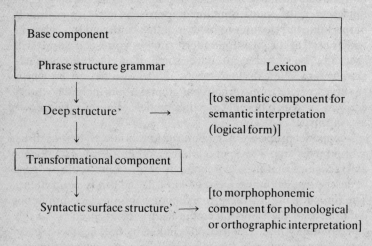

Figure 5:5

The base component aims to capture generalizations about basic constituent structure. It consists of a set of phrase structure rules of the sort that we have discussed in 5.2 and has access to the lexicon in order that lexical items can be inserted into the structures it generates. The output of the base component is a 'lexicalized phrase marker', the (syntactic) deep structure discussed in 5.1.

The deep structure is perhaps the most important single construct in the entire system since it acts as the essential bridge between the syntax and the semantics. This crucial position is reflected in the fact that it is made available to the semantic component for semantic interpretations and it is the input to the transformational component. We have seen that the nature of the deep structure is such that it contains, as it were, the seeds for the growth of a particular sentence insofar as it contains elements that the transformational component will use to determine, in coordination with the lexicon, what transformations will and what will not apply in a particular derivation. It also contains the essential ingredients for the construction of a semantic representation.

The transformational component not only accounts for surface forms, but is also the component which is primarily responsible for accounting for structural relatedness between sentences. It consists of a set of transformational rules of the kind discussed in 5.1, formulated as structural operations which can add, delete or move constituents. It, too, needs access to the lexicon to ensure that transformations are not inappropriately applied to trees containing particular lexical items (the case of RESEMBLE mentioned in 5.1 or BELIEVE in 5.2). Each rule operates on an input structure and produces a derived structure, which may itself be the input structure to a further transformation. The final derived structure after the operation of all the transformations is the syntactic surface structure. This structure is made available to the morphophonemic component for a phonological or orthographic interpretation.

The semantic component operates on the syntactic deep structure to produce a representation of certain aspects of the meaning of the sentence. In order to do this it, too, will need access to the lexicon, which it will use in the way outlined in 5.1.

Two important points should be made about these semantic representations. The first, which we have already drawn attention to, is that it should not be forgotten that the system is a 'competence' grammar and hence the semantic representation only captures some of those rather limited aspects of meaning that are held to belong to competence, characteristically cognitive meanings of the sort outlined in Chapter 1. The sorts of meanings that can be accounted for will thus be limited, but the semantic component will, in conjunction with the syntax, be able to account for certain types of ambiguity, paraphrase and partial paraphrase. The second is that, given the position adopted at the end of the last section, transformations will not affect meaning. All meaning-bearing elements will be present in the deep structure either as lexical items or as items like *whether* which will trigger transformations and be available for semantic interpretation. This is a very strong condition and we will explore some of its consequences in the next chapter. A brief comment should also be made on the form of meaning representation we have chosen. In fact in earlier versions of 'standard theory' grammars no systematic semantic representation was supplied, though the semantic representation, whatever it would look like, was certainly supposed to be interpreted from deep structures. More recently semantic representations have been provided in a modified form of predicate calculus, rather along the lines we have been using, and we will continue to show semantic representations in this way. Given a representation of this kind, the semantic component will be able to perform further operations on the representations, including particularly those which involve the rules of logical inference.

The morphophonemic component will operate on the syntactic surface structure to produce a phonological or orthographic representation of the sentence. Since we discussed word formation at some length in Chapter 4 we will not discuss it again here. We should however make one comment: the morphophonemic component, like the other components, will need access to the lexicon.

Derivations along the lines proposed naturally raise a number of questions. Two of the most fundamental are: why, with three components and lexicon, is the descriptive burden carried in the syntactic component, which the diagram at the beginning of the section shows to be the 'core' to the system? And why do we choose a two-stage derivation for sentences, the first producing a 'basic' structure and the second transforming this into a surface structure?

Part of the answer to the first question lies in the historical development of the model. It grew out of a formalization of the constituent structure grammars proposed by the 'structural' linguists of the 1940s and 1950s: cf. Lyons (1977a). For them, grammars were descriptions of the formal distribution of linguistic items, and semantics was excluded on principle. Chomsky's *Syntactic Structures* (1957), the first widely available transformational grammar, followed in this tradition, although it does contain a final chapter envisaging a link between syntax and semantics. As the transformational model developed towards the standard theory there was a growing interest in integrating semantics into the description, most notably in Katz and Postal's *Integrated Theory of Linguistic Descriptions* (1964). Although the principle of an integrated description was accepted within the transformational school by the time of Chomsky's *Aspects of the Theory of Syntax* (1965), the basis of the standard theory, there was no general agreement on what form a semantic representation should take or just what work it should do, and indeed this very issue was the cause of much acrimonious debate. It is perhaps for these reasons that the burden of the description falls on the syntax. In Chapter 6 we shall see that recent developments have, for a variety of reasons, redistributed the descriptive burden, enriching the power of the phrase structure component or the semantic component or the lexicon or all three at the expense of the syntax.

Our second question was, why should we choose to derive sentences by a 'two-stage' procedure, the first producing a 'basic structure' and the second transforming this structure into a surface structure? The declared aim of the description is to relate forms to meanings, and consequently there are two prongs to arguments for such a procedure, one relating to questions of syntactic structure *per se*, to the distribution of linguistic items in structural configurations, and the other to questions of semantic interpretations. In this model both turn on the notion that the structure underlying the active declarative structure is in some sense basic. We will examine each in turn.

Semantic arguments tend to cluster round questions of paraphrase, ambiguity, the identity of understood elements and so on. If transformations do not change meanings then if a set of surface sentences can be derived from a single deep structure, they must be paraphrases, and the fact of a single deep structure seems to account for this. The converse holds for ambiguity since here transformations operating on two or more distinct deep structures will obliterate the distinctions between them to yield a single surface structure. As to understood elements, if these are specified in deep structure and subsequently deleted, their identity is available at the deep structure level from which semantic interpretations are constructed.

Syntactic arguments are based on the notion that language is structured, and that a linguistic description should seek to capture the most illuminating generalizations about these structures. The PS rules capture basic generalizations about co-occurrence formulated in structural terms, and define certain basic structural relations like subject and object – a matter to which we will return in Chapter 7. The transformations are formulated as structural operations, designed to encapsulate generalizations about structural relatedness. Arguments then tend to cluster around such questions as the alleged inadequacy of phrase structure grammars, the desirability of capturing important structural generalizations and derivational simplicity.

Arguments about the capturing of generalizations intertwine with those about derivational simplicity. Consider again the six sentences we looked at in 5.1.

1. The cat has killed the mouse (affir; act; declar)
2. The mouse has been killed by the cat (affir; pass; declar)
3. The cat hasn't killed the mouse (neg; act; declar)
4. Has the cat killed the mouse? (affir; act; interrog)
5. Which cat has killed the mouse? (affir; act; wh(subject) interrog)
6. Which mouse has the cat killed? (affir; act; wh(object) interrog)

Sentences 2, 3 and 4 are each derived from 1 by changing one feature of the description. Thus the 'affirmative, active, declarative' 1 is changed to an 'affirmative, passive, declarative' in 2, to a 'negative, active, declarative' in 3 and so on. These changes can obviously be compounded, and our rules have taken this into account. We will, for example, wish to derive a 'negative, passive, interrogative' as in *Hasn't the mouse been killed by the cat?* In principle it is perfectly possible to do this by a single complex rule, which the reader is invited to try and formulate, but to do so would miss some of the generalizations of the step-by-step approach we have adopted, and it would also lead to a very large number of individual rules, one for each possible combination of the features recognized in our original description. Our description has the further virtue that all sentences of a given type, *wh* interrogatives for example, have gone through the *wh* movement rule. The more complex formulations would split information about this single rule up into an array of pieces; there would be no *wh* movement rule as such, but instead a variety of different rules, all of which combined parts of this rule with some other set of characteristics. It is simpler and more revealing to do the complex derivations in a series of small steps and it also involves a smaller number of simpler rules.

A further advantage flows. Each of the proposed rules applies to structures other than those illustrated. For example, the rule of subject-auxiliary inversion proposed for the derivation of interrogatives applies unmodified to various other types of sentence: *Had I known that she was coming* (compare *If I had known . . .*); *Seldom have I enjoyed a film so much* (compare *I have seldom enjoyed . . .*). Similarly the rule of *wh* movement applies to other structures containing *wh* items, even though they are not themselves interrogatives, for example relative clauses, where *wh* pronouns must be initial in their clauses, *the man who Mary married*, and certain kinds of exclamatory sentences like *What a nice man Harry is!* Subject-aux inversion and *wh* movement are then independent of each other. If we refer to these small transformations as elementary transformations, since each performs a single elementary task, then we see that the elementary transformations can be compounded in a variety of ways to produce a variety of sentence types. It gives some support to the notion that transformations capture structural generalizations if one rule captures a structural regularity which recurs from construction to construction in different combinations with other rules. In principle it would be desirable for there to be a small set of transformations each of which accomplished one single small change, and each of which could be compounded with other transformations to produce complex changes. This approach also offers another reason why the active declarative is considered to be the most basic sentence type: if we tried this procedure using any other sentence types as basic, the description would be much more complicated.

Another set of arguments for derivational simplicity concerns the nature of the constituent structure rules that would be required if we sought to generate each of the structures independently. In early writings on transformational grammar, it was generally claimed that it was literally impossible to account for the distributional facts of language by means of a phrase structure grammar: cf. Postal (1974). Given the kinds of restrictions we have hitherto placed on PS grammars this is probably true, as we noted in 4.3. Furthermore, generating all structures separately misses the very generalizations that lie at the centre of this model. Some recent work, which we will look at in the next chapter, shows that both of these claims are incorrect for phrase structure grammars more generously conceived.

Two further arguments should be mentioned, both of which relate to the question of lexical insertion. The first involves the matter of 'selection restrictions' which we raised in 4.1. Wherever these are handled it seems that the restrictions for a whole set of transformationally related sentences can be captured most economically by formulating the restrictions as they apply to the basic sentence type, and then letting these restrictions generalize to all the transformationally related sentences. For example, the selection restrictions on passive sentences seem to be the mirror image of the restrictions on the related active sentences. So, if *John planted the beans* is well formed, then so too is *The beans were planted by John*, conversely, if *These beans planted John* is deviant, then so too will be *John was planted by these beans*, as indeed will be all the other transformationally related sentences. If this is true, and it seems to be very plausible, then a single statement of selection restrictions is obviously a great economy.

The second argument concerns the categorial environments into which a lexical item can be inserted. We have considered transitive verbs like KILL to occur in the environment [− NP], yet in the surface sentence *Which mouse has the cat killed?* this environment is apparently not met, since KILL is not followed by an object NP. The transformational solution to this will suppose that the expression *which mouse* is generated 'in place' in the deep structure as the object of KILL (*The cat has killed which mouse*) and is moved to its final position by transformation. This accounts for the fact that KILL occurs in a perfectly well-formed sentence and yet has, apparently, no surface structure object.

The late 1960s and early 1970s saw a great flurry of activity using this model. It seemed to offer a powerful and insightful way not only of describing the surface forms of language but also of accounting for intuitions about many aspects of the structure of language, that some strings of words are and others are not sentences of the language, that simple active declarative sentences are in some sense 'basic' both from a structural and from a semantic point of view, that some sets of sentences are systematically related both structurally and semantically, that sentences with markedly different structures can realize the same meaning, that other sentences are clearly ambiguous and so on. The transformational view of language seemed to offer some account of all these insights in terms of the two-level description, and the choice of the terms 'deep' and 'surface' structure seemed to be particularly appealing, since a description in these terms appears to see into the heart of things! Furthermore the notion that a small set of base phrase structure rules coupled with a restricted set of transformations that can be combined in different ways to produce an enormous variety of sentence types has an intuitive appeal. It is after all rather like the notion in science that a small number of atomic particles can combine in a restricted number of ways to produce the infinite variety of the physical world. In addition, the model offered explicit claims about the nature of language and the nature of the rules necessary to generate a language, and the emphasis on the necessity of a formal and explicit description meant that it was publicly testable. Here was a traditionally arts subject that could perhaps lay claim to the rigour of the 'hard' sciences.

We can relate some of these remarks to our observations in 2.5 about the nature of models. Transformational grammar appeared to offer a powerful *descriptive* tool for the classification and manipulation of large amounts of complex data. More than this, it also proved to be a fruitful source of hypotheses about language, and hence an invaluable guide in the search for new data. It seemed also to offer a particularly insightful way of relating forms to meanings, providing one was prepared to accept the initial hypotheses about linguistic competence. At the time many people were prepared to do this, and there was a wide acceptance of Chomsky's view that an understanding of performance would follow from an understanding of competence, and was indeed logically dependent on it. It was this faith that led to the development of notions like variable rules that we mentioned in 2.3, as a possible way of relating 'grammatical' to 'communicative' competence.

Perhaps more excitingly, transformational grammar seemed to be an *explanatory* tool, offering explanations at various levels of abstraction. Within one language it seems to offer 'explanations' to some of the problems raised above: Why do active declarative sentences seem to be 'basic'? – They are the sentences that most directly reflect the deep structure. Why do some sentences with strikingly different surface structures paraphrase each other? – Because they derive from the same deep structure, the elements of which have been moved around, some may have been deleted and others added. Why are some sentences ambiguous? – Because they derive from distinct deep structures which by the operation of transformations have been collapsed together into the same surface structure. How is it that in a sentence like *I want to go*, we unambiguously interpret *I* as the semantic subject of both verbs? – Because the configuration is found in the deep structure, and the subject of the second verb is deleted during the derivation, and so on.

More exciting still, the model makes large claims to explain the very nature of language itself by offering a number of 'universalist' claims about the nature of the formal systems of language and about psychological processes that involve language.

The universal claims stem from Chomsky's hypothesis (1965: 27ff) that language can be characterized by a set of 'formal' and 'substantive' universals. The 'substantive' universals are a set of categories common to all languages, lexical categories like noun, verb, adjective and so on, and a set of grammatical categories like tense, number and gender. The claim for lexical categories is that the possible set is finite. A language might not choose the whole set, so some languages, like Japanese, might not draw a syntactic distinction between verb and adjective, or others, like Latin, may not have articles, but a language cannot 'invent' a new and unique lexical category. This in itself is an old idea, and language descriptions have always drawn on a small set of such categories, but transformational grammar opened up the prospect of a formal definition of these basic lexical categories. The same kind of claim is made for grammatical categories. All languages have ways of referring to time and this may be grammaticalized in different ways in different languages into the category of tense. Similarly, all languages have ways of referring to 'oneness' and 'more than oneness' and this may be grammaticalized as the category of number, again in different ways in different languages. If grammatical categories of this sort correspond to semantic or perceptual categories, and if these are universal, then a strong claim is being made both about the nature of perception and about the nature of language. Furthermore, in this respect languages will not, as the 'structuralist' school had claimed, vary in arbitrary ways from each other. The 'formal' universals are formal properties of grammars. All grammars will have PS rules and a set of transformations. The PS rules will have certain common properties of the kind we looked at in 4.2: lexical classes will be distributed into phrasal classes, the structures defined will be hierarchical, the rules will be recursive and so on. The transformational rules will be structure-changing rules, and there may indeed be particular types of transformation that are universal. Claims of this sort naturally lead to the possibility that at an abstract enough level perhaps there is a deep structure common to all languages.

We shall do no more than mention the psychological claims although they have been very influential and are extremely controversial. They relate to the acquisition of language by children, and to the storage and processing of language by any speaker. As far as children are concerned, it seems fairly uncontroversial to suppose that if animals are genetically programmed for various kinds of quite complex communicative behaviour, then so too are humans. Language is an immensely complex system, yet children are able to master it in a comparatively short time even though they have no formal instruction and their only apparent source of information is a random sample of the speech of adults. Perhaps, then, they have some genetic inheritance to assist them in forming their internal grammars? Just what the nature of this genetic inheritance might be is highly speculative. Chomsky's very controversial proposal is that some structural principles of universal grammar are innate. The second area we mentioned concerned the mental storage of language, and the processing and production of speech. Here transformational grammar offers the hypothesis that if the most suitable description of language involves the use of transformations, then perhaps they are the analogues of some mental capacity. Do we, perhaps, perform transformations as we speak and process language? The hypothesis is obviously extremely provocative and stimulated a good deal of psychological investigation. Whether claims of this sort can be substantiated or not, and there seems in fact to be little evidence that they can, there is no doubt that the very fact that they were advanced was important because they stimulated a great deal of research activity in the attempt either to substantiate or to disprove them. We will return to some of these matters later.

When transformational grammar of this type seems to be so insightful, so intuitively appealing and to have such interesting psychological implications, we will clearly be interested to enquire why its influence and appeal has so diminished in recent years. Many former advocates have moved away to other models and those that have remained faithful have, over the last decade, introduced radical changes. The principal shift has been away from an interest in the way particular rules are to be formulated towards an interest in the general system of principles which lie behind the rules. This has led, among other things, to the virtual abandonment of the central feature of the system we have just been discussing, the syntactic transformation. Why this should have happened will be the question we address in the next chapter.

6 The Rise and Fall of Transformations

> The number of rational hypotheses that can explain any given phenomenon is infinite.
>
> (R. M. Pirsig)

At the end of the last chapter we saw that the 'standard theory' model provoked a great flurry of research in the late 1960s and early 1970s, and the prospects opened up by this powerful new tool seemed to offer the hope that vigorous research into the syntax of English and other languages might force a particular language, and perhaps language in general, to yield up its secrets. Unfortunately for this naive optimism, the more areas of language that were subjected to investigation, the more clearly did it emerge that the problem was more complicated than might have been expected! It also became clear that the model itself was not without problems. In this chapter we will see what some of these problems are and trace some of the more recent developments of the transformational model. In particular we will see how it has come about that 'transformational' grammars have now abandoned most of the transformations that were so eagerly welcomed when the model was first introduced.

It will be recalled that the aim is to link sounds and meanings. The general structure of the standard theory model and the relationship between the various components proposed was set out in Figure 5:5. The model envisages a central syntactic core which generates syntactic structures, and two 'interpretive' components which assign semantic and phonological representations. The syntactic component comprises a set of base rules and a battery of transformations and has access to the lexicon. The 'deep structures' generated by the base rules and lexicalized from the lexicon are made available to the semantic component, which in its turn will need access to the lexicon in assigning a semantic representation. The 'syntactic surface structure', the output of the syntactic component after the operation of the transformations, is made available to the phonological component for interpretation into a phonological structure, and it too will need access to the lexicon. In this way the link is made between sounds and meanings.

The central feature of this account is that the syntax is the 'core' of this system, and the most prominent part of the syntax is the transformational component. Although the standard theory envisages a semantic component, the nature of the component is not clearly defined and so little attention is paid to the role it might have in a total description. The standard theory also envisages a lexicon, but the nature of this is not well defined either and it is, in fact, little more than a list of lexical items. This means that the bulk of the descriptive work is performed by the phrase structure component and, crucially, by the syntactic transformations.

The proposal that the syntactic component should play such a prominent role raises a number of questions. We will be particularly concerned with three. First, questions obviously arise concerning the centrality of the syntactic component and hence the 'directionality' of the relationship between it and the various other components: why should these other components be interpretive of structures that arise in the first place in the syntactic component? Second, the proposal to put the bulk of the descriptive work in the syntactic component rather than distributing it among the different components raises the question as to whether the burden could not with advantage be distributed. Third, questions arise concerning the power of the syntactic transformations which lie at the heart of the central syntactic component.

The first question, concerning the 'directionality' of the relationship between the various components, was the cause of much speculation and argument in the late 1960s. As outlined above, the syntactic component is the core and the other two components are interpretive of the structures produced in the syntax. It is clear, however, that the directionality of this relationship can be reversed. In particular, if the semantic component is taken seriously and a proper semantic model developed, then it is possible to see the syntactic component as interpretive of structures deriving in the first place from the semantics. This approach is, for obvious reasons, known by the general label of 'generative semantics' and can be contrasted with the 'interpretive semantics' approach of the standard theory model. We will look briefly at some of the insights and problems of this approach in 6.1, and see why it has now been largely abandoned.

The second question we raised concerned the 'division of labour' between the various components of description: the syntactic and semantic components and the lexicon. As we have noted, the standard theory model assumes that the main burden of description is borne in the syntax and particularly in the transformational component of the syntax. However, for a variety of reasons which we will explore in the various sections of 6.2, it is clear that this is not the only possible way to handle these matters. If the lexicon and the semantic components are given as much attention as the syntactic component itself, it soon becomes clear that many descriptive tasks can be handled in any of the three, or divided up among them. This being so, it is important to have some views on the nature of these components and the sort of work they might do. We can then decide whether there are principled reasons for handling some task in one place rather than another.

It is worth briefly exemplifying what is at issue here. Consider, therefore, the question of paraphrase. In a standard theory model much of this is dealt with by using syntactic transformations. Indeed paraphrase is a principal justification of the transformational approach. The supposition is that the syntactic base rules generate a deep structure which will receive some particular semantic interpretation, and syntactic transformations then shuffle the elements of the structure to yield a set of distinct surface structures. These are paraphrases by virtue of the fact that they derive from the same deep structure. So, in 5.2 the paraphrase relationship between active and passive surface structures is accounted for by assuming a common deep structure and proposing a passive transformation.

It is, however, a pity to restrict the notion of transformation to syntactic operations alone. If the notion were to be more liberally interpreted then it could still be seen as involving a systematic relationship between one structure and another, but the structures in question could as easily be semantic or lexical as syntactic. From this point of view, it is perfectly possible to envisage the semantics or the lexicon as performing 'transformations', or taking on, in one way or another, some of the descriptive tasks assumed in the standard theory by the transformational component.

For instance, we could suppose that the base rules directly generate as many distinct strings as the language needs, including one for the active structure and another for the passive. If we then assume that the semantic representation of both active and passive will require the order of the arguments for the verb to be in the 'logical' order VERB (SUBJ, OBJ), we could propose a semantic rule which recognizes a passive sentence, assigns the NP in the surface structure *by* phrase to logical subject and assigns the surface structure subject NP to logical object. Now, the rearrangement of the arguments into the requisite logical structure has been performed by a semantic 'transformation'. We still have the relation of paraphrase, but the descriptive burden of accounting for the paraphrase is shifted from the syntax to the semantics. Some of the powerful semantics models now available do just this.

Yet another way in which the balance between the components can be altered is to remove some of the descriptive burden to the lexicon. For example, in earlier transformational grammars, when linguists were just beginning to flex their transformational muscles, much of the 'derivational morphology' that we proposed in 3.1 as the province of the lexicon was treated by transformational rules in the syntax. So, for instance, the structure underlying the sentence *Wellington defeated Napoleon* was regarded as the deep structure source not only of the independent sentence, but also of NPs like *Wellington's defeat of Napoleon*, *the defeat of Napoleon by Wellington* and indeed of the 'passive NP' *Napoleon's defeat by Wellington*. Given an acceptance of the transformational 'paradigm' of description, it will perhaps seem 'natural' to treat data of this sort in this way. But just as we can imagine semantic transformations, so too we can conceive of lexical 'transformations'. Indeed many of the productive derivational rules we examined in 3.1 can be thought of in precisely these terms. In 6.2a we will see how we can transfer this particular task from the syntax to the lexicon.

These remarks about the 'division of labour' raise a number of general questions. Are there any principled reasons for locating the descriptive burden in one component rather than another, and if so what are they? Or, since it is often convenient for reasons internal to the model to transfer material from one component to another, is the matter to be settled in 'empirical' terms? Some possible answers will emerge in the discussion.

The third question we raised is perhaps the most damaging to a transformational view of language since it questions the adequacy of the very notion of a syntactic transformation. Transformations are, as we have seen, rules that take as their input a particular structural configuration and by adding and deleting constituents or moving them around yield another structure. These are powerful abilities. In the first flush of enthusiasm transformations seemed to offer a solution to almost any problem and many transformations were proposed, some to deal with very general problems, others to deal with quite small and specific problems, and often with very little apparent thought about the problems that an uncontrolled battery of transformations would pose. A favourite apocryphal illustration of the indiscriminate use of transformations is the answer to the question 'How do you derive *Michael* from *Moses* using two rules?' The answer is the ordered transformations of '*oses* deletion' and '*ichael* insertion'! The example may be facetious, but the problem is a real one, for transformations clearly cannot be treated as a magic wand, and if they are, linguistic descriptions will find them as useful as mathematics finds 'Flannagan's finagling factor': 'that quantity which, when multiplied by, divided by, added to, or subtracted from the answer you get, gives the answer you should have got'. If the potential power of transformations is not controlled then they will be little other than *ad hoc* devices of little descriptive use and of no explanatory value. We will consider this general problem and some ways of constraining transformations in 6.2b.

These three general questions are, as it were, internal to the transformational model itself. There were also disruptive influences from outside this particular paradigm, particularly a growing interest in 'functional' approaches to linguistic descriptions. In Chapter 5 we noted that a structure-based grammar (and transformational grammars are structure-based) treats functional notions like 'subject' and 'object' as of secondary importance. If the description needs to call on them, they are defined in terms of structural configurations. But this is not the only way in which a grammar can account for functional notions, and in Chapter 8 we will be examining approaches which take function rather than structure to be basic. This means that basic syntactic configurations will be defined in functional rather than categorial terms, and categorial structure will be seen as interpretive of functional structure rather than the other way round. We shall also see that although a few functional grammars maintain the notion of syntactic transformations in the derivation of sentences, others abandon syntactic transformations (or never had them in the first place) in favour of other devices, like 'serialization rules'. Although many transformationalists have been publicly sceptical about functional models, it is interesting to find that many prominent functional grammarians are in fact refugees from a transformational approach. Furthermore, many of the insights of the functional approach have, over the years, been silently incorporated into transformational grammars. One such is some of the modifications to the base component associated with the 'Xbar theory' of phrase structure rules. Another is the adoption of terminology relating to relational notions like 'agent', 'patient' and so on which have found an important place in lexical entries, as we shall see in 6.2a.

We will briefly mention two further kinds of problem, neither of which we shall have the space to discuss properly. The first is connected with the question of the 'psychological reality' of models of linguistic description. Chomsky has always claimed that a description is an attempt to account for our linguistic abilities – see, for example, Chomsky (1966), where he claims that linguistics is a branch of cognitive psychology. If this is the case, then an obvious question is whether a linguistic model should attempt overtly to reflect what psycholinguistic investigations suggest about our linguistic capacities. Many psychologists are, however, extremely sceptical of whether any psychological correlates can be found for much of the descriptive machinery of transformational grammars, and in particular the notion of syntactic transformations. There have, however, been attempts to devise 'psychologically real' grammars. The second kind of problem concerns the relationship between 'pragmatics' and syntax, and in particular whether a 'syntactic' solution to the problem of accounting for linguistic structure is either possible or desirable. We will return to this question again in more detail in Chapter 8.

From these remarks it will be clear that the general theme of this chapter is how and why transformations have fallen from favour and how the model has coped with this. The reader will, of course, be aware that the problems involved are complex and in the discussion to follow we can only give an outline of what is at issue. What we will try to do is to raise the various issues involved and then see how 'mainline' transformational grammars have coped with them in moving towards the current model.

6.1 Generative semantics

One of the earliest, and certainly one of the liveliest and most provocative, developments out of standard theory was 'generative semantics'. In 5.3, it will be recalled, we discussed the principle that 'transformations do not change meaning'. If this principle is rigidly adhered to it must follow that all elements of meaning are accounted for in deep structure, and if this is the case then this stance will have substantial implications for the nature of the model. In particular, it now becomes important to enquire whether there is any real difference between the deep structure representation of a sentence and its semantic interpretation. If there is no difference between these two types of representation (and the generative semanticists claimed that this was the case) then two things follow. First, rules 'interpreting' deep structures into semantic structures will be superfluous: if all meaning is accounted for in deep structures, and these are isomorphic with semantic structures, then semantic structure will, as it were, be deep structure and there is no need for a distinct level of deep structure. Second, if deep structure is semantic structure, then the function of transformations will be to interpret semantic structures into surface structures: hence 'generative semantics'.

If this approach is to be taken seriously, then clearly major attention must be paid to the nature of semantic representations. For the generative semanticists this meant borrowing insights from logic and devising semantic representations based on the formulae of the predicate calculus. Such representations can be rather easily interpreted in terms of tree structures with the same general characteristics as the familiar analysis trees generated by phrase structure grammars: cf. McCawley (1981). This being so, transformations may be thought of as an appropriate way of 'translating' such representations into surface sentences.

We will look at an example of this in the analysis of quantifiers. Quantifiers are items like *all*, *some* and *few* that occur as modifiers of nouns within NPs like *all boys*, *some men*, *few books*. Their analysis has been of particular interest to philosophers and logicians for many years because they pose peculiarly interesting analytical problems. It will hardly be surprising therefore that they also offer problems for linguistic descriptions. We can appreciate the nature of the problems by considering an example. In terms of the grammar we looked at in Chapter 5 the two sentences

1. Few students read many books
2. Many books are read by few students

are related by the passive transformation, and if transformations do not affect meaning then they should be paraphrases of each other. But are they? There is an element of meaning that remains constant: who is doing the reading and what is read. There is however another element of meaning that appears to change: the most natural intepretation of 1 is 'there are few students of whom it is the case that they read many books' and of 2 'there are many books of which it is the case that few students read them'. These interpretations are different, so there are two meanings. We should also notice that it is, in fact, possible to get both readings from each sentence, but that each sentence has a preferred reading.

Two things at least are at issue. First, if two meanings are involved then, if we adhere to the principle that transformations do not affect meaning, we must find an appropriate deep structure representation to account for the difference. Secondly, we need to have some hypothesis about the 'focusing' effect of word order. It seems that the dominant meaning for each of our examples is determined by which of the quantifiers comes first: first mention therefore seems to have the effect of bringing the meaning associated with that particular constituent into 'focus'. We need to find an appropriate way of representing this.

As far as the first of these problems was concerned, the generative semanticists hit on the predicate calculus as a possible solution. Hitherto we have represented the logical structure of a sentence like *The student reads the book* with the formula READ (STUDENT, BOOK). It will now be necessary to be more precise. We will therefore modify our representation to:

STUDENT (X), BOOK (Y), READ (X, Y)

Here the two arguments of READ are specified as the 'variables' X and Y, and each of these variables is then 'bound' by statements that specify the 'value' of each variable: the value of X is specified as STUDENT and that of Y as BOOK. In logic, quantifiers are treated as operators, with a status similar to that of the operators QU and NOT introduced in 5.1. These operators can then themselves have arguments, rather as verbs have arguments, and if the arguments are variables, then the value of the variables can be specified in exactly the same way as we have specified the values of the variables for the verb READ. So, for example, the NP *few students* can be represented as FEW (X), STUDENTS (X). In these terms the sentence *Few students read books* will have the logical representation:

FEW (X), STUDENTS (X), BOOKS (Y), READ (X, Y)

In a comparable fashion *Students read many books* will be:

MANY (Y), BOOKS (Y), STUDENTS (X), READ (X, Y)

In both cases the predication READ (X, Y) is said to be 'within the scope' of the quantifier and this is shown in this logical representation by order. This order is also reflected in sentences of English where the NP containing the quantifier is topicalized by being brought to the front of the sentence. So *There are few students that read books* corresponds to the first formula and *There are many books that students read* corresponds to the second.

So far so good. But what happens when, as in 1 and 2, there are two quantifiers? The difficulty now is that one quantifier must be within the scope of the other: in our representation one must precede the other. This brings us to the problem we started with. One possible ordering will be

FEW (X), STUDENTS (X), MANY (Y), BOOKS (Y), READ (X, Y)

Here *few* has scope over *many*: a reading that is reflected in the topicalized sentence *There are few students who read many books*. It is also the preferred reading for sentence 1, where *few students* is the subject expression. The other case will then be

MANY (Y), BOOKS (Y), FEW (X), STUDENTS (X), READ (X, Y)

where *many* has scope over *few*: a reading reflected in *There are many books read by few students*. This is the preferred reading of sentence 2, where *many books* is the subject.

We now have semantic representations which can account for both the element of shared meaning, the arguments of READ, and the difference in meaning, the ordering of the quantified NPs. We can also say why one sentence prefers one meaning and the other the other: the preferred meaning interprets the first quantified NP as having scope over the rest of the sentence. However, since the passive is not an overtly topicalized structure, in contrast to the sentences with *there* which are overtly topicalized, either interpretation will be available given an appropriate context, though out of context one will be dominant.

If this is an acceptable interpretation, we should now enquire what the grammar is going to do about it. If we maintain the principle that transformations do not affect meanings, then we will need to establish as many deep structures as there are meanings: the 'generative semanticists' opt for this solution and we will look at it in a moment. Before doing this, we will briefly mention two other possible ways of looking at the problem. One is to weaken the principle that transformations do not change meaning and say that some transformations do affect the meaning of some types of deep structure constituents. So, for example, we might say that since the functional relations of both the active and passive sentence remain identical under transformation, this is the element of meaning that transformations do not change. Transformations could, however, be permitted to change the scope of quantifiers. This 'hybrid' approach was adopted by some transformational grammarians in the early 1970s but it seems to be rather a patch-up job and entails the semantics having to keep track of the transformational history of a derivation. Another solution, currently widely accepted in the transformational camp, is to say that sentences like those in our example do indeed derive from the same deep structure and that the difference in meaning is accommodated by operations in the semantic component.

We now return to the generative semantic approach. This, you recall, supposes that since two meanings are involved, two underlying structures must also be involved. One of these structures, that for the dominant reading of *Few students read many books*, might, following the logical formulae introduced above, be along the lines of Figure 6:1.

Here the quantifiers *few* and *many* are, as the discussion above suggested, treated in underlying structure like verbs, and the nouns they modify in surface structure are treated as their arguments. The scope of a quantifier in this representation is represented by a dominance relation: a quantifier in a higher sentence will have scope over all lower sentences. In the figure *few* is the highest quantifier and hence the rest of the sentence will be in its scope. This will correspond to the first of our logical

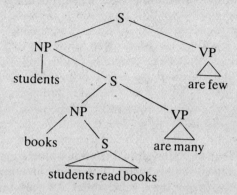

Figure 6:1

representations and to the sentence *There are few students who read many books*.

Given that this is a satisfactory underlying semantic representation, we will now need machinery to derive the appropriate surface structure. This is a transformation of 'quantifier lowering'. This transformation moves a quantifier from its predicate position, and 'lowers' it on to the noun phrase it is to modify in the surface structure. In Figure 6:1, since *few* is in construction with *students*, it will be lowered on to the NP *students* in the bottommost sentence and the topmost mention of *students* will be deleted. If we do the same with *many*, the transformation will have the effect of 'flattening' this quite elaborate structure into the simple NP VP structure appropriate for the surface sentence *Many students read few books*. This is, however, a complex transformational operation, a point to which we will return.

This may be a satisfactory account of the scope difference between these sentences, and an appropriate syntactic machinery for relating the underlying and surface structures, but we have still to account for the 'focusing' effect of word order. One way of doing this might be to propose that superordinate to the topmost S is yet another S, as in Figure 6:2:

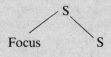

Figure 6:2

Focus might then be developed to contain some marker which will determine the relevant difference in meaning and consequently trigger any word order changes that may be necessary. We will not attempt to discuss what this might be.

One further generative semantic analysis in the same spirit is worth a mention. This is the analysis of 'inchoative' and 'causative' verbs. What is at issue can be briefly explained as follows. Consider first an adjective like BROKEN which can be used to describe a state of affairs, as in *The bottle is broken*. Let us suppose this can be represented by the formula 'BOTTLE BE BROKEN'. Many stative adjectives like BROKEN can be related to intransitive verbs which are 'inchoative', or describe a 'change of state'. Thus, the stative adjective BROKEN is related to the intransitive inchoative verb BREAK, as in *The bottle broke*. Now, the change-of-state verb implies, as a result, the stative adjective – the result of 'a bottle breaking' is that it 'is broken'. This could be represented by the formula 'BOTTLE CHANGE (BOTTLE BE BROKEN)', where the stative meaning is embedded under an abstract marker, CHANGE, of the inchoative nature of the event concerned. We could also propose that CHANGE could, in appropriate circumstances, be realized by a distinct item of its own, usually the verb GET or BECOME, as in *The bottle got broken*.

There is yet a further relationship to be accounted for. Many intransitive inchoative verbs have a corresponding causative verb which introduces the 'agent' responsible for the change of state: in the case of the intransitive BREAK this is the transitive

BREAK as in *The drunkard broke the bottle*. By analogy with the previous analysis we could represent this as 'DRUNKARD CAUSE (BOTTLE CHANGE (BOTTLE BE BROKEN))'. As before, the abstract item CAUSE can, under appropriate conditions, receive its own realization as the verb MAKE or CAUSE: *The drunkard made the bottle break*.

If an analysis of this kind correctly captures the semantics of sentences of this kind, then it is straightforwardly translatable into the tree diagram of Figure 6:3.

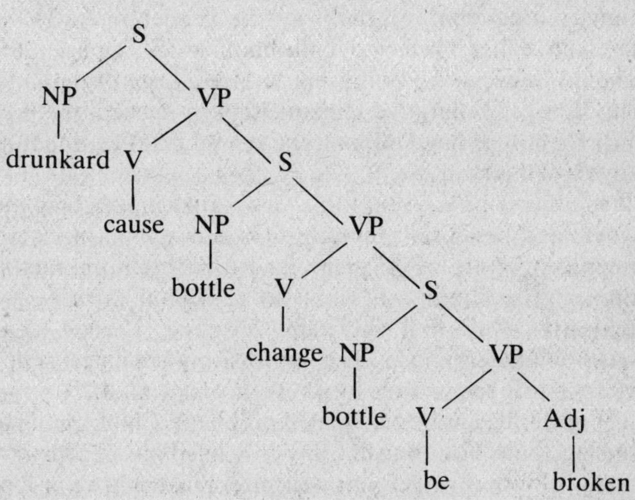

Figure 6:3

We now need to propose a set of transformations to relate this structure to appropriate surface sentences. A transformation called 'predicate raising' is proposed. This takes either a 'real' or an 'abstract' verb and 'raises' it on to the next highest verb, incorporating both into a complex predicate which will later be lexicalized. So, for example, starting from the bottom, we can raise BE on to CHANGE, producing the complex item CHANGE-BE: this we will suppose is lexicalized as GET yielding *The bottle got broken*. If we raised the adjective as well, yielding CHANGE-BE-BROKEN, this would lexicalize as BREAK, yielding *The bottle broke*. Raising all the verbs will yield CAUSE-CHANGE-BE-BROKEN, lexicalized as BREAK in *The drunkard broke the bottle*. Relationships of this kind between stative, inchoative and causative verbs are very common, and not only in English, and the generative semantic approach, while certainly not without its critics, drew attention to many features of this relationship. We shall be examining them in a little further detail in Chapter 7.

Space dictates that we can offer no more than this rather summary treatment of the way the model operates. (The interested reader is referred to the books noted on pages 266–7). It should, however, be sufficient to give a taste of the kinds of issues that the generative semanticists approached, the ways in which they were handled, and the types of problem that assail analyses of this kind.

It must first be said that this view of language stimulated a serious, and beneficial, investigation into many aspects of the semantic structure of language, and the mutual interaction of syntax and semantics. It was also presented in a lively and provocative way that inevitably inspired a good deal of discussion and acrimony. This aggressively polemical style was perhaps partly responsible for its eventual downfall.

There are also more substantial problems. Chief among these is the fact that it is hard to find any principled way of constraining either the kinds of underlying structures that might be proposed, or the number and nature of the transformations that are to relate these very complex abstract structures to simple sentences. As far as the underlying structures are concerned, consider what would happen if we were to combine the different kinds of analysis offered above: the structure becomes so elaborate that it is difficult to control. Furthermore there is no reason why we should stop here, and the structure can easily become yet more elaborate if we attempt to integrate other aspects of meaning, and the representation is designed to capture all kinds of meaning. An inevitable consequence of these excessively complex structures is an equally uncontrolled growth of transformational power. Each new structure seems to require a corresponding transformation to flatten it out again! So, in addition to 'quantifier lowering', and 'predicate raising', which we have mentioned above, we will need a whole host of other transformations, each with rather special properties. It all quickly begins to look rather *ad hoc*! The consequence is that after the excitement of the early years, back in the late 1960s, the influence of the generative semantic school has largely receded in favour of more sober models suited to a more sombre age, and these tend to preserve the distinction between a semantic and a syntactic component, and handle the kinds of problem we have discussed above in other ways.

6.2 Towards a new model

In this section we will be working towards an outline description of the general architecture of recent proposals for a transformational model of description, the 'revised extended standard theory', REST for short. In comparison with the flamboyance of the generative semantics approach that we looked at in the last section, with its bevy of transformations, this model will seem excessively chaste in its abandonment of literally dozens of transformations. It may also, perhaps, seem to be of baroque complication in that it has abandoned the rather straightforward relationship between the components proposed by the standard theory in favour of a set of very general principles dispersed among the various components. To understand how this has come about we will begin by looking at two general points raised at the beginning of this chapter. First, if syntactic transformations are treated as some kind of 'magic dust' that can be sprinkled over any structure to create the desired surface structure, then they lose whatever explanatory power they might otherwise have. One of our preoccupations will, therefore, be with ways in which they can be constrained. Second, it is not essential to concentrate all descriptive power in the transformational component of the syntax. It is equally possible, given the suitable development of other components of the description, to distribute this power. The two matters are clearly interrelated since reducing the power of the transformational component inevitably means transferring some descriptive power to the other components of description. Equally, when we begin to pay proper attention to the other components, we will find that we want to entrust some part of the total description to them at the expense of the transformational component. This is exactly what has happened. The consequence is that all but a few transformations have been abandoned, and that the focus of research attention has tended to move away from questions relating to syntactic transformations themselves and into other areas. We will need to see where the descriptive power has gone, and what replaces transformations as a focus of interest.

The necessity for restricting the power of transformations can be shown both at an abstract theoretical level and at the practical level of language descriptions. The theoretical reasons have to do with the mathematical properties of grammars, and we will do no more than mention this issue. Since its inception, many transformational grammarians, including notably Chomsky himself, have been concerned to explore the mathematical properties of the grammars proposed. The mathematical properties of phrase structure grammars, which as we have seen in 4.2 are a highly constrained system, are now well known. The mathematical properties of grammars with transformations, however, are much less clearly understood, but investigations in this area yield the gloomy result that if unconstrained they are quite without explanatory power. There are equally compelling practical reasons for constraining grammars. If they are not constrained they will 'overgenerate' wildly. This means that the grammar will define as well formed infinite numbers of sentences which quite clearly are not well formed. This must obviously not be allowed to happen.

How then is the power of transformations to be constrained? The most radical solution would be to do away with them entirely. This course has, indeed, been advocated by many people, and we will return to this point of view in 6.3. We shall also see in Chapter 7 that many functional models of description do quite nicely without any transformations. It is not, however, altogether surprising that the suggestion has not been taken up by transformational grammarians. Many transformations do indeed disappear as the descriptive burden is reallocated among the various components, but, for reasons which will appear in 6.2b, there are some kinds of transformation that persist. The task then will be to see what principles can be invoked to ensure that these remaining transformations are kept within tight bonds.

In Chapter 5 we saw that transformations are operations that change one structure into another. They do this by inserting, changing, moving, or deleting items or pieces of structure or both. We will look briefly at each kind of operation and consider whether any can be dispensed with, and if not what sorts of limitations need to be imposed on those that remain.

Rules that insert constituents need particular care: it would obviously be absurd to have a rule that derived *I like hot coffee* from *I like coffee* by an 'evaluative adjective-adding rule', since a rule of this sort would play havoc with any attempt to produce a coherent semantics. There is therefore a general principle that no transformation can insert items with semantic content. This restriction will mean, in effect, that none but entirely predictable items can be introduced by an insertion transformation. It will also mean that these transformations cannot change meaning. An example of a permissible operation within this restriction would be the insertion of the 'dummy' subject *it* in sentences like *It is raining* or *It is amazing that any transformations are left*. Another possible example is the passive transformation: this specifies the addition of an agent phrase and particularizes the relevant preposition as *by*, which is thus defined as having no semantic import. A more severe restriction on additioning transformations would be to stipulate that they cannot create syntactic structure. This more stringent condition would still permit us to introduce the dummy *it*, but would disallow the passive as a transformation, because it creates structure in the *by* phrase. Later in the chapter we will discuss other ways of handling the passive construction that will conform to the stronger restriction.

Rules that change constituents need a comparable restriction to outlaw rules which replace one lexical item with another. The general principle will be that items with semantic content cannot be changed, and then these transformations too will be unable to change meanings. We do not want to derive *I like bananas* from *I hate bananas*, or even *I dislike bananas* from *I do not like bananas*. The relation between LOVE and HATE, or LIKE and DISLIKE, will be handled in the lexicon and the semantics, as will other relations of this kind between words. A strict application of this restriction will even disallow rules that change the form class of lexical items, thus ruling out a transformational treatment of the kind of nominalization, mentioned at the beginning of this chapter, which changes a verb like DEFEAT (*Wellington defeated Napoleon*) into the noun DEFEAT (*The defeat of Napoleon by Wellington*). This is, in fact, a desirable conclusion: we saw in 3.1 that operations of this kind differ in several ways from syntactic operations, and they often have idiosyncratic semantic side-effects. For reasons of this sort, they are more insightfully formulated as derivational rules in the lexicon, and we will see in 6.2a how this might be accomplished.

The principle that items with semantic content cannot be changed by transformation can be extended even further. In a standard theory account, some pronouns are derived transformationally by replacing a 'full' NP by the corresponding pronoun. Thus *John1 hated John1* will, by a rule of 'reflexivization', yield *John1 hated himself1*: the numerical indices to the two mentions of *John* are intended to indicate that the same 'John' is at issue. Similarly, *John1 thinks that John1 is clever* will, by a rule of 'pronominalization', yield *John1 thinks that he1 is clever*. However, if we stipulate that transformations cannot change items with semantic content, such an operation will be denied us and we will need to think of other ways of accounting for the relationship between a pronoun and its antecedent. REST concludes that the proper place for operations of this sort is the semantic component. In brief, what is suggested is that all pronouns should be generated in the underlying structure in the very positions in which they will be found in the surface structure, and that the semantic component should contain a set of principles which will relate pronouns to their antecedents. This is one area that has recently generated a lot of interest.

We have now looked briefly at two rule types, replacement and insertion rules. In each case we have concluded that they should be constrained so that they cannot affect items with semantic content or make structural alterations to trees. These constraints are so stringent that it becomes, in fact, almost impossible to conceive of operations that might usefully be performed by transformations of this kind!

This now leaves us with two classes of rule – movement rules and deletion rules. Both still seem to be required. Movement rules can be illustrated by the passive once again. This is an operation that forms the subject of an active sentence into a *by* phrase and moves it to a position following the verb, and moves the object NP into the now vacant subject position. The question that arises with movement rules is whether any constituent can be moved, and whether it can be moved anywhere. In the case of the passive it is clear that the answer to both of these questions is no – particular constituents are involved and they must move to quite specific places. Although we cannot consider movement rules in detail because they involve a number of rather special considerations, section 6.2b is devoted to a discussion of some of the issues they raise. In anticipation let us merely say that the discussion will provoke a radical reorganization of the whole structure of the grammar.

The last set of transformational rules to be considered are 'deletion rules'. We have seen that insertion and changing rules need to be constrained so that they do not change meaning. A comparable constraint is needed for deletion rules because if we can freely delete anything we like, then we will never get a systematic relationship between meanings and forms since almost any form can be related by deletion to almost any other: we could, for example, derive *I like bananas* from *I like pineapples but can't stand bananas* by deletion of the string *pineapples but can't stand* – this is clearly absurd. For this reason deletion transformations are generally constrained by imposing a condition of 'recoverability': that is, the identity of the deleted item must be uniquely recoverable. In *I like pineapples but not bananas* we can quite unambiguously reconstruct the second part as *I do not like bananas*: it cannot possibly be understood as *Stalin's mother does not like bananas* or *I have not bought bananas for months*. This recoverability condition will mean that the transformation will require identity between the 'controller' of the deletion and the 'victim': this is the case in the example.

Deletion rules will remain necessary because, given the kind of PS rules we currently have, there seems to be no way of satisfying the recoverability condition by any means other than deletion.

At this point we should briefly raise the issue of rule ordering, because this matter has been the subject of considerable attention in recent years. We saw in 5.1 that even the limited battery of transformations proposed there required to be ordered. The necessity for ordering was illustrated by showing the interaction between passive and negative: one order produces the desired sentences, and the other leads to ungrammaticality. It will clearly be the case that ordering problems will multiply as the number of transformations multiplies. It is then hardly surprising that when large numbers of transformations were thought to be necessary, the question of whether transformations should or should not be ordered and what consequences sprung from either position occupied a good deal of space in the academic journals. Fortunately we need not pursue this matter here. The REST model has abandoned all but a few transformations, and consequently ordering is no longer the burning issue it once was. Furthermore, Chomsky's recent proposals (cf. Chomsky, 1981) suggest that the two kinds of rule that remain, movement and deletion, should be separated into distinct components. We shall see some reasons why this should be so in 6.2c. The components are themselves ordered, the movement component preceding the deletion component, and various other operations intervene between them. In these circumstances ordering becomes something of a non-issue.

So much then for constraints on the operation of transformations. We will close this section by briefly mentioning yet another device to prevent the grammar overgenerating. This is a set of 'filters', devices that scan surface structures to ensure that they are in fact well formed. One example will suffice. In a sentence like *I think that Mary is coming to dinner* the complementizer *that* is optional. Let us then suppose that *that* is deleted by a 'complementizer deletion rule'. In the example, this rule can be considered optional since the sentence is grammatical either with or without *that*. But this is not always the case. In some circumstances it is obligatory to delete: *Who do you suppose —— is coming for dinner?* is well formed, but *Who do *you suppose that* —— *is coming for dinner?* is not. In others it is obligatory not to delete: *That Mary is coming to dinner is unfortunate* is well formed, but **Mary is coming to dinner is unfortunate* is not. There are two courses open to us. We could either impose a series of very specific conditions on the operation of the complementizer deletion rule, or we can allow the rule to operate freely, and propose a set of filters to declare particular outputs illegal. To cope with the two examples above, we could envisage filters like this: 'If the subject has been moved out of a subordinate tensed clause, then the complementizer node must be empty': this will mark as ungrammatical **Who do you suppose that is coming for dinner?*; and 'If a subordinate sentence is initial in the whole sentence, then the complementizer node must be full': this will mark as ungrammatical **Mary is coming to dinner is unfortunate*. REST chooses to use filters. Filters of this sort serve a useful function in that they enable the transformations to be formulated as exceptionless. If the transformation overgenerates because of this, the filters then subsequently declare any anomalous structures to be illegal. This is all very well, except that we now need some theory of filters to ensure that they are not merely *ad hoc* devices to patch up inadequately formulated rules: we will not pursue this issue further here.

In the sections which follow, we will see how some of these general principles work out in practice. We will look at two areas: the lexicon in 6.2a and movement rules in 6.2b. In 6.2c we will attempt to summarize the new model.

6.2a Enriching the lexicon

The lexical entries that we used in Chapter 5 looked like this:

$$\text{GIVE} \quad \text{V,} \text{——NP}_{PP}(\text{to NP})$$

$$\text{NP1(agent)} \text{——NP2(patient) to NP3(goal)}$$
$$\text{'GIVE'(NP1, NP2, NP3)}$$

The first line specifies the relevant subcategorization environment: GIVE is a verb that can take both a 'direct' and

an 'indirect' object, as in . . . *give* —— *the book* —— *to Mary*.
The second line gives a functional specification of these various
'arguments': the subject is assigned the function of 'agent', the
person who does the giving; the object that of 'patient', the thing
given; and the indirect object that of a 'goal', the person to whom
the thing is given. The third line represents a 'logical' account of
the various arguments. REST assumes that the lexicon includes
a set of principles which will determine how functional relations
are assigned to the various arguments of a verb: in 7.1a we will
look at some of the issues involved. We saw in Chapter 5 how
representations of this kind will permit us to relate the syntactic
and semantic representations.

In a standard theory grammar, as we have seen, the burden
of accounting for systematic relationships between sentences
falls largely on the transformational component. GIVE, for
example, occurs in two environments:

NP1 (GIVE) NP2 to NP3   John gave the book to Mary
NP1 (GIVE) NP3 NP2   John gave Mary the book

(The NPs are numbered to keep track of the relationships
between them in the two structures.) A standard theory
grammar takes the first structure as basic, the 'deep' structure,
and handles the relationship between the two structures by a
syntactic transformation, called 'dative movement'. This
transformation derives the second structure by deleting the
preposition and reordering the arguments of the verb. Since the
semantic interpretation is derived from the common deep
structure, this and the transformation capture the syntactic and
semantic relationships between the two structures.
Furthermore, since the second structure is derived from the first
by a syntactic transformation, the lexical entry for GIVE at the
head of this section need cope only with the first structure.

The transformation of dative movement applies to a number
of verbs other than GIVE, including OFFER, SEND and
TAKE. It is not, however, universally applicable, and there are
a number of verbs which it must be prevented from applying to,
including BROADCAST and TRANSMIT. These verbs occur
in the first structure – 'NP1 BROADCAST NP2 to NP3' (*Radio*

Moscow broadcasts propaganda to the West) – but not in the second – (**Radio Moscow broadcasts the West propaganda*). In a standard theory account the transformation is stopped from applying to the latter verbs by an annotation in their lexical entries. BROADCAST, for example, will have an entry parallel to that for GIVE shown above, but it will also contain a feature [−dative]. The transformational rule will be sensitive to this feature and will not operate on structures containing a [−dative] verb. In this way the transformation itself is stated in general terms and the exceptions to the rule are treated as a lexical matter.

A syntactic transformation is not the only possible way of handling relationships of this kind, and the restrictions on such relationships. We will now explore the possibility of transferring this potential from the syntax to the lexicon. An obvious way of doing this is simply to list the various environments concerned for each verb. So we might reformulate the entry for GIVE along the following lines:

GIVE V, —— NP$_{PP}$(to NP)

   NP1(agent) —— NP2(patient) to NP3(goal)
   —— NP NP
   NP1(agent) —— NP3(goal) NP2(patient)
   'GIVE' (NP1, NP2, NP3)

This entry shows both of the relevant structures, and a functional specification is provided in full for each. There are two reasons for this. First, the annotations on the NPs show how the two environments are related: for instance, that the NP in the PP in the first structure bears the same relationship to the verb as the NP immediately following the verb in the second. Secondly the identification of the NPs in this way allows the construction of a common 'logical' representation which explicitly shows that the two structures are held to be paraphrases of each other.

Note that all the semantic and syntactic relations that were originally done by the syntactic transformation are now coped with quite adequately by the lexical entry. The disadvantage seems to be that we no longer have an explicit formulation of the relationship, and furthermore, since the entry is specific to GIVE, we have no way of knowing that other verbs like OFFER and SEND share the same kind of relationship. We can remedy this by proposing a derivational rule in the lexicon itself. So, we could propose the following rule:

Any V which occurs in the structure

NP1 —— NP2 $_{PP}$(to NP3)

also occurs in the structure

NP1 —— NP3 NP2

Since we shall be proposing that the lexicon contains other derivational rules of this kind which redistribute the arguments of a verb, we will assume that there is a general convention for rules of this kind that the functional roles associated with the various NPs in the source structure are maintained by these NPs when they are redistributed in the derived structure. If we now let this rule apply to our initial entry for GIVE, at the head of the section, we will derive the second fuller entry.

Let us now identify the rule in the way we identified the morphological rules discussed in Chapter 3. We could for instance retain the name of the transformation and call it the 'dative derivational rule'. Now the annotation we used to stop verbs like BROADCAST going through the dative movement transformation will instead stop BROADCAST from going through this new lexical rule.

We should now enquire whether we can generalize this treatment to other syntactic transformations. What about what we have hitherto regarded as the passive transformation? We might propose a derivational rule of the following kind:

Any V that occurs in the structure

NP1 —— NP2

also occurs in the structure

NP2 BE PassPart$_{PP}$(by NP1)

where 'PassPart' is the 'Passive Participle' of V

Given the convention, mentioned after the lexical 'dative' rule, about the redistribution of the functional arguments of the verb in the derived structure, once again we can account for the appropriate syntactic and semantic relationships. The interaction of the two rules will also provide for us appropriate structures for the various possible forms of 'passive dative' (*The book was given to Mary by John* etc.) and associate them with appropriate semantic interpretations.

Rules of this kind have further advantages. In the proposed derivational rule the '*by* phrase' is optional: this is to cope with 'agentless passives' like *John was killed*, where an indefinite agent is 'implied'. In a standard theory model, sentences like this are derived from the corresponding active structure with an indefinite subject expression, perhaps '*someone*' *killed John*. This is passivized to *John was killed by* '*someone*', and the indefinite agent phrase is then deleted by a transformation of 'non-specific agent deletion' to yield the agentless *John was killed*. In this new model all this machinery is unnecessary: agentless passives are derived directly by simply not selecting the optional agent phrase: i.e. the underlying structure of *John was killed* is *John was killed*! The semantics of these sentences can be accounted for by adding a rider to the derivational rule to the effect that 'if the "*by* phrase" is not chosen, then the logical representation will be of the form "There is an X such that V (X NP2)"'. Under our general rules for constructing semantic representations, the sentences *Bill killed John* and *John was killed by Bill* will now both receive the same logical interpretation – 'KILL' (BILL, JOHN) – which was what we originally proposed in Chapter 5. Our new lexical rule, together with the rider we have just introduced, will now interpret *John was killed* as 'There is an X such that 'KILL' (X, JOHN)'. The lexicon has acquired additional semantic powers.

A derivational rule of this kind in the lexicon has other advantages too. It can, for instance, be supplemented in a rather straightforward fashion to account for 'get' passives, like *John got killed*. It will also allow us to offer a sensible account of the relationship between passives and those quite numerous items that behave like passives, but for which there is no active counterpart: *The Antarctic is uninhabited by man*, *John was untutored*, etc. Such items can simply be entered as they are, and their relationship to verbs like INHABIT and TUTOR covered by the same kind of general rules of implication as will be used for other formal and semantic relationships within the lexicon.

Operations of this kind can be extended further. In early transformational grammars a good deal of derivational morphology was dealt with in the transformational component because, at the time, it seemed somehow 'natural' to make use of the powerful new transformational machinery to account for the relationships between a sentence like 1 below and NPs like 2a–2d.

1. The teacher assessed the pupils
2a. The teacher's assessment of the pupils
   b. The assessment of the pupils by the teacher
   c. The pupils' assessment by the teacher

Under our new approach, however, relationships of this sort can be readily dealt with in the lexicon by using a derivational rule of the type we have just been discussing. Assume, for example, a lexical entry for ASSESS along these lines:

ASSESS V, ——NP
         NP1(agent)——NP2(patient)
         'ASSESS'(NP1, NP2)
      N, By *-ment* nominalization rule

The first three lines of this entry parallel those for GIVE at the beginning of the section. The final line is a pointer to a derivational rule of the following kind:

-ment nominalization rule
$_N(V+\textit{-ment})$

NP1 to prenominal genitive (e.g. *the teacher's assessment*) or

to PP with *by* (e.g. *assessment by the teacher*)
NP2 to prenominal genitive (e.g. *the pupils' assessment*) or
to PP with *of* (e.g. *assessment of the pupils*)

The rule which derives the nominalization will now also account for the distribution of the arguments of the verb into the appropriate nominal modifiers, and if we maintain the convention about the way in which the functional roles of the verb are distributed in the derived structure, we get an appropriate semantic reading.

What is proposed is a substantial transfer of descriptive potential from the transformational component to the lexicon. The effect of a thoroughgoing approach of this kind, which is now widely followed, is to enrich the power of the lexicon at the expense of the transformational component. The advantages are considerable. It simplifies the transformational component, thus disposing of some of the artifactual difficulties created by the nature of the model, like rule ordering. It results in an increase in descriptive power with no loss of any of the insights which transformations were devised to capture. All those are still in place, though captured in a different way. Finally, it brings together in one place, in the lexicon, a set of operations that are similar. The operations concerned are those that involve the rearrangement of the arguments of a lexical item within basic structures. Sometimes, but not always, such operations will also involve a change of form class. We have examined one case (dative movement) where the lexical item is a verb, the basic structure is a simple proposition, and no form class change is involved; another (passive) where the lexical item is a verb, the basic structure is a simple proposition and a form class change is involved in that the verb becomes a passive participle; and a third (nominalizations like that for ASSESS) where a form class change from a verb to a noun is involved and the basic structures are a proposition and an NP.

In summary, it is proposed that the lexicon should contain a list of lexical items, each categorized for its syntactic co-occurrence potential (i.e. whether it is transitive, intransitive etc.), and its functional and logical interpretation. It will also contain a set of rules which will account for the ways in which the arguments of a verb can be rearranged within a basic structure, and any morphological and semantic consequences of this. The lexicon is now no longer a simple list of lexical items at the disposal of the phrase structure and transformational rules: it now has a significant part to play in a total description.

6.2b Constraining movement rules

Movement rules are those syntactic transformations which move constituents. If we adopt the view proposed in the preceding section, that rules, like passive, which have the effect of rearranging the arguments of a verb within a simple sentence, should in general be dealt with in the lexicon rather than in the transformational component, then a large number of what used to be syntactic transformational movement rules disappear and become derivational rules of the lexicon.

An obvious question now follows: can we dispense with syntactic transformations that move constituents altogether? Chomsky's answer is no, we will need to retain those movement rules that have the ability to move constituents out of simple sentence structures. There are a number of such rules, but we will restrict our discussion to a consideration of just one, the rule of *wh* movement, which is the principal formation rule for *wh* questions. The arguments are quite complex, but it will be worth while following them in order to see why recent versions of transformational grammar look so different from standard theory models.

When we first discussed *wh* movement in 6.1 we offered some arguments to suggest that *wh* NPs should be generated 'in place' and subsequently moved to the front of the sentence. These arguments are still relevant for this section, and we will offer another argument in a little while. Given this position, *What is John giving —— to Mary?* derives from *John is giving what to Mary?*, and *Who is John giving the book to —— ?* derives from *John is giving the book to who?* and so on. In these examples, and others to follow, '——' indicates where the relevant *wh* NP was originally generated, and hence where it has been moved from. (And, in order to simplify what is already complicated enough, we will disregard problems connected with the inversion of subject and auxiliary in questions: *John is* to *is John* in the example above. We will simply supply inversion silently wherever necessary.)

In 5.1 we postulated that all sentences develop from an Sbar node dominating an S and a 'Comp' node. We proposed that *wh* movement moves the *wh* NP into this comp node. Figure 6:4 illustrates what is at issue for the sentence *What is John giving —— to Mary?* and indicates how *wh* movement applies. In line with our analysis in 5.1, [+wh] in the Comp node indicates that the resultant sentence will be interrogative. With embedded interrogatives the [+wh] Comp node will be filled with the complementizer *whether* (*I don't know whether John is giving a present to Mary*). *Whether* does not occur with main clause interrogatives, and 'e' in the Comp node indicates that it is 'empty'.

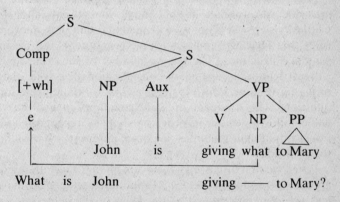

Figure 6:4

Figure 6:4 deals with a simple sentence, and what is going on here looks superficially like the kind of rearrangement of the arguments of the verb that we have proposed to entrust to the lexicon. If, however, we turn to complex sentences, sentences that have other sentences embedded in them, then a quite different picture emerges. Consider a sentence like

$$_{S1}(\text{What do you think}_{S2}(\text{John is giving} \underline{\quad} \text{to Mary?}))$$

Here, on the assumption that *what* derives originally from '——', *what* has moved out of its own sentence, S2, and into the superordinate sentence S1. *Wh* words can move even longer distances:

$$_{S1}(\text{What do you think}_{S2}(\text{John said}_{S3}(\text{he is giving} \underline{\quad} \text{to Mary?}))$$

Who was it you told me your mother said she wanted to be quite sure you would never consider speaking to —— again?

Long-distance movement of this kind is quite different from the kind of movement we were discussing in the last section. That involved rearrangements within a simple sentence. This involves moving constituents across sentence boundaries, and, furthermore, there seems no way in which we can constrain the distance a *wh* word can move (in the last example the *wh* word has moved over seven simple sentences).

These facts suggest that the machinery we used in the last chapter to rearrange the arguments of a verb within a simple sentence is not an appropriate way of dealing with long-distance movement of this kind. It also offers additional support to the proposal that the *wh* word should be generated 'in place': i.e. in those sites we have marked with '——', where the item is understood. To do otherwise would present formidable difficulties for our current conception of phrase structure rules. It seems, then, that long-distance movement rules will have to be dealt with by a syntactic movement transformation.

We now need to ask two questions about such rules: can any constituent be moved and can a constituent be moved anywhere? The answer to both of these questions will be no, and the consequence of our investigation into the reasons for this will involve a radical revision of our conception of what transformations can do and hence of the structure of a grammar.

The first question we posed was: can any constituent be moved? Simple sentences do not pose problems. As far as the

simple sentence illustrated in Figure 6:4 is concerned, it is clear
that any of the NPs could be replaced by a *wh* word and that this
could then be moved to Comp. This will yield *Who —— is giving
the book to Mary?*, *Who is John giving the book to ——?* and so
on, depending on which NP contains the *wh* word.

Complex sentences, that is sentences which themselves
contain a sentence embedded as a constituent, are, however, a
different matter. Here there are restrictions on what can be
moved. Consider first a sentence like *The rumour that John gave
a book to Mary is untrue*. In this sentence the subject expression
the rumour that John gave a book to Mary has a head noun
rumour modified by a 'noun complement' sentence *that John
gave a book to Mary*. Let us assume that this sentence has the
structure schematically represented in Figure 6:5.

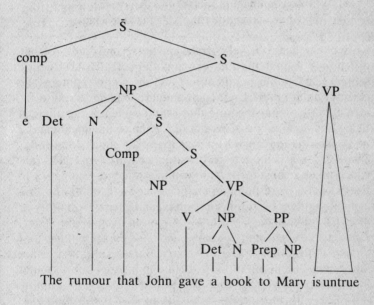

Figure 6:5

We can question the subject NP as a whole – *What is untrue?*
What we cannot, however, do is to question any of the NPs in

the subordinate sentence which forms the complement clause modifying *rumour*. So if *John* were replaced by a *wh* word, this cannot be moved to comp or we shall derive the patently impossible **Who is the rumour that —— gave a book to Mary untrue?*. The same is true for the other NPs in the complement clause since **Who is the rumour that John gave a book to —— untrue?*, **What is the rumour that John gave —— to Mary untrue?* are equally unacceptable.

Before considering what the conditions are that inhibit movement, we should note that complexity of structure as such is not at issue. We have already observed what *wh* movement can operate over long distances. Furthermore if we compare the following pair of sentences:

a) Who do you imagine John claims to have met —— ?
b) *Who do you imagine John's claim to have met —— ?

we find that the first is well formed and the second is not, yet they differ only in that the first contains the verb CLAIM with a sentence functioning as its object and the second contains the corresponding noun CLAIM with a noun complement clause.

We should in passing note that *wh* movement is not alone in being unable to move items out of a noun complement clause: no transformation can move a constituent out of such a structure. There is, for instance, a transformation known as 'topicalization' which takes a constituent from within a sentence and puts it to the front. So corresponding to *John gave the book to Mary* we can derive the topicalized *The book, John gave —— to Mary* or *Mary, John gave the book to ——*. We can even derive *Harry, I imagine John claims to have met ——* corresponding to *I imagine John claims to have met Harry*. But topicalization cannot take a constituent out of the structure in Figure 6:5: we cannot have **Mary, the rumour that John gave a book to —— is untrue* nor **The book, the rumour that John gave —— to Mary is untrue*. Nor, parallel to the examples at the end of the last paragraph, can we have **Harry, I imagine John's claim to have met ——*. What we have said about *wh* movement and topicalization is also true of other movement rules, though this must be taken on trust as we do not have the space to demonstrate that this is so.

What seems to be at issue is that some types of constituent form 'islands'. Constituents in these islands are, as it were, stranded. They are unable to escape from their islands by movement rules. There is no inhibition on the constituents moving around within the permissible limits within the island – so we can have a passive constituent sentence with no trouble: *The rumour that Mary was given a book by John is untrue*. What we cannot do is extract NPs from island constructions.

Noun complement sentences are not the only island structures. We cannot extract items from relative clauses:

$\bar{S}(_{Comp}(e)_S(_{NP}(\text{The book}_{RelS}(\text{which John gave to Mary}))_{VP}(\text{was expensive}))))$

*Who was the book which —— gave to Mary expensive?
*Who was the book which John gave to —— expensive?

Nor can we extract items from the complements of verbs like ASK when they contain the complementizer *whether*.

$\bar{S}(_{Comp}(e)_S(\text{He asked}\bar{S}(_{Comp}(\text{whether})_S(\text{Mary gave the book to John})))$

*Who did he ask whether Mary gave the book to —— ?
*What did he ask whether Mary gave —— to John?

As in noun complement clauses, the constituents are trapped in their islands and unable to escape.

The answer to the question 'Can any constituent be moved?' is, then, 'no'. Some constructions form islands out of which nothing can be moved. It follows therefore that we will need to constrain movement rules to stop the derivation of impossible sentences like those in the examples.

When 'island constraints' were first noticed, it was proposed that there should be a series of such constraints of the form 'noun complements form islands', 'relative clauses form islands' and so forth. It is, however, natural to ask whether all island constructions have anything in common. If this were the case then we could propose one general constraint to cover them all. In his more recent work Chomsky has proposed such a generalization. He notes that in all the island constructions we have examined the *wh* word would have to 'cross' at least two NP or S nodes to get to the Comp node at the front of the sentence. Thus, in Figure 6:5, if we replace any of the NP nodes with a *wh* word, it will have to cross the S node dominating *John gave a book to Mary*, the NP node dominating *the rumour that John gave a book to Mary* and the S node dominating *The rumour that John gave a book to Mary is untrue*. What is at issue is illustrated schematically in the labelled and bracketed diagram below, which can be compared with the tree in Figure 6:5.

$$\bar{S}(_{Comp}(e)_S(_{NP}(\text{the rumour}_{\bar{S}}(_{Comp}(\text{that})_S(\text{Who gave a book to Mary})_{VP}(\text{is untrue}))))))$$

      └3-2————————————1┘

    *Who is the rumour that —— gave a book to Mary untrue?

Chomsky proposes that if we identify NP and S nodes as 'bounding nodes' for movement rules and stipulate that no movement rule can cause a constituent to cross more than one bounding node, we will have a generalization that will effectively trap constituents in the island constructions we have illustrated. The reader is left to apply this generalization to the other island constructions illustrated earlier in the section.

This proposal may serve to identify island constructions, but as it stands it seems to create another problem: if a *wh* word cannot cross more than one bounding node, how is long-distance *wh* movement possible at all? Chomsky's ingenious answer is to propose that empty Comp nodes become 'escape hatches'. Note that in defining bounding nodes as NP and S we carefully avoided stipulating that Sbar is also a bounding node. There was a reason for this. Let us assume that *wh* movement operates on simple sentences but that it applies 'cyclically'. This means that it will start on the most deeply embedded Sbar, moving the *wh* word into Comp. This crosses only one bounding node. It will then apply to the next most deeply embedded Sbar, moving the *wh* word to Comp again. This too involves crossing only one bounding node. If this process is iterated cyclically right up to the root Sbar, we will be able to move *wh* words over long distances, and successive movement from Comp to Comp will not now offend the constraint about crossing more than one bounding node. Comp operates as the escape hatch to permit this. This can be illustrated schematically in:

$\bar{S}(_{Comp}{}^{(e)}{}_{S}{}^{(you\ think(}\bar{S}({}_{Comp}{}^{(e)}{}_{S}{}^{(John\ said(}\bar{S}({}_{Comp}{}^{(e)}{}_{S}{}^{(he\ is\ giving\ wh\ to\ Mary)))}$

What do you think John said he is giving —— to Mary

This solution will get the right answers in the examples we have looked at: the islands will remain islands and constituents will be trapped in them and the cyclical application of the transformation using Comp as an escape hatch will allow *wh* words to move long distances in the appropriate circumstances. The reader will hardly be surprised to learn that this account is somewhat simplified! As it stands it will not do all the work that needs to be done for a complete account, and further refinements will be necessary. To pursue this particular matter further, however, will take us too far out of our way, and what has been presented should be enough to show the direction in which the new model tends.

We must now turn to the second question posed at the beginning of this section: can a constituent move anywhere? The discussion has, in fact, already provided an answer to this question for *wh* movement. *Wh* movement will move a *wh* NP into the Comp node at the head of its sentence. Indeed, one of the reasons why we postulated that every S should be in construction with a Comp node was precisely in order to have an identifiable location for *wh* words to move to. Figure 6:6 shows this schematically:

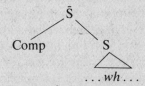

Figure 6:6

The structure provides a site for the *wh* NP to move to, and a ready-made node label to dominate the moved constituent.

An important feature of the way the transformation is formulated is that it does not create any new structure: it only moves a constituent to an already existing site. Transformations like this, which do not create new structure, but only rearrange constituents within an already existing structure are, for obvious reasons, known as 'structure-preserving'. We have only discussed *wh* movement, but if all movement transformations could be made structure-preserving, then we would have a very strong limitation on the form of possible movement transformations. Although we have not examined any others, and have no space to do so, it seems that it may indeed be possible to reformulate almost all movement rules as structure-preserving. An exception is the inversion transformation associated with question formation: there seems no sensible way to reformulate this as a structure-preserving operation, and we will have to be content with marking a few identifiable named operations like this as exceptions to the general principle.

At this point it is worth briefly referring back to the discussion of the dative and passive rules in the previous section. Clearly when these were syntactic transformations, as in our original formulation in Chapter 5, neither was structure-preserving: the passive spectacularly not so in its ability to create a new piece of structure in the agent phrase that accommodates the former subject NP of the active sentence. If we accept the stipulation that all syntactic movement transformations are to be structure-preserving then neither of these two operations can survive as syntactic transformations. This is yet another good reason for handling operations of this kind in the lexicon.

If we accept the proposal that movement transformations are to be structure-preserving, then we can add one final refinement. Suppose that when a constituent moves it leaves behind it a 'trace' of its former presence. We will represent such traces as 't'. Suppose also that the trace is 'co-indexed' with the moved constituent. We will now have a complete and unambiguous record of what has moved and where it came from. There is an example of the use of traces in Figure 6:7 below, and the reader can readily construct 'traced' versions of the other examples we have looked at.

Several consequences flow from this new proposal. One is that if we are to have a site for the trace, a movement rule cannot obliterate the site from which something is moved, otherwise there will be no home for the trace. Structure-preserving with traces will then neither create structure (items only move to already empty sites) nor destroy structure (a trace will be left behind in the vacated site), it will only move items around within already established structures.

Another consequence is that if all movement transformations are structure-preserving then the derived structure after the operation of the movement transformations will, like a well-preserved archaeological site, contain a complete record of the original deep structure. Chomsky calls traced structures that are the result of movement rules 'S structures'. They have a particularly important place in the REST model, as we shall see. The principal difference between an S structure and deep structure from which it derives will be that the deep structure will contain empty nodes, to accommodate potential movement, and the S structure will contain the traces of movement transformations. What this proposal involves is shown schematically (and ignoring inversion once more) in Figure 6:7.

Deep structure: $_{\bar{S}}(_{Comp}(e)_{S}(\text{you would like}_{NP}(wh \text{ book})))$

S structure: $_{\bar{S}}(_{Comp}(wh \text{ book}1)_{S}(\text{you would like}_{NP}(t1)))$

Figure 6:7

At this point the reader may be tempted to wonder whether we need bother with transformations at all: after all, if transformations neither change nor create structure, and if the sole effect of movement transformations is to move items around within existing structures leaving traces behind, why not generate S structures directly? Some models do indeed move in just this direction: that is, they conceive of structures like the 'S structure' of Figure 6:7 as being directly generated. It should however be noted that if we adopt this position then we will need to devise machinery to relate the traces to the relevant item in comp: these 'binding' conditions are the subject of considerable study today.

Let us now summarize the position we have arrived at, because we have erected a number of important principles. All movement transformations, with a few named exceptions like auxiliary inversion, will be structure-preserving: that is, they will neither create nor destroy structure. Transformations will operate cyclically 'bottom up' from the most deeply embedded sentence to the root sentence. Movement will be constrained by identifying NP and S as bounding nodes and stipulating that no movement transformation may move an item across more than one bounding node. The comp node will, however, function as an escape hatch for *wh* words. All movement transformations will leave behind a trace co-indexed with the moved item: this will provide in the S structure a complete record of all movements that have taken place.

These new proposals are quite radical. They redefine the notion of a movement transformation and constrain it very severely, and the consequences for the total model are considerable at all levels. To begin with, the phrase structure rules will have to be modified in such a way as to ensure that they generate the necessary structures in the first place, including the sites to which movement is permitted. We will not pursue this matter here, but merely note that the kind of modification that will be needed will be the sort of thing we did to accommodate a comp node.

The lexicon will also need modification. The principal consequence of this will be an enriched lexicon. In the last section we discussed various ways in which this comes about, and we now see some additional reasons why it is necessary.

There will also be far-reaching effects on the relationship between the syntax and the semantics. Chief among these is the fact that semantic interpretation can now be carried out at this new level of S structure rather than at the level of deep structure. This has some advantages, chiefly the fact that S structure contains a record both of where moved items came from and where they end up. The former information is important because we need to know where items came from in order to link them up correctly with the verbs they 'belong' with. The latter information, where the moved items end up, can also be important, particularly in the case of questions, as can be seen by comparing the two sentences

Did you tell your mother what you want t for Christmas?
What did you tell your mother you want t for Christmas?

In both cases we need to know that *what* was originally the object of WANT. For each sentence, however, the final position of *what* is important for the semantic interpretation.

Perhaps the most surprising effect of this new arrangement, however, is that transformations largely disappear, and the effect of those few that remain will be largely predictable. This makes it possible for Chomsky to propose that, as far as movement rules are concerned, it may be possible to reduce them all to a single rule!

Before closing the section we should briefly mention the place of deletion transformations in this new model, which, it will be recalled, are now to be separated into separate components. Under these new arrangements movement transformations will operate on deep structures to produce S structures, and deletion transformations on S structures to produce the level of syntactic surface structure familiar from the standard theory model.

The architecture of the model will thus be along the lines shown in Figure 6:8.

We have come a long way. We started off with standard theory grammars where the transformational component was rich in rules, and where the solution to almost any descriptive problem appeared to be to propose another transformation. We end up with much of this power transferred elsewhere in the grammar and a transformational component which may contain but a single transformation!

6.2c 'Revised extended standard theory'

We began this section by observing that one of the characteristics of the new model towards which we have been working is that

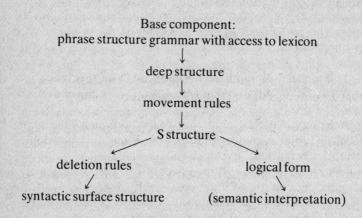

Figure 6:8

the descriptive power of the grammar is no longer, as in standard theory, concentrated in the transformational component of the syntax, but is distributed among a variety of components. In the various subsections above we have looked at some of the principles which determine what sort of information should be handled in which component. Figure 6:8 shows the relationship between the components, and we should now summarize the characteristics of the new model.

The base component is a version of phrase structure grammar known as 'Xbar'. We have not discussed this because the general principles which govern grammars of this type do not differ substantially from those enunciated in 4.2, except insofar as they are enriched by taking explicit account of 'dependency' relations between constituents.

The characteristics of the lexicon were summarized at the end of 6.2a where we saw that it accounts for certain kinds of basic and derived syntactic environments and is responsible for assigning the functional specifications associated with lexical items from which a semantic representation can be built.

The structures produced by the phrase structure rule and lexicalized from the lexicon are, as in standard theory, 'deep structures'. The function of this level of structure is, however, vastly reduced. As before, it has the task of defining the environments into which lexical items are inserted, and it provides a locus for the definitions of 'logical' subject and object. Where it differs from the standard theory level of deep structure is that it is no longer the input to the semantic component.

The transformational component containing the movement rules is, as we have seen, vastly restricted in scope. The movement rules are few in number and highly constrained, both as to what constituents they can move and where they can move them to. Movement is 'structure-preserving', neither creating nor destroying structure, and all moved items leave 'traces' behind in their original sites. The output of the movement rules will be an 'S structure'. Since the movement rules neither create nor destroy structure, configurations at this level will be the same as those at the deep structure level, except that the various terminal nodes may be differently filled, since items may have moved, leaving traces behind them.

S structures are now open to two different types of operation. One is to receive an interpretation in terms of 'logical form', and subsequently perhaps a fuller semantic representation. We have already noted, and it is worth mentioning again, that the interpretation assigned at this level is of a strictly limited nature, as is indicated by the fact that it is referred to as involving a representation in 'logical form'. This is usually taken to mean a version of the predicate calculus, along the lines we have been using, and will include a representation of the way pronouns and traces may be 'bound' by an antecedent within the sentence. For a full semantic representation yet other machinery, of a kind which is not explored within this model, would need to be devised.

The S structure will now go through the deletion component. Deletions are governed by the principle of recoverability mentioned in 6.2. Since semantic interpretation takes place before a string enters the deletion component, it will be clear why recoverability is an important constraint on operations of this kind. The output from the deletion component will, finally, be checked for well-formedness by a set of filters of the kind mentioned on page 168. The output is now a 'syntactic surface structure' and ready to enter the phonological component for a phonological specification. Once again we have a model that relates meanings to surface forms.

The account presented above is, in fact, somewhat of an oversimplification since a number of further principles are proposed which we have not had the space to explore. It will, however, serve to show the way the model is conceived – as a set of interlocking components each of which is governed by a set of principles which determine the kinds of phenomena that are to be handled in this part of the description and constrain the ways in which this can be achieved.

In some obvious ways this new model appears to be vastly more complicated than the model we looked at in Chapter 5. In many ways, however, it is, in fact, much more straightforward. It identifies a number of different kinds of problem that the description of a language needs to address, and articulates a set of very general principles for each. The principles are formulated in general terms because it is claimed that they are part of 'universal grammar'. This means that all languages should reflect the principles, though, of course, different languages may interpret them in somewhat different ways. One example of what is at issue will suffice. We saw in 4.1 that phrasal and lexical categories could be related in the phrase structure component by rules of the general form XP –> . . . X . . ., where 'XP' is a phrasal category – 'noun phrase', 'verb phrase' and so on – and 'X' is the corresponding lexical category – 'noun', 'verb' etc. The notation '. . .' indicates that the category in question may be modified by further material to its right or left or both, but the general schema does not specify which. Suppose that we accept this as a general principle for the construction of phrase structure rules in any language, i.e. as a principle of universal grammar, then we are proposing that in all languages there is a particular relation between phrasal and lexical categories, but that individual languages have the liberty to determine the order of the appropriate modifiers within some particular 'XP'. So, for instance, we would need to specify for English that adjectives typically precede the noun within the NP, whereas in French they typically follow it; in English the object typically follows the verb, whereas in Turkish it normally precedes it, and so on.

There is a striking difference between this new way of looking at the description of a language and that articulated in standard theory. The difference may perhaps be summed up in Chomsky's own words:

> The problem has always been to discover the elements that interact to yield the full complexity of natural language. Early transformational grammar was in part on the wrong track in attributing the complexity to the variety of phrase structure rules and transformations . . . I think we may now be a good bit closer to identifying these fundamental elements: principles of the kind I have been outlining, which are now being investigated and developed in work that I think has already been quite fruitful and that raises many intriguing questions for further study. (Chomsky, 1982a:89)

6.3 The retreat from transformations

One way of avoiding the kinds of problems that transformations present is to abandon them altogether, and with them the constraints, filters and so on that are still needed to control even the reduced number of transformations that remain in the REST model. A number of ways have been canvassed for doing this, including putting even more of the descriptive burden in the lexicon, and developing a more extended theory of phrase structure grammar. In this section we will look briefly at the latter proposal, and see how a developed phrase structure grammar, of a kind that has come to be known as 'generalized phrase structure grammar', can account for the complexity of structure found in a language, without sacrificing any of the appropriate generalizations about the way these structures interrelate and how they are interpreted. As in other sections, our account will, of necessity, be somewhat oversimplified.

Many of the general principles governing PS rules that we set up in Chapter 4 will apply to this form of PS grammar too, though we will also need to introduce some new conventions as we go along. We will begin by assuming a set of phrase structure rules that define tree structures of the sort that are already familiar:

1. S → NP VP
2. VP → V   (runs; eats)
3. VP → V NP   (eats biscuits; killed John)
4. VP → V NP PP[to]   (gave a book to Mary; sent a present to Jane)
5. VP → V NP NP   (gave Mary a book; spare me a minute)
6. VP → V S   (thinks John is clever)

When we first met rules of this sort in 4.2, we saw that they could be collapsed into a single complex rule. This time, we will keep the rules separate, and identify each by a number. There are two reasons for this. The first is concerned with the way in which the various structures generated by the rules are related to semantic interpretations. In a fully articulated version of the grammar, which we do not have space to present, each of the phrase structure rules will be associated with a rule of semantic interpretation. Each of the rules should therefore properly be presented as a 'triple' consisting of the number of the rule, the structure developed by the rule (we have these in the rules presented above), and the semantic interpretation of this structure (which is not shown in the rules above). Given that each rule is associated with a distinct semantic interpretation, each will obviously need to be presented separately. The effect of associating individual rules of syntax with semantic rules for the interpretation of the structure they develop is that the semantics of a sentence will be constructed along with its constituent structure. This means that there is no distinct 'semantic component' associated with this grammar – syntax and semantics are developed side by side, though just how this is accomplished is no concern of ours here.

The second concerns the way lexical items are categorized. In previous discussions we have supposed that a lexical entry contains an annotation to identify the structures that it can enter, thus KILL has been given a categorization '—— NP', GIVE a categorization '—— NP PP' and so on, indicating that KILL can enter the structure generated by rule 3, GIVE that by rule 4 and so on. We still need this information, but now, instead of listing the environments a verb can enter, we will identify the structures it can occur in by referring to the appropriate phrase structure rule: thus KILL will be a '3' verb, indicating that it can enter the structure generated by rule 3, GIVE a '4' and '5' verb, indicating that it enters both of these structures, and so on.

Both of these points can be illustrated by considering the categorization of GIVE as entering two structures, 4 and 5. In a standard theory transformational grammar the paraphrase relation between structures 4 and 5 with a verb like GIVE is accounted for by assuming a common deep structure, that generated by rule 4, and the 'dative transformation' to produce the structure generated by rule 5 as a 'derived' structure. This solution is not open to us now because the grammar we are developing has no transformations. In 6.2a we coped with this matter in a different way and assumed a derivational rule in the lexicon. This model offers yet another solution. As far as GIVE is concerned, this is that the semantics associated with rule 4 will eventually yield an interpretation which will be the same as that derived from rule 5.

Rule 4 introduces another feature of rules in this kind of grammar. Syntactic categories at all levels are treated not simply as node labels, as we have regarded them hitherto, but as having some internal structure. This is represented in a feature notation. With the few rules that are illustrated here, this notation can hardly be developed very far, but rule 4 shows the kind of thing that is at issue: the rule stipulates that the PP to be developed must contain the preposition *to*, and this is shown by ascribing the feature [to] to the category. The implications of this notation are shown in Figure 6:9, where it can be seen that as the PP is developed, the feature is passed down from the 'mother' category to that of 'daughter', which is the head of the resultant construction, where it is 'discharged' by being realized as the preposition *to*. This machinery will doubtless remind the reader of one of the morphological models mentioned in 3.2, where a similar proposal was made.

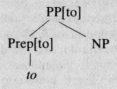

Figure 6:9

Let us now see how this grammar copes with a familiar problem: the derivation of passive sentences. One way of handling this would be to propose additional phrase structure rules:

7.   VP → V[pass] (PP[by])   (was killed (by Bill))
8.   VP → V[pass] NP (PP[by])   (was given a book (by John))

(The feature [by] on the PP will pass down through the structure developed under the PP just as in Figure 6:9. The feature [pass] will operate in a comparable fashion, being passed down to its daughters until it is discharged in a passive verb form.) As stated, these rules clearly do not capture some relevant generalizations, as for instance that there is a systematic relationship between the structures developed by rules 3 and 7 and rules 4 and 8, and so on, and that the class of verbs that enters rule 3 is the same as the class that enters the corresponding passive rule. It is proposed to cope with this problem through a set of 'metarules'. Metarules are statements that relate together particular phrase structure rules. A passive metarule might look like this:

IF there is a rule: n, VP→V NP X

> (where 'n' stands for the number of the rule, and 'X' in the body of the rule stands for any VP constituents following the object NP. As before, we have omitted the semantic specification.)

THEN there is a corresponding rule: n, VP→V[pass] X (PP[by])

If we apply this metarule to rules 3 and 4 then it will give us rules 7 and 8, and in doing so capture the relationship between the two kinds of structure. (It should also be mentioned that the metarule will also specify the semantics of passive VPs, but this will not concern us here.) It is important to note that this is not a transformational rule, but a correspondence rule: transformations, as we have seen, are rules that change structures into other structures, rearrange items within structures and so on, but that is not what is happening here. What the metarule states is that if there is a VP rule which introduces an object NP, perhaps followed by other constituents, represented by 'X', then there is a corresponding VP rule which introduces the same class of verbs in their passive form, followed, where appropriate, by the same other constituents, represented by 'X', and an optional *by* phrase. Note that the rule number, represented as 'n', does not change: given the convention that the structures a verb can enter are identified by the number of the rule that develops the structure in question, this captures the fact that those verbs that will enter an active structure will also enter the corresponding passive structure.

We will close by considering how a grammar of this kind can deal with 'long-distance' dependencies. That is, in a sentence like *Who did you say your mother told you never to talk to ——?* how can a phrase structure grammar show that *who* is to be understood as the object of the preposition *to*, from which it is separated by a considerable distance? We saw in 6.2b that sentences of this sort constitute a major reason why the REST model needs to retain movement transformations: it has no other way of accounting for the dependency other than assuming that the *wh* word is generated as the object of the preposition and subsequently moved to the front of the sentence.

The solution is extremely ingenious. Suppose we think of the problem in two parts. The first involves generating a *wh* word at the front of the sentence and the second a corresponding 'hole' at the position in the sentence where the *wh* word 'belongs'. The position of the 'hole' is represented by '——' in the example in the preceding paragraph.

Let us start by considering the simple sentence *What is John thinking about* ——*?*, and suppose, as a first approximation, that it can be analysed as shown in Figure 6:10: the analysis is deliberately simplified and contains the as yet unspecified nodes 'X' and 'Y':

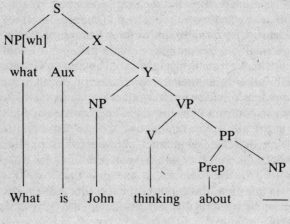

Figure 6:10

Generating a *wh* word at the front of this structure is relatively straightforward. We can suppose that there is a phrase structure rule of the form

n, S → NP[wh] X

If features 'trickle down' on to their daughters, then NP[wh] will generate the *wh* NPs that we need. When we have seen how 'X' in the rule is to be developed, we will return to see that we can produce such phrase structure rules by metarule.

'X' must now be developed to produce *is John thinking about* ——. Consider first the hole. We have supposed that the *wh* word is an NP, and if this is so, then if the hole has a category, it must be an NP too. This is the supposition shown in Figure 6:10.

Consider now what the function of this NP is: it is the object of the prepositional phrase *about* ——, so the prepositional phrase is 'a PP with an NP hole'. Let us represent this as PP/NP (in words, 'PP slash NP') where the slash notation indicates that the constituent to the left of the slash lacks, somewhere in its structure, the constituent to the right. Note that the slash notation does not specify where the hole is to come, merely that there is a hole. Now consider the VP constituent. If the PP constituent lacks an NP somewhere in its structure, then the VP which contains this PP also lacks an NP somewhere in its structure. The VP can thus be considered to be 'a VP with an NP hole'. Using the slash notation again, we have a representation VP/NP. This account immediately suggests a parallel with the features mentioned earlier: just as a feature can trickle down from some category to its daughter, and then from the daughter to the daughter's daughter and so on, so a slashed constituent can, as it were, pass its slash down to a daughter. Given this, we can see that the slash NP on the VP will pass down to become a slash NP on PP, and then it will pass to a daughter of PP and become a slash NP on NP. We now have an NP consisting of an NP hole. This is just what we require: the slashed NP has been discharged by becoming an NP hole.

We can now extend this notation to 'X' and 'Y'. They too must be categories slashed with NP. For our purposes we will represent these two categories as, respectively, 'S1/NP' and 'S2/NP'. The slashed NP indicates that the structures contain, somewhere, an NP hole. The representations 'S1' and 'S2' are intended to relate to the structures necessary to accommodate the inversion of subject and auxiliary: this can be coped with in this model, but, as with our previous discussion of question formation, we will ignore in this brief discussion just how this is done. Incorporating this information into Figure 6:10 will yield the derivation of Figure 6:11.

Let us now return to the original PS rule for questions. The form of this rule, we can now see, must be

$$S \rightarrow NP[wh]\ S/NP$$

That is, a *wh* word followed by a sentence with an NP hole. The

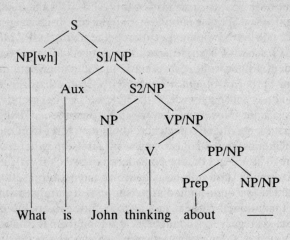

Figure 6:11

semantic specification for this rule will ensure that the *wh* NP is given an interpretation in the NP hole, wherever that may turn out to be. This is, of course, exactly what the traces we discussed in 6.2b were designed to ensure. We have now managed to achieve the same effect without recourse to a movement transformation! Given our previous observations about metarules, we can now propose a metarule of the following kind to accommodate *wh* questions:

IF there is a rule:　　　　　　　　　n, S → X

(where 'X' stands for any sentence expansion)

THEN there is a corresponding rule: n, S → NP[wh] S/NP

This rule will then ensure that for every sentence there is a corresponding *wh* interrogative structure consisting of a *wh* word followed by a sentence with an NP hole.

Another point to note is that the notation S/NP, and the other slashed notations, do not specify where the hole should be, simply that there should be one. In the example we have been working with, the slashed NP discharges itself as a hole in a PP. It might equally easily, however, have been discharged in the subject position, yielding a sentence like *Who is —— thinking about Christmas?* Nor is there any reason why a slashed NP should not be carried down into an independent sentence, yielding perhaps *Who did your mother say you were never to talk to ——?*

We will not pursue the derivation of complex sentences any further. We should not, however, conclude without mentioning that the very same machinery can insightfully be extended to an account of the kind of data that is accounted for by deletion transformations in a transformational account. For example, in a sentence like *John went to London and Charlie —— to New York*, the hole in the second conjunct is understood as *went*: this suggests that the second conjunct is a sentence lacking a verb, i.e. S/V: the semantics specifying the identity of the missing item.

We have not had space to do justice to phrase structure grammars, but several points emerge from even this brief summary. The first relates to a claim that used to be made by transformational grammarians: this was that the nature of language is such that it is literally impossible to describe it in phrase structure terms, and an additional level of transformational description is therefore necessary. This claim was doubtless true of the particular kind of phrase structure grammar espoused by those who made the claim (essentially the kind we looked at in Chapter 4); it is clearly not true if more elaborate phrase structure grammars are used. There seems no reason to doubt that the powerful phrase structure models we have just been glancing at have no less generative capacity than transformational grammars and have a number of advantages over them. To begin with they have no transformations, obviously, and consequently are not encumbered with the constraints and filters that even a single transformation seems to entail. Furthermore, since in the generalized phrase structure model we have been examining the semantic and syntactic rules work hand in hand, the model does not have the variety of distinct components characteristic of the transformational model. For reasons of this kind, it seems likely that generalized phrase structure grammars will, over the next few years, attract an increasing amount of attention.

We began this chapter by looking at some of the problems raised by the notion of a syntactic transformation and have seen how it has been suggested that the model can be modified to take account of these problems. We have also looked briefly at one other kind of model, a generalized phrase structure grammar, that does away with transformations altogether. We should now turn to look at models of syntactic structure that start from a rather different point of view, and consider syntactic function rather than syntactic structure as primary: this will be the subject of the next chapter.

7 Functional Relations

Now any linguistic phenomenon may be regarded either from without or from within, either from the outward form or from the inner meaning. In the first case we take the sound (of a word or of some other part of a linguistic expression) and then enquire into the meaning attached to it; in the second case we start from the signification and ask ourselves what formal expression it has found in the particular language we are dealing with.

(Otto Jespersen)

Thus far we have been looking at linguistic units primarily in 'categorial' terms. We have identified categories, like noun or noun phrase, in terms of their internal structure and their distribution within other structures. Thus the phrase structure grammars we looked at in Chapter 4 defined sentences in terms of the distribution of items into categories within structures, and the transformational relationships we looked at in Chapter 5 were defined in structural terms, the rules identifying some particular structure and changing it into some other structure.

This is not the only way in which sentence constituents can be viewed, and in this chapter we will consider a different approach. This time we will be concentrating primarily on the functional relationships that can be contracted between constituents. After an introduction to the general problem, we will turn to a central concern of functional grammars, the nature of the relationships between the verb and the various NPs and other constituents in the sentence. Here we will look at two approaches to description, one describing the various relations established with labels like 'agent' and 'patient' and the other with labels like 'subject' and 'object'. In 7.2 we will see what grammars that take these relationships as primary might look like, and how they differ from the constituent structure grammars we have hitherto been concerned with. Finally, in 7.3 we will look at some of the 'universalist' implications of this type of analysis.

Functional approaches can, in some ways, be considered to be the inverse of the categorial approach we have adopted thus far. We saw in Chapter 5 that when categorially based grammars need to call on functional relationships they are treated as being of secondary rather than primary importance. What this means is that if a description is couched primarily in categorial terms (configurations of constituents like noun, noun phrase, verb, verb phrase and so on), then functional notions will either be derived by an interpretation of some categorial configuration, which was how we defined subject and object in 5.1, or they will be derived from lexical entries, which was how we treated relations like 'agent', 'patient' etc. with verbs like KILL in 6.1. From this perspective, categorial structure is primary and functional structure secondary. This time, although we shall of course still be interested in constituent structure, we shall consider functional relationships as primary and constituent structure as interpretive of functional structure. One consequence of the difference of approach will be that the notion of a syntactic transformation will generally be abandoned in favour of other ways of handling sentence relatedness.

Let us first consider the general question of grammatical relations. A traditional view distinguishes between 'paradigmatic' and 'syntagmatic' relations, and we can exemplify the difference between the functional and the categorial approaches by contrasting the way in which they approach this distinction. Paradigmatic relations are essentially relationships of substitutability, the relation between an item in a particular syntactic position and other items that might have been chosen in that syntactic position but were not. We called on this relation in Chapter 4, when establishing lexical and phrasal categories. Syntagmatic relations are essentially relationships of co-occurrence, the relations contracted between an item in a particular position in the sentence and other items that occur in other positions in the same sentence. We used this relationship too in Chapter 4, particularly in the discussion of subclasses: for example, a verb is transitive or intransitive depending on whether it does or does not need a following NP. The relations are clearly interdependent and all syntactic categories need to be classified in terms of both kinds of relation.

In this chapter we shall be primarily interested in syntagmatic functional relations. In this case, instead of being primarily concerned with the distribution of constituents, we will be primarily interested in the 'dependency' of one constituent on another. In almost all constructions one constituent can be considered to be the 'head' and the others 'dependants' of the head. The head will 'govern' its dependants and mark this government in various ways. We can see what is at issue by looking at some examples of dependency in the English noun phrase.

In noun phrases with the categorial structure [Det (Adj) N (PP)], like *the large cat* or *the cat on the mat*, the noun is the 'head' of the construction and the adjective, determiner and preposition phrase its 'modifiers'. The modifiers are dependent on and governed by the head. The dependency reveals itself at all levels of linguistic structure. Semantically the head is the salient constituent, and modifiers will restrict its potential reference. With adjectives like *large* the semantic dependency of the adjective on the noun is particularly marked since, as we mentioned in 1.2, the interpretation of 'scalar' adjectives crucially depends on the noun modified: 'large' for a cat is larger than 'large' for a mouse, but smaller than 'large' for an elephant.

Syntactically the dependency is shown in a number of ways. To begin with, the head is obligatory, whereas modifiers are normally optional. So we can find NPs with only a head noun, as in *Cats sit on mats*, but we will not find NPs consisting only of modifiers, as in *The sits on the mat*, or *The large sits on the mat* (except in the latter case in special circumstances, where a head noun is 'understood').

Dependencies of this kind are often also overtly marked, and when they are, it is the head that governs the marking. Three kinds of marking are typically found, morphological marking, the use of special particles or other words like prepositions and marking by word order. Morphological marking in the NP is usually in the form of 'concord' or 'agreement': a particular grammatical category of the head is copied on to the dependants.

English does not have a great deal of morphology, and consequently has few concordial constructions, but where they do exist it is clearly the head that determines the concord. So, those determiners that vary for number (*that:those*; *this:these*) take their number from the head noun: *those cats* not **that cats*. More highly inflecting languages than English show more complex patterns of agreement. In French, articles agree in number and gender with the head noun, so we find NPs like *la table* not **le table*: it would hardly be appropriate to claim that the latter is ill formed because the head noun is in the wrong gender! In Latin, adjectives concord with the head noun which governs their number, gender and case, as we saw in the short example in 3.2.

English has few special particles reserved as markers of dependency apart from the 'apostrophe *s*' used to mark the dependent 'genitive' in structures like *John's book* or *the man next door's car*. The language does, however, make extensive use of prepositions for this purpose, as in the other 'genitive' structure in English, *pint of milk* or *President of the United States*, and in 'postnominal' PP modifiers like *man in the moon* and *holidays in Greece*.

The third important marker of dependency is word order, and here again it is the head that is the determining factor, the order of the modifiers being determined relative to the head, rather than the other way round. In English determiners and adjectives generally precede the head and PP modifiers invariably follow it, as the examples show. In other languages the order may be different but a description of the ordering relation will always specify the position of the modifiers in terms of the head. Thus in French we may say that articles precede and adjectives normally follow the head, as in *une chatte large*.

It will be obvious that languages differ in the way they mark NP dependencies. English, with its relatively restricted morphology, typically chooses word order: adjectives precede the noun they modify, and this is how, in a sentence with several adjectives, we know which adjective to associate with which noun. By contrast Latin, with its elaborate morphology, will permit adjectives to occur either before or after the noun, or indeed quite separate from the noun, and we know which adjective is associated with which noun because of the number, gender and case markers.

Identifying the function of various constituents in this way does not lessen our interest in the syntactic category of constituents, and it is hardly surprising that dependency and categorial relations share many similarities. Two points of similarity are worth a mention, because they also demonstrate the difference in emphasis between the two approaches. First, there is typically a strong correlation between syntactic category and grammatical function. Characteristically, nouns function as heads and adjectives as modifiers, as in the examples we have been considering. But this is not invariably the case, and it is interesting to see what happens in atypical constructions. When we meet an NP consisting of two or more nouns the pressure of the modifier-head pattern invites us to interpret the last as head and the others as modifiers: so a *bus station* is a type of station and a *station bus* is a type of bus. Similarly if we encounter an NP with two adjectives and no noun, as in *the undeserving poor*, it too will be interpreted as a modifier-head construction, *poor* being construed as the head and *undeserving* as its modifier. Indeed, in order to maintain the form-function correlation between head and noun, and modifier and adjective, descriptions frequently say about an NP like *the filthy rich*, either that the adjective *rich* has been 'recategorized' as a noun, or that there is an 'understood' noun. But this confuses category and function, and it is interesting to observe that it is generally the dependency structure and not the lexical class that determines the interpretation and analysis.

Secondly, we saw in 4.1 that coordination is an important criterion for class membership. It is equally important when we are discussing dependencies. We have already seen that conjuncts are normally of the same category: nouns coordinate with nouns, verbs with verbs, NPs with NPs, VPs with VPs and so on. 'Cross-category' coordination, noun with verb, NP with VP and so on, is usually unacceptable. Dependency structures show similar restrictions, and cross-dependency coordination is usually as infelicitous as cross-category coordination. So, we can coordinate subject expressions (*John and his brother bought a house*) or object expressions (*John bought a car and a house*).

We can also, though perhaps less felicitously, find coordinations like *That vase, my grandmother gave me and I cracked*, where the topicalized constituent *That vase* is construed as the object of both GIVE and CRACK. We cannot, however, coordinate subject and object expressions. So a sentence like *That vase, my grandmother gave me and cracked*, where the topicalized *that vase* is to be understood as the object of GIVE but the subject of CRACK, is impossible. In this respect, dependency is in fact sometimes more crucial than category. We can find cases where it is in fact permissible to coordinate unlike categories, providing they have the same dependency. So, for example, it is possible to coordinate adjectives and PPs providing they are both 'complements' (a term to be explained in the next section): *The baby is in bed and asleep* (PP and adj), *I am going home and to bed* (N and PP). In text, cross-dependency coordination is sometimes exploited for a particular rhetorical effect known as 'zeugma', as in *Mr Pickwick took his hat and his leave*. Such examples derive their effect precisely from the 'creative' disregard of the 'normal'.

7.1 The verb and its dependants

In this section we will be concerned with what has traditionally been regarded as one of the most important sets of functional relationships to be found in any language: those between a verb and the various NP and PP constituents with which it co-occurs. These relationships can be viewed as a set of dependencies, parallel to the modifier-head dependencies discussed in the previous section. We will first consider some of the general problems of description, and then in the following two subsections examine two approaches to description. We shall, as in the previous section, be interested both in the general nature of the relationships and also in the ways in which they are syntactically marked.

Any discussion of the dependencies between the verb and the NPs etc. with which it co-occurs meets with an immediate problem. The dependencies operate at various linguistic levels, and at each level the relations are somewhat different. We will consider three levels: a 'surface' level of word forms in a sentence, a 'deep' level of semantic or logical relations, again within a sentence, and a 'textual' level, which involves relationships both within and between sentences. It will not be entirely surprising to find that there are close relationships between these various levels, or indeed that some of the terminology involved is sometimes applied to all three levels. Such a variable use of terminology can, however, introduce some confusion if we are not careful.

It will be helpful to start the discussion by distinguishing between the different levels. Consider the sentence *The farmer is killing the ducklings*. A 'surface' description will obviously be interested in a categorial description of surface structure of the kind we have discussed in previous chapters. It will, however, also be concerned to identify dependency relations at this level of structure, since various facts of word order, morphological marking and so on hang on these dependencies. So, for instance, we will want to identify *the farmer* as the 'grammatical subject' and *the ducklings* as the 'grammatical object'. The word 'grammatical' is used to indicate that in this case we are dealing with surface grammatical structure. The grammatical subject is an obligatory constituent, it precedes the verb, concords with it in number and is the governor of the concord (in the example we have *the farmer is* . . . and not *the farmer are* . . .). Furthermore, if the subject is a pronoun, it will be in the 'base' form *he* rather than the 'oblique' form *him*.

The grammatical object is also an obligatory constituent when we are dealing with a transitive verb like KILL in an active sentence. It will immediately follow the verb, and, if it is a pronoun, will be governed by the verb in the 'oblique' form *them* rather than in the 'base' form *they*. Other dependencies are sometimes marked by word order and sometimes by other markers, particularly prepositions. The 'indirect object' (*Mary* in *John gave the book to Mary/ gave Mary the book*) can either follow the object, and then it will be marked with the preposition *to*, or it can precede the object, and then it will have no prepositional marker. Instrumental expressions are marked with the preposition *with* (*The farmer killed the ducklings with an axe*). Benefactive expressions are marked with the preposition *for* (*The farmer killed the ducklings for his wife* and so on). At this level of description we can regard the subject as the head of the sentence as a whole, with the VP as its modifier; and within the VP we can regard the verb as the head and its objects etc. as modifiers.

Next, consider our example from the point of view of a 'deep' description. Since such descriptions are usually more influenced by semantic or 'logical' factors than they are by factors relating to distribution and surface constituency, it is perhaps hardly surprising that there are different views on what a representation at this level should look like. The transformational model assumes that the representation should be in categorial terms, essentially of the same kind as those used in the surface description. A functional model, on the other hand, will usually assume that at this level the description should be in relational rather than categorial terms. If we take the latter point of view, and have a deep representation in dependency terms, then it will not be surprising that the relations in question turn out to be rather different from those at the surface. At this level, the verb itself is usually regarded as the head of the construction and all the various NPs etc., including the one that will eventually become the grammatical subject, as its dependants. These dependants are often referred to as the 'arguments' of the verb. In these terms, instead of talking about 'transitive' and 'intransitive' verbs, as we might do in a surface categorial description, we will describe verbs in terms of the number of arguments they take. Thus, DIE will be a 'one-place verb' since it occurs with only a single argument (*The ducklings died*), KILL will be a 'two-place verb' since it needs two arguments (*The farmer killed the ducklings*), GIVE will be a 'three-place verb' (*The farmer gave some grain to the ducklings*) and so on.

Given this approach to verb classification, if a verb has more than one argument, as in the case of KILL, it will clearly be important to distinguish between them: there is a clear difference of meaning between *The farmer killed the ducklings* and *The ducklings killed the farmer*! There are a number of ways in which this might be done. One, which we look at in more detail in 7.1b, is to characterize each argument with a label like 'agent', for the performer of the action, 'patient' for the sufferer of the action, 'goal' for the beneficiary of the action and so forth. These descriptions can then be associated with the various arguments, perhaps along the following lines:

> DIE (patient ——)
> KILL (agent —— patient)
> GIVE (agent —— patient, goal)

The lexical entries developed in Chapter 5 were partially along these lines.

Another way of distinguishing between the various arguments is to use labels like 'logical subject', 'logical object' and so on, the modifier 'logical' indicating that these relations hold at a 'deep' semantic level of description rather than at the 'surface' level of grammatical description. We will look at this approach in more detail in 7.1b. In these terms, since we assume that all verbs have a logical subject, the single argument associated with a one-place verb must be the logical subject. With two- and more place verbs there are various ways in which we might distinguish the arguments. The simplest is to label them as logical subject, object and so on: FARMER[LS], KILL, DUCKLINGS[LO]. Alternatively, we can establish a convention that, in representations at this level of description, the order in which the various NPs are shown identifies their relation. So, for example, we can identify the first argument as the logical subject, the second as the logical object and so on. This approach has been implicit in the logical representations we have used in previous chapters: thus in KILL (FARMER, DUCKLINGS), corresponding to *The farmer killed the ducklings*, FARMER is logical subject and DUCKLINGS logical object, and in KILL (DUCKLINGS, FARMER), corresponding to *The ducklings killed the farmer*, DUCKLINGS is logical subject and FARMER is logical object.

Let us now turn briefly to the third level mentioned at the beginning of the section. This, it will be recalled, was concerned with textual structure. At this level, people sometimes talk about the 'psychological subject' or 'topic' of a sentence. A description of this kind relates to the everyday notion of 'what someone is talking or writing about', as, for example, when someone enquires *What is the subject/topic of* The Times' *main leader today?* The notions of 'topic' or 'psychological subject' are rather different from the other types of subject we have looked at, principally because they cannot reasonably be restricted to a consideration of individual sentences in isolation in the way that the notions of agent etc. or logical and grammatical subject necessarily are. Rather, they involve the concept of a 'text', or 'discourse'. Because of this difference, we will leave consideration of these notions to Chapter 8. It will, however, be useful to have some idea of what is at issue. When we meet a sentence in isolation we typically construe the first NP as the 'psychological subject'. Thus, characteristically, we interpret an active sentence like *The farmer is killing the ducklings* as a comment on the activities of *the farmer*, and the corresponding passive *The ducklings are being killed by the farmer* as a comment on the fate of *the ducklings*. In cases of this sort, grammatical and psychological subjects coincide because the grammatical subject is the first NP constituent in the sentence. It is, however, possible to construct examples where this is not the case, as in *The ducklings, the farmer killed*. In this example, order is not the only marker of the psychological subject, since structures of this kind are usually also associated with particular intonational features.

So far, then, the discussion has suggested that there are at least three different levels of description involved, and that they need to be kept apart. This is particularly important when we are using the terms 'subject' and 'object', since they are used at all three levels.

Before we turn to examine the two approaches to description we will be looking at in this section, we should briefly consider two general questions that apply to both approaches. First, how do logical arguments correspond to grammatical constituents? And second, how many logical arguments can a verb have?

As far as the first question is concerned, we will find several types of relationship. In the most straightforward cases, each logical argument will correspond to a surface constituent. If a verb has only a single argument, as in the case of DIE, then this will become the grammatical subject. If there are two, then either argument can become the grammatical subject, but the particular choice will have syntactic consequences. With KILL, the choice of agent, or logical subject, as grammatical subject will yield an active sentence, *The farmer killed the ducklings*, and the choice of the patient, or logical object, as grammatical subject will yield the corresponding passive, *The ducklings were killed by the farmer*.

Each logical argument does not always correspond to a surface constituent. Sometimes a logical argument has no surface realization, and when this happens descriptions often speak of an 'understood' argument. This is the case, for example, in 'agentless' passive sentences like *The ducklings were killed*. Here, since 'killing' implies a 'killer', it seems that an agent is 'understood'. Sentences of this sort are often used either when an unknown agent is involved or when the identity of the agent is 'recoverable' from the context. We might informally represent this in some such terms as KILL('X' DUCKLINGS), where 'X' represents the understood subject, either recoverable or indefinite.

We can also find the converse situation, where there are more surface constituents than there are logical arguments. In these circumstances descriptions often speak of a 'dummy' constituent. To see what is involved here we must briefly return to the other two cases. In the first case, each argument is realized by an NP or PP containing a lexical noun or pronoun which can be said to refer to some object in the real or imagined context. So we can say *The cat died* or *It died*, and in the latter case it will make sense to ask *What died?* In the second case, although there is no lexical realization for the understood argument, otherwise it would hardly be 'understood', it nevertheless makes sense to question its identity. So, if you say *The ducklings were killed*, it makes sense for me to ask *Who killed them?* Consider now a verb like RAIN in a sentence such as *It is raining*. Here it makes no sense to ask *What is raining?* since *it* does not refer to anything at all. At the logical level RAIN can be considered to be a 'no-place verb', a verb with no logical arguments. Since there are no arguments, none can be realized by a lexical noun or pronoun, and furthermore there is no argument that can be assigned to grammatical subject. In these circumstances, since a grammatical subject is necessary in all sentences in English, the language has available a special 'dummy' subject, *it*. Sentences of this kind are sometimes said to involve an 'impersonal subject'.

Let us now turn to the second question. How many arguments do we want to associate with a verb? We have seen that it is possible to categorize verbs as 'no-place', 'one-place', 'two-place' and so on in terms of the number of arguments that co-occur with the verb. We have also seen that there is no necessary correspondence between logical and grammatical structure. It is also clear that sentences can have large numbers of constituents, as for example

This morning – I – cut – my chin – while I was shaving.

We should now enquire whether CUT is a 'four-place' verb, or whether some of these constituents do not 'count' in the categorization, and if so which ones and why. We can begin to answer this question by drawing a distinction between 'nuclear' and 'circumstantial' constituents. Nuclear constituents will be those that have a particularly close tie to the verb, both syntactically and semantically. Syntactically the tie is revealed by the fact that the constituents involved are usually obligatory and cannot be omitted without yielding an ungrammatical sentence: it is these constituents that are the grammatical subject, object etc. Semantically, the nuclear items will be particularly closely related to the kind of action etc. described by the verb. These constituents are the arguments of the verb, and we can say that the verb and its arguments constitute the 'propositional nucleus' of the sentence. Circumstantial constituents characteristically refer to the circumstances of time and place in which the proposition is set, and have a looser tie to the sentence. Syntactically they are usually optional, and so can be omitted without affecting grammaticality: constituents of this kind are usually classified as 'adverbs', of place, time etc. Semantically, they will be related to the propositional nucleus as a whole, rather than to the verb in particular. By these criteria, in the example sentence *I* and *my chin* will be nuclear, and *this morning* and *while I was shaving* circumstantial.

Unfortunately it is not always quite as simple as this, and there are in fact often considerable problems in distinguishing between nuclear and circumstantial constituents. The heart of the problem is that there is a conflict here between a grammatical and a functional characterization. At the functional level, if we define as nuclear those constituents which are crucially involved in the type of event etc. described by the verb, then we will frequently find that at the grammatical level some such constituents are syntactically optional. In the example, the 'cutter' and the 'thing cut' are nuclear at both levels. Equally clearly the temporal expressions are circumstantial at both levels. Suppose, however, we were to add an 'instrumental' expression? In the example, an instrument is implied by the adverbial context, since one shaves with a razor, but this is not always so. Consider a sentence like *I cut myself with the potato peeler*, or *He cut the cake with a ceremonial sword*. In these cases the instrumental expression seems to be functionally nuclear but categorially optional. We shall meet other similar cases as we proceed.

What we have been trying to do in this section is to identify different levels of functional analysis, a 'surface' level, a 'deep' or 'logical' level, and a 'textual' level. We have also noted that these levels do not necessarily coincide. In the sections that follow in this chapter we shall be primarily interested in the first two of these levels as they affect the structure of individual sentences. In Chapter 8 we will look briefly at sentences in texts.

7.1a Agents and patients

In this section we will look in more detail at one of the ways mentioned at the beginning of this chapter of describing the functional relationships between a verb and the various NPs etc. with which it can co-occur in a proposition. There are a number of ways in which this can be done, and the description here follows the approach of Brown and Miller (1982). This approach characterizes the 'role' each argument plays in the sentence in terms of notions like 'agent', 'patient', 'goal' and so on, and in addition characterizes the verb in any predication in terms of one of a number of 'process' types, which describe the type of state or event the verb refers to. We will begin with an informal description of the kind of phenomena that are of interest, leaving to section 7.2 a consideration of how such phenomena are to be accommodated in a model of description.

Let us start by considering the sentences

1. The door opened
2. John opened the door

Both can be used to refer to an 'event', so we will characterize the process type of OPEN by a feature 'event'. 1 and 2 can be compared with the sentence

3. The door is open

which will typically be used to describe a state of affairs rather than an event, so we will propose a feature 'state' to characterize the process type of the verb BE, and characterize the adjective OPEN as 'descriptive'.

What now of the roles of the various NPs? We will consider first the NPs in the 'event' sentences and return to the 'state' sentence in a moment. In 2 *John*, as the instigator of the action, can be described as an 'agent' and *the door*, the object which 'is affected by the verb', as a 'patient'. In fact, for reasons which will appear, it will be more helpful to describe the semantic role of *the door* in more general terms as 'neutral'. Turning now to sentence 1, the semantic role of *the door* in this sentence is plausibly regarded as the same as that of *the door* in 2, since it is once more the 'object that is affected by the verb'. We can represent these observations as:

1′ Neut(ral)   Event
2′ Ag(ent)   Event   Neut
3′ Neut   State   Desc(riptive)

Let us now widen the data base to include:

4. John opened the door with a key
5. A key opened the door

The additional argument in 4, *a key*, can be ascribed the role of 'instrument' – the 'object used in the performance of the action described by the verb' – and this role is preserved in 5. So these two sentences can be characterized as:

4′	Ag	Event	Neut	Inst(rument)
5′	Inst	Event	Neut	

We now have the beginnings of a set of participant roles, 'agent', 'neutral' and 'instrument'. As we meet with other role types, this set will need to be extended further. We also have two basic verb process types, 'state' and 'event'. We will now expand our description of the verb process types a little further. Both state and event verbs can be further subclassified in terms of the type of state or event that is involved. We have already described the adjective OPEN as a 'descriptive' adjective, and it will then be reasonable to describe the verb OPEN as a descriptive verb. Descriptive event verbs can now be further subclassified to describe more precisely some significant features of the event at issue. Two of the most common further classifications are shown in the examples. Sentence 1, *The door opened*, contains an 'inchoative' or 'change-of-state' verb (used to describe circumstances where a participant changes from one state to another) and sentence 2, *John opened the door*, a 'causative' verb (used to describe a situation where one participant causes a change of state in another).

With 'descriptive' verbs and adjectives, we often find triplets involving a state, an inchoative event and a causative event, as shown in Figure 7:1.

This relationship has consequences for lexical, syntactic and semantic structure. The lexical consequences can be seen in the relationship between the adjectives of the leftmost column and the verbs of the other two columns. A variety of relationships can be observed, depending on the particular lexical item involved. In the case of OPEN, there is a simple class change from the adjective in the left column to the inchoative and causative verbs of the middle and right columns. With RIPE the verbs of the middle and right columns are derived from the adjective in the left column by a derivational rule affixing *-en*. With HOT, there is the corresponding causative verb HEAT, in the right-hand

State	Event, Inch	Event, Caus
Neutral——	Neutral ——	Agent —— Neutral
The door is open	The door is opening	John opened the door
The fruit is ripe	The fruit is ripening	The sun ripened the fruit
The food is hot	The food is getting hot	Mary is heating the food
The grass is dead	The grass is dying	The drought killed the grass

[The first line of descriptors relates to the type of state or event, the abbreviations are Inch(oative) and Caus(ative). The second line of descriptors relates to the role relations of the various NPs.]

Figure 7:1

column, but this is not generally used as an inchoative and instead we use the 'periphrastic' form GET HOT. In the last example we find an instance of another common type of relationship involving distinct, but semantically related, lexical items. So we find the adjective, DEAD, the morphologically related intransitive verb, DIE, that is not used causatively except in jokes (*He deaded me!*), and the quite distinct lexical item, KILL. In this case the semantic relationship is preserved even though lexical identity is not, since DEAD:DIE:KILL is parallel to HOT:GET HOT:HEAT or RIPE:RIPEN:RIPEN.

There is a variety of syntactic consequences of the relationship. To begin with, there are different syntactic restrictions on each type of sentence. State predications do not normally occur with the verb in the 'progressive' form: so we will not find sentences like *The door is being open* or *The grass is being dead*. Nor do state predications usually occur in imperative sentences: *Be ripe (oh fruit)*. There is no such restriction on the causative sentences where *John is opening the door* and *Open the door, John* are perfectly well formed. Causative predications will also occur freely with instrumental expressions (*John opened the door with a key*) but these do not occur freely with state expressions (*The door is open with a key*). We should also note another very general relationship between these sentence types. The subject of the intransitive state or inchoative sentences 'becomes' the object of the corresponding transitive causative sentence and a new agentive subject is introduced: we will return to this relationship later.

In a semantic description, there is an equally clear relationship between the three types of predication. This can be highlighted by using a representation in which we postulate 'abstract' predicates, CHANGE to correspond to the process feature inchoative, and CAUSE to correspond to the process feature causative. We have already met an analysis of this sort in 6.1, when we were discussing 'generative semantics'. (In the representation 'P' stands for an embedded predication.)

The plates are warm   WARM(PLATES)

The plates are warming   CHANGE(PLATES P)
                                    /
                              WARM(PLATES)

Mary warmed the plates   CAUSE(MARY P)
                                    /
                              CHANGE(PLATES P)
                                    /
                              WARM(PLATES)

In these representations the element CHANGE and the embedded predication WARM(PLATES) are intended to show that the 'change of state' involved in 'warming the plates' leads to a state where the 'plates are warm'. Similarly CAUSE represents the fact that the agent, 'Mary', 'causes' the 'change of state'. In this way we can explicitly draw the logical implication that if someone 'warms plates' they 'change to a state of being warm'.

This relationship between state and event predications is one of the fundamental relationships in any language, and its influence is, as we have seen, pervasive at many levels of linguistic structure. A description involving verb processes and nominal roles is an insightful way of describing them. The relationships are particularly clear in English with descriptive verbs because of the clear lexical and syntactic parallelisms. They can, however, be illustrated by verbs of other process types.

With verbs of 'place' and 'motion' we find triplets like:

State, place		John is in bed
Event, motion, inch		John is going to bed
	caus	The doctor sent John to bed
State, place		The ball is under the table
Event, motion, inch		The ball is rolling under the table
	caus	John rolled the ball under the table

and verbs of 'possession' exhibit a similar set of relationships:

State, poss		I have a banana
Event, poss, inch		I am getting a banana
	caus	John gave a banana to me
	caus	John took a banana from me

Unfortunately, there is no space to develop this kind of analysis further, and the interested reader is referred to the Further Reading at the end. The discussion should, however, give an idea of the kind of data in which an analysis of this kind interests itself, and the kind of generalizations it draws about linguistic structures. The basis principle is that verbs are subcategorized into a number of process types (and further classification can be readily imagined), and that NPs are classified into a number of role types (and again further classification can be thought of). In 7.2 we will see how information of this kind can be incorporated into grammatical descriptions.

7.1b Subjects and objects

In this subsection we will consider another way of describing the dependency between the verb and other sentence constituents. This involves the traditional relations of 'subject', 'object' etc.

We have already noted that the terms have been used to apply to several different levels of description and the traditional use of the terms does not always keep the different levels very strictly apart. In what follows we shall, initially, follow this tradition.

At the grammatical level of description, subject is the least problematic function to identify since all simple declarative sentences of English must have one, even if it is only the 'dummy' subject associated with no-place verbs like RAIN. At the logical level, subject causes no problems with one-place sentences, since the single argument will, by definition, be the logical subject. Sentences with several arguments can sometimes be problematic. There are, however, various rules of thumb for deciding which argument will be the logical subject. Primary among these is perhaps the fact that it seems that an argument that is typically realized with a human NP is more likely to be logical subject than one which is not. So, if there is an agent, and agents are characteristically human, then this will be logical subject. When it comes to realization at the grammatical level an agent will usually be chosen as grammatical subject in preference to other arguments, and when some other argument is chosen in preference to an agent, the choice is usually 'registered' by the use of passive morphology in the verb. If there is no agent, then there might be an 'experiencer', and if so, this will usually be considered to be the logical subject. This can, however, result in a mismatch between logical and surface relations. With verbs relating to sense perception, like SEE and HEAR, and with some other verbs such as LIKE, HATE and RELISH, the experiencer is indeed normally realized as the grammatical subject: *I can see the stars*, *I like linguistics*. There are, however, many verbs – EXCITE, AMUSE, INTEREST among them – where the experiencer is realized as grammatical object: *Linguistics interests me*. There seems to be no alternative in such cases other than to record such matters in the lexicon.

Objects are less easy to define because a number of different kinds of dependency can be contracted between a verb and its object. Traditionally this was recognized by identifying a number of different types of object, each with a different semantic interpretation and different syntactic behaviour. The most straightforward object type is the 'direct' or 'affected' object exemplified in a sentence like *John beat the donkey*. Such object expressions are typically interpreted as 'undergoing the action described by the verb', hence the description 'affected object'. It is this type of object that occurs with transitive verbs (where traditionally the 'action of the verb' is said to 'pass over' – hence 'transitive' – from the subject to the affected object). The most clear-cut cases of transitive verbs are verbs of 'violence' like BEAT and KILL, and perhaps one reason why such verbs are so frequently used in linguistic examples is because they are the clearest cases of an object expression. In English, the principal syntactic marker of this dependency in a simple sentence is word order: the object immediately follows the verb with no other marking (except in the case of pronouns). Two further syntactic characteristics are worth mentioning. One we have already met: this is the relationship between the 'direct object' of an active sentence and the 'subject' of the corresponding passive: the relationship is indeed often described in some such terms as 'the object of the active sentence "becomes" the subject of the corresponding passive sentence, and the subject of the active sentence is relegated to a syntactically optional prepositional phrase'. It will be noted that this characterization does not draw a clear distinction between the levels of analysis involved. It is, however, clear enough what is at issue. The second is the reasonably systematic relationship between transitive sentences and others involving the verbs DO(TO) and HAPPEN: *John beat the donkey*: *What John did to the donkey was beat it*: *What happened to the donkey was that John beat it*.

Another type of object is the 'object of result' or 'effected' object. In this case, the object expression can be thought of as being, as it were, 'created' by the 'action of the verb', hence its name. Examples are: *God created the world*, and *Leonardo painted the Mona Lisa*. Objects of result resemble direct objects in some respects – for example they have passive counterparts (*The world was created by God*, *The Mona Lisa was painted by Leonardo*) and differ from them in others – for example there are no corresponding HAPPEN and DO(TO) sentences (**What happened to the world was that God created it*, **What God did to the world was create it*). Sentences with verbs that take objects of result are often loosely paraphrased by others involving

MAKE: *Mary wove this cloth: Mary made this cloth*. Such paraphrases are hardly thinkable with verbs involving direct objects (*John beat the donkey* has no relation at all with *John made the donkey*). Individual verbs differ as to which type of object they take: verbs like HIT and KILL only occur with direct objects, and verbs like WEAVE and CREATE only with objects of result. Other verbs can co-occur with either type of object: *The spy burned the documents* (direct object); *The cigarette burned a hole* (object of result); *Rembrandt painted a self-portrait* (object of result); *I painted the bathroom* (direct object). We have already observed that functionally different constituents cannot be coordinated without producing a deliberate effect: *I would like to have Hockney paint my portrait and the bathroom*.

Yet another traditionally recognized type of object is the 'indirect object', *Mary* in *John gave the book to Mary* or *John gave Mary the book*. Semantically indirect object expressions are understood as being the 'recipient' or 'beneficiary' of the action described by the verb. Syntactically the indirect object can occur either in a PP with the preposition *to* following the direct object, or between the verb and its direct object with no preposition. In the latter case this creates a structure which has apparently two objects and consequently two passive forms (*Mary was given the book by John* and *The book was given (to) Mary by John*) and two sets of HAPPEN sentences (*What happened to Mary . . .*, and *What happened to the book . . .*).

A discussion of the indirect object leads inevitably to a mention of a heterogeneous collection of functional relations, often collectively referred to as 'oblique objects'. This is the area that is primarily responsible for the difficulty in drawing a clear distinction between nuclear and circumstantial constituents that we mentioned at the beginning of this chapter. Functionally, oblique objects are nuclear in that they provide information important to a full interpretation of the verb. Syntactically, however, they are frequently optional, and when they occur they are found in prepositional phrases, usually with a quite specific preposition, the identity of which will need to be noted as part of the lexical entry for the verb in question since it is often not predictable. They do however have one syntactic peculiarity that sets them apart from adverbs and other constituents that can occur in prepositional phrases, and it seems to be related to their status as functionally nuclear. This is that the NP in the prepositional phrase can be 'promoted' to oust the direct object and take its place. The former object will then be 'demoted' to a prepositional phrase, again often requiring a lexically specified preposition, and often optional. The general pattern will remind us of the passive construction where the object is 'promoted' to become subject, and the previous subject is 'demoted' into an optional prepositional phrase. This means that we will find pairs of sentences, in one of which there is an object NP following the verb and itself followed by an oblique object PP, and in the other the NP from the oblique object has been promoted to become the object and the original object demoted to a PP. An example is:

The commissioner presented a badge to the boy scouts
The commissioner presented the boy scouts with a badge

The identification of *a badge* as the deep object is reflected in the fact that for both sentences it is an appropriate answer to the question *What did the commissioner present?* (he can hardly be held to have presented *the boy scouts*!). Similarly, *the boy scouts* is in both cases an indirect object, an appropriate answer to the question *Who did the commissioner present a badge to?*

It is now interesting to note that the NP which has 'become' the direct object also inherits the other syntactic potentialities of object NPs: it is, for instance, available for further promotion as subject of the corresponding passive sentence:

Badges were presented to the boy scouts by the commissioner
The boy scouts were presented with badges by the commissioner

This relation can be observed with a wide variety of verbs, and is acceptable to varying degrees with different verbs. Traditionally these new objects have been distinguished in terms of the function from which they may be considered to have been promoted. So we find:

Benefactive object: John baked Mary a cake
                                (cf. John baked a cake for Mary)

Instrumental object: John shot an arrow at the apple
                                (cf. John shot the apple with an arrow)

Locative object: John planted the garden with trees
                                (cf. John planted trees in the garden)

What seems to be involved from both a syntactic and a semantic point of view is a 'hierarchy of objecthood': direct objects are most 'object-like' and oblique objects the least. The more object-like an argument is, the more closely it will be tied to the verb, both syntactically and semantically, and the less object-like it is, the looser will be its syntactic and semantic ties to the verb, and the more it will resemble a simple adjunct. A verb, it seems, must have a subject, but can have one or more object-like expressions, providing each is different.

We should briefly mention a third nuclear function, 'complement'. This can be illustrated in sentences like

Jane is an engineer
They became engineers

Here the relation between the NP and the verb is radically different from that of any of the object constructions just discussed. Syntactically, such sentences have no passive counterparts and cannot occur in HAPPEN sentences (*An engineer was become by Jane*, *What happened to an engineer was that Jane became it*). Semantically, the relationship between the two NPs and the verb is also quite distinct from that of any of the object types. A complement typically ascribes an attribute to, or describes a characteristic of, some other NP in the sentence. This is reflected in the fact that the complement agrees in number with the expression to which it is complementary.

We have now looked at two different ways of describing the verb and its arguments at the 'deep' level. One approach involves labels like 'agent' and 'patient', and the other labels like 'logical subject' and 'logical object'. In both cases a description will need to relate the various items involved to a 'surface' description involving 'grammatical' subjects, objects and so on. The two approaches are to a degree complementary, but they do not entirely overlap. The 'role' relations have the advantage that they are more detailed and hence allow for subtler distinctions to be drawn. In particular, a description in terms of role relations demonstrates quite clearly that the relations of logical subject and object are not semantically homogeneous. This can be seen by comparing the roles of the subjects and objects in *The ducklings* (patient) *died*, *The farmer* (agent) *killed the ducklings* (patient), *John* (experiencer) *loves Mary* (goal), *Edinburgh* (location) *is windy* (attributive complement). On the other hand, a description in terms of role relations is difficult to constrain since it is not clear what principles might limit the set of relations that are available: some descriptions settle on only two or three 'basic' roles, others permit a larger number. From this point of view, a description in terms of logical subject etc. may seem more desirable, since the set of relations at issue can be restricted to three, or (including the various complement types) to four. This corresponds to a traditional view that there are 'intransitive' (one-place), 'transitive' (two-place) and 'ditransitive' (three-place) verbs: and it does indeed seem to be the case that the propositional nucleus is restricted to a small number of arguments. In the next section we will see how these notions can be incorporated into a description.

7.2 Functional grammars

In this section we will be concerned with the question of how dependency structure might be reflected in a grammar. There are many ways in which this might be done and we clearly cannot look at all of them, so we will look briefly at three somewhat different models. In what immediately follows we will consider a 'dependency grammar' to accommodate the kind of material we discussed in pages 203–4. In the next subsection we will look at 'case grammars', which reflect the approach we adopted in 7.1a. And in 7.2b we will look at 'relational grammars', which attempt to accommodate the kinds of insights we developed in 7.1b. Although in each of these approaches we will largely concentrate on the kind of material first introduced in the corresponding section, it will be clear that each model makes much more comprehensive claims which we do not have space to consider.

We have already remarked that when categorially based grammars need to make use of functional relations, they generally interpret them out of structural configurations. It is, for example, possible to interpret some dependency relations out of the phrase structure rules of Chapter 4. Thus we could stipulate that in any rule of the kind XP → . . . X . . ., the 'X' in the right-hand side of the rule will be the head of the construction on the left-hand side of the rule. So, in a rule like NP → (Det) N (PP) we will identify N as the head of the NP. Xbar phrase structure grammars have indeed been developed to accommodate just such information.

In this section we will consider a more radical approach, which introduces a quite different way of constructing analysis trees. This time, instead of showing dominance relations, as constituent structure trees do, the analysis trees will be based on dependency relations. And instead of having 'nodes' and 'branches' dominating constituent structure configurations, they will have 'arcs' relating constituents to each other. In particular, such trees will show which constituent is head and which are dependants on the head. A typical tree showing relations in the NP of the kind we discussed at the start of the chapter is shown in Figures 7:2a and 7:2b.

The tree in Figure 7:2a is a generalized dependency structure for a NP, and that in 7:2b is an analysis in these terms of the NP *The big cat on the mat*. In the example, the head of the construction, the noun, is shown as having three dependent modifiers: a determiner, an adjective and a PP. In the case of the PP, the preposition is shown as head and its NP modifier as dependent on it.

In the particular example, the tree also reflects surface structure ordering. This is not a necessary feature of a dependency representation, and the representation would be no different if we assumed that the items were unordered. Indeed, from a dependency point of view there are some advantages in

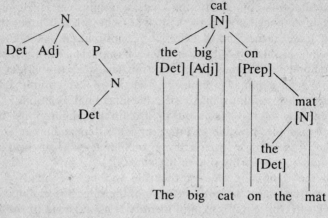

Figure 7:2a   Figure 7:2b

making this assumption because we can then treat all markers of dependency (word order morphology and so on) equally. Ordering relations can be specified by 'serialization' rules. For English these might take the form:

Prepositions govern nouns to the right.
Nouns govern determiners and adjectives in that order to the left and prepositions to the right.

These rules are not syntactic transformations because transformations operate on ordered categorial structures and these rules assume unordered dependency structures. These rules are, rather, rules which interpret constituent order from functional structure. Observe too that it is possible to envisage different languages with the same, or similar, underlying dependency structures but with different serialization rules.

Morphological markers of concord are perhaps best represented in trees of this kind with a morphological model which uses features: we briefly exemplified such a model in 3.2. In the generalized example in Figure 7:3a, a feature of the head, represented as [f], is shown as having 'trickled down' on to both of the modifiers. What features trickle down and on to what modifiers will, of course, be specified in the grammar of a par-

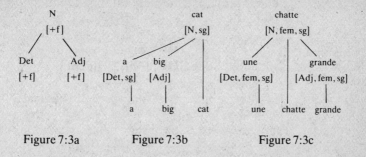

Figure 7:3a   Figure 7:3b   Figure 7:3c

ticular language, and will differ from language to language. In English, only features of number trickle down, and then only on to certain determiners: this is shown in Figure 7:3b. In French, features of both number and gender trickle down on to both determiners and adjectives; this is shown in Figure 7:3c.

Government can be handled in a similar way, except that this time the head will not be marked for the feature involved, but will govern a feature on its dependant. This is shown in Figure 7:4, where [obl] indicates the 'oblique' form of the pronoun, in English *me, him* etc.

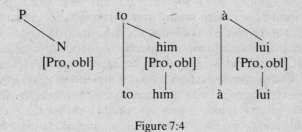

Figure 7:4

Analyses of this kind can with advantage be extended to sentence structure. We could, for instance, represent a sentence like *The cat sat on the mat* by an analysis tree of the kind shown in Figure 7:5.

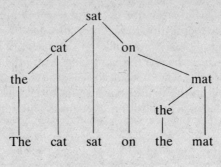

Figure 7:5

7.2a 'Case' grammar

In this section we will consider models of description that explicitly incorporate the relations we have been referring to as 'role' relations. Among the best known are models called 'case' grammars, which largely develop from the work of Fillmore (1968). The 'cases' involved are what we have been referring to as 'roles'. In order to avoid confusion with 'morphological' case ('nominative', 'accusative' and so on) we will continue to use the term 'role' for functional relationships at the 'deep' level and restrict the term (morphological) 'case' for variations in word form at the surface level.

Fillmore's 'case' grammar was originally introduced as a modification of 'standard theory' transformational grammar of the kind we developed in Chapter 5. Where it differed most strikingly from standard theory models was in the proposal that the most basic level of underlying structure should explicitly contain functional information. This was handled by developing a structure containing a verb node and a series of nodes labelled with role relations like 'agent', 'neutral' and 'goal'. These relational nodes in turn dominated a categorial structure containing a node labelled K, for 'Kasus' (or case), and an NP. The K node can be regarded as the site for the morphological or other marker of the relation in question. In English the markers are prepositions, since prepositions frequently have this function: in other languages the K nodes might dominate morphological case labels like, say, 'nominative', 'accusative' and so on. A 'deep structure' in these terms would look like Figure 7:6. The preposition for agent is shown as *by*, which does indeed turn up in passive sentences in the 'agent phrase' (*John was killed by Bill*). *To* is a frequent marker of goal (*John gave a book to Mary*). The neutral NP is shown with a 'zero' preposition, '∅' in the figure, because in no transformation of the sentence does a preposition ever mark this function with verbs like GIVE.

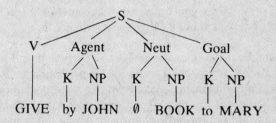

Figure 7:6

There are a variety of ways in which a structure of this kind might be related to a surface sentence. In the original case grammars it was seen as an ordered structure of the kind to which transformations can be applied, and the reader can see that transformations could be devised to relate this structure to a variety of surface forms: *John gave the book to Mary*, *Mary was given the book by John* and so on.

Another way of looking at the structure is to consider it as an unordered relational structure. In this case, we will need a set of 'serialization' rules to derive surface structure. Perhaps along the following lines:

Active (a) Verb to second constituent
     (b) Agent to subject (no prepositional marker)
     (c) Neutral to object (no prepositional marker)
     (d) Goal to either (i) between verb and object (no preposition)
             or (ii) in PP with *to* and sentence final

Given suitable definitions of the surface relations 'subject' and 'object', choosing a, b, c and di will yield *John gave Mary the book*, and choosing a, b, c and dii will yield *John gave the book to Mary*. In this spirit the same structure will relate to passive sentences with rules like:

> Passive (a) Verb to second constituent and passive in form
> (b) Either (i) neutral to subject (no preposition)
> or (ii) goal to subject (no preposition)
> (c) If bi – neut to subject – then goal to PP with *to*
> If bii – goal to subject – then neut to object
> (d) Agent in PP with *by* and sentence final

As they stand, these rules are rather too particular and further generalizations clearly need to be made: for instance, Verb is always second constituent, Agent will be subject of an active sentence if there is one, and so on. Nor is this the only way in which a case grammar can be conceived. There are models that use a dependency structure rather like that introduced in 6.2 but with the addition of role information on the dependency nodes. We will not, however, go into such models here since space forbids.

Yet another way of looking at role relations is to consider them as a lexical rather than primarily a grammatical matter. Under this view, whatever model of grammar is chosen, lexical entries for verbs would be augmented with information about the functional relationship between the verb and its arguments. Lexical entries can then become extremely informative about the types of semantic, and syntactic, relationships which can be formed between sentences. For example the three uses of the lexeme OPEN which were described in Figure 7:1 might be specified as:

OPEN   Adj;Desc   (Neut Vb——)
                         State: (Neut 'OPEN')

     V;Desc   ——#   (Neut Vb——)
                         Event: (Neut 'CHANGE' (Neut 'OPEN'))

     V;Desc   ——NP   (Ag——Neut)
                         Event: (Ag 'CAUSE' (Neut 'CHANGE' (Neut 'OPEN')))

In the first of any pair of lines, the first column identifies the form class (Adj, V etc.), the second the process class (Descriptive etc.), the third the syntactic selection frame (for example, —— NP for a transitive verb), and the fourth the role of the various NPs etc. (for example, Agent —— Neutral). The second of each pair of lines shows a semantic analysis of the item in question, and how the particular lexical item is related to others. Thus the 'stative' use of OPEN is explicitly related to the inchoative and causative uses. From this lexical entry, given a sentence like *John opened the door* we can derive the implication that *The door opened* and so on. With an item like RIPE, where there is a morphological relationship between the adjective and the various verb forms, we can envisage a parallel representation:

| RIPE | Adj;Desc | (Neut Vb——) |
| | | State: (Neut 'RIPE') |

V by rule affixing *-en*

| | V;Desc | —— | (Neut ——) |
| | | | Event: (Neut 'CHANGE'(Neut 'RIPE')) |

| | V;Desc | ——NP | (Ag —— Neut) |
| | | | Event: (Ag 'CAUSE'(Neut 'CHANGE'(Neut 'RIPE'))) |

Where different lexical items are involved we might envisage representations of the form:

| DEAD | Adj;Desc | (Neut Vb——) |
| | | State: (Neut 'DEAD') |

| DIE | V;Desc | —— | (Neut ——) |
| | | | Event: (Neut 'CHANGE'(Neut 'DEAD')) |

| KILL | V;Desc | ——NP | (Ag —— Neut) |
| | | | Event: (Ag 'CAUSE'(Neut 'DIE')) |

The meaning of KILL can be ascertained by consulting the meaning of DIE which in turn is determined by consulting the meaning of DEAD.

Representations of this sort can be made extremely flexible.

So, we might envisage entries for GIVE and TAKE along the following lines:

GIVE   V;Poss   ——NP PP(to)   (Ag/Source——Neut Goal)

Event: (Ag 'CAUSE'(Neut 'CHANGE'(Goal 'HAVE' Neut))) and (Source 'HAVE' Neut) before event, and (Goal 'HAVE' Neut) after event.

TAKE   V;Poss   ——NP PP(from)   (Ag/Goal——Neut Source)

Event: (Ag 'CAUSE'(Neut 'CHANGE'(Goal 'HAVE' Neut))) and (Source 'HAVE' Neut) before event, and (Goal 'HAVE' Neut) after event.

The entries explicitly relate GIVE and TAKE, and they also contain other information, particularly about the location of the object during the events described. In both cases the 'source' has the object before the occurrence of the event, and the goal has the object after the occurrence of the event. The verbs differ in whether the source or the goal is also the agent.

7.2b 'Relational' grammar

In this section we will consider models that take logical relations like subject and object as basic. It will be sensible to begin by recalling the distinction between 'logical' and 'grammatical' subjects and objects that was drawn in 7.1. Grammatical subject and object relate to features of surface grammar: the grammatical subject precedes the verb and controls number agreement on it, the grammatical object follows the verb and is governed in the 'oblique' form when it is a pronoun. Logical subject and object, by contrast, relate to deep structure. We can illustrate this by referring once again to the sentence *The cat has killed the mouse.* With a verb like KILL the logical subject is the 'killer', *the cat*, and the logical object is the NP that is 'affected by the action of the verb', *the mouse.* In active declarative sentences, as in the example, grammatical and logical subject and grammatical and logical object coincide; in the correspond-

grammatical and logical object coincide; in the corresponding passive sentence, *The mouse was killed by the cat*, they do not.

Given this outline description, it would seem that from a functional point of view both sentences can be given an identical representation, and that this will follow the logical rather than the grammatical relations. To show the relationships involved we will use the type of dependency representation used in a model of description known as 'relational grammar'. As with 'case grammar', we can hardly do justice to a complete theory of grammar in a page or two, but we will hope to be able to impart the general flavour of the model. It proposes deep structures like that in Figure 7:7.

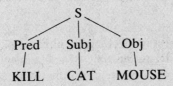

Figure 7:7

The representation follows the 'logical' representation we used in Chapter 5 in that it shows the predicator at the left-hand end of the tree followed by its arguments. In this representation each 'arc' hanging from or 'depending' on the S node is labelled with a functional relation, subj, obj etc. These labels are to be understood as labels on the arcs themselves defining the functional relations involved, and not as nodes which dominate constituents. To relate structures of this kind to surface forms we will, as before, need a set of realization rules to 'serialize' the various constituents involved and to specify morphological details. Perhaps along the following lines:

1. The subject argument will precede the verb as an NP and will control number agreement on it.
2. The object argument will immediately follow the verb as an NP (and will be in the oblique form if it is a pronoun).

Given these rules and the structure in Figure 7:7 we will derive the surface sentence *The cat killed the mouse*.

Relational grammars assume a further set of rules which can reassign dependency functions. Such rules assume that the relations recognized are ordered in a hierarchy: subject, object, indirect object, oblique object. A reassignment rule can take an item on the hierarchy and 'promote' it to a higher position in the hierarchy. The promoted item will then enjoy all the privileges of the position to which it has been promoted; it may, for example, be eligible for further promotion. The consequence of promotion is that some other item must be 'ousted'. The 'ousted' item will become a 'chômeur' (French for 'unemployed'), and will lose any entitlement to promotion. Chômeurs will normally be realized in prepositional phrases. The passive can be viewed in this light:

Passive: (i)   Promote object to subject
       (ii) Reassign the ousted subject to a 'subject chômeur'
      (iii) Mark the verb as passive

The result of these operations will yield the developing tree of Figure 7:8.

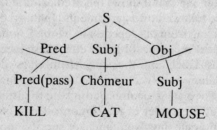

Figure 7:8

If we now supplement the realization rules we already have with the rule

3. A subject chômeur will occur in a PP with *by* and this will be the sentence final constituent

and pass the bottom line of the structure in Figure 7:8 through our realization rules, we will derive the surface passive sentence *The mouse was killed by the cat*. It will be clear that many of the phenomena we discussed in 7.1b can be accommodated in a description of this kind, since many of them dealt precisely with the promotion of various constituents and the consequences of this promotion.

We do not, unfortunately, have space to see how a model of this kind would deal with other types of construction. What is, however, more important is that it should be appreciated that the sorts of operations that are involved call on neither a categorially defined deep structure nor on syntactic transformations. Instead they involve a functionally defined underlying structure and a series of operations which reassign functions according to particular rules and a set of realization rules which order constituents and assign morphological markers.

7.3 Functional universals and language typologies

We have seen in previous chapters that there is currently considerable interest in the question of language universals. In this section we will look at this matter from the point of view of functional models because they offer interestingly different perspectives on this question, and insightful ways of constructing language typologies.

Let us begin with an example from the point of view of an approach that uses roles or 'deep case'. It seems not totally unreasonable to suppose that human experience can universally be conceived of as involving agents acting on patients with particular goals and so on. If this is so, then we would expect that it would be possible to make an analysis of any language which called on functional roles like 'agent', 'patient' and the like. It will then be interesting to see how such functional relations are reflected in surface grammatical features and to enquire how different languages or groups of languages make the connection. We saw in 7.2a that this was one of the matters that motivated case grammars. It raises the obvious question of what the relationship is between functional 'deep' cases, which might be universal, and the 'surface' grammatical category of 'morphological case', which quite clearly is not universal.

In most Indo-European languages which have a category of morphological case, a distinction has traditionally been drawn between 'grammatical' and 'local' case. Local cases, as the name suggests, are those cases that are used principally to indicate location, and movement into or out of locations. The notion of location is readily extendable from place, in a literal sense, to persons, so that it is possible to analyse 'verbs of giving' as well as 'verbs of motion' as involving 'sources' and 'goals': this is what we did in 7.1a. In this instance there seems to be a reasonably direct relationship between the semantic functions of particular cases and their morphological realization.

Grammatical case, by contrast, is traditionally held to be related to the functions of grammatical subject and object. So, to return to Latin again, the most characteristic use of the nominative and accusative cases is as grammatical subject and object respectively. The general pattern is:

> intransitive: nominative verb
> transitive: nominative verb accusative

With this arrangement of cases, if the subject must be nominative and the direct object accusative, it seems that there can be no essential connection between case and the functional role of the item involved. Not all case systems operate like this. There is a group of languages, often called 'ergative' languages, where all morphological case marking seems to be more closely related to deep role relations than to surface grammatical function. In an ideal such language the distinction between local and grammatical case would disappear. So, for instance, a patient NP would always be realized in the same morphological case, usually called the 'absolutive', regardless of whether it occurred in a transitive or an intransitive sentence. Similarly, an agent NP would always occur in the same case, usually called the 'ergative' (hence the name for this kind of language). The pattern is thus like this:

    intransitive: absolutive
    transitive: ergative verb absolutive

Ergative languages are found in many parts of the world: Basque, many of the languages of the Caucasus and some Australian aboriginal languages. As an example, consider the following from Yidiny, an Australian language:

    yiŋu   bulmba   bala+ŋ
    this+abs house+abs open+pres [abs(olutive), pres(ent)]
    'this house is open'

    waguja+ŋgu yiŋu   bulmba   bala+ŋa+l
    man+erg   this+abs house+abs open+transitivizer+pres
                                           [erg(ative)]
    'the man is opening up this house'

(The absolutive form is the root form of the noun, hence there is no separate case marker, the case marker of the ergative is -ŋgu. It should also be noted that the verb itself has a special 'transitivizing' affix, -ŋna-.)

    The two situations have been somewhat simplified for the purposes of exposition, but give an idea of what is involved. The reader will also doubtless see that with only a little imagination an 'ergative' analysis can be extended even to languages which do not show the relationships as overtly as does Yidiny. English indeed can, and has been, interpreted in this light: the analysis which was presented in 7.1a was slanted in this direction. The difference between English and Yidiny might then be seen as being a difference between a language that marks the ergative relation with morphological case, and one that marks it, inter alia, in verb derivation (RED:REDDEN, CLEAR: CLARIFY).

    Let us now turn to the kind of universalist claims that can be advanced on behalf of a functional description that interests itself in deep 'logical relations' like subject and object. In 7.2b we saw that it was possible to regard a 'deep' description as involving an unordered series of these relations, and a grammar as involving a set of serialization rules, morphological realization rules and so on. Given this, it will be possible to claim that there may be constructions that are functionally identical (i.e. they have the same functional deep structures), but which have widely different surface structure realizations in different languages. It has been claimed that the 'passive' construction is one such. Not all languages have a construction that is identifiable as 'passive', but for those that do, the surface forms that realize this relationship differ widely. The English passive construction differs from its active counterpart both in word order and in morphology. In Basque active and passive have the same word order, though there is a change in the form of the verb:

Piarresek egin   du etchea
Peter+erg make   has house+abs   [erg(ative), abs(olutive)]
'Peter made the house'

Piarresek egina   da etchea
Peter+erg made   is house+abs
'the house was made by Peter'

A different situation holds in Chinese: here word order changes, but the verb form remains the same:

Zhù   lǎoshi píyèle   wǒde   kǎoshi
      Prof.   mark+past   my   test
'Prof. Zhu marked my test'

wǒde   kǎoshi bèi   Zhù   lǎoshi píyèle
my   test   by   Prof.   mark+past
'My test was marked by Prof. Zhu'

From examples of this sort, which can be multiplied, it would seem that an attempt to define the active:passive relationship in purely categorial terms is doomed to failure, since different languages realize the relationship in different ways. There seems to be no single rule, or set of rules, that can be held to be universal. What does, however, seem to be universal, and this is why the term 'passive' has been used to describe widely different structural forms, is the fact that there is a correspondence between the logical object of the active and the logical subject of the passive and between the logical subject of the active and some NP associated with the passive. A categorially defined transformation seems to have no hope of universality, whereas a functionally defined operation (with particular realizations for each language) may have.

We will end the chapter with a brief look at a particularly interesting typological question that has recently attracted a lot of attention. It is concerned with the ordering relations between modifiers and their heads. It will be recalled that in discussing modifier-head relations at the beginning of this chapter we noted that the head of a construction can be seen to govern its modifiers, and that one marker of government is word order. To begin with, let us look at word order relations in four construction types in English:

1. The verb and its object: the governed object is to the *right* of the verb:
   e.g. (John) sold $\rightarrow$ the car,   (Harry) ate $\rightarrow$ a banana

The arrow, '$\rightarrow$', here and in subsequent examples points from the head, the verb *sold* in this case, to the dependant, in this case the object NP *the car*. The position of the subject relative to the verb is not at issue in the present discussion, and hence is shown in brackets in this and in other examples.

2. The 'adposition' and its object: the governed NP is to the *right* of the adposition. The general term 'adposition' is used to cover both 'prepositions', which precede their objects and hence govern them to the right, and 'postpositions', which follow their objects and hence govern them to the left: we will come to some examples of postpositions in due course:
   e.g. in $\rightarrow$ the purse,   to $\rightarrow$ the police station

3. The noun and its modifying adjective(s): the governed adjective is to the *left* of the noun:

e.g. the big ← eagle,   an intelligent ← girl

4. The noun and its modifying genitive: English has two constructions. In the more common the governed genitive bears an 'apostrophe *s*' marker and is to the *left* of the noun:

e.g. the cat's ← head,   the girl's ← room

In the other genitive construction, the governed genitive is in a PP with *of* and is to the right of the noun:

e.g. the head → of the cat,   the son → of the king

Since in English prepositional modification in the NP is always governed to the right this construction follows the general pattern for prepositional phrase modification.

As far as these four constructions are concerned, English is not totally consistent: it governs to the right with prepositions and verbs, and to the left with genitives and adjectives. Some languages are more consistent: as Greenberg (1966:76), the father of typological studies of this sort, remarks: 'Linguists are . . . familiar with the notion that certain languages tend consistently to put modifying or limiting elements before those modified or limited, while others just as consistently do the opposite.'

An example of a language that consistently modifies to the right is Scots Gaelic. The four constructions exemplified for English would be:

1. Verb and object: the governed object is to the *right* of the verb:

e.g. Reic (Seumas) → an car
      sold (James)   the car   'James sold the car'

2. Adposition and its object: the governed object is to the *right* of the adposition (a preposition):

e.g. anns → an   sporran
      in   the   purse   'in the purse'

3. Noun and its modifying adjective: the governed adjective is to the *right* of the noun:

e.g. an   iolair → mhor
      the eagle   big   'the big eagle'

4. Noun and its modifying genitive: the governed genitive is to the *right* of the noun:

    e.g. ceann → a'chait
        head   of-the-cat(genitive)   'the cat's head'

A language that consistently modifies in the opposite direction, to the left, is Turkish. Here our four constructions would be:

1. Verb and its object: the governed object is to the *left* of the verb:

    e.g. (Ahmet) otomobili ← aldı
        (Ahmet) the car   took   'Ahmet took the car'

2. Adposition and its object: the governed object NP is to the *left* of the adposition (a preposition):

    e.g. karakola   ← yakıin
        police-station   near   'near the police station'

3. Noun and its modifying adjective: the governed adjective is to the *left* of the noun:

    e.g. zeki   bir ← kız
        intelligent   a   girl   'an intelligent girl'

4. Noun and its modifying genitive: the governed genitive is to the *left* of the noun:

    e.g. kızların ← odaları
        girls   their-rooms   'the girls' rooms'

Given data of this sort, it seems that some languages are more 'consistent' than others in their patterns of word order modification. Gaelic and Turkish are consistent in that they consistently modify in one direction or the other, and English is mixed in that it governs in one direction in some constructions and in the other in others. Let us first see whether we can give a syntactic definition of a consistent language. A categorial description of consistency can be offered in terms of phrase structure rules. In Chapter 4 we developed phrase structure rules of the form XP → . . . X . . ., to be interpreted as 'an "X phrase" dominates a construction containing an "X", where "X" is the head of the construction'. This means that '. . .' in the rule will contain the modifiers of the head X. In a consistent language all modifiers will be on the same side of the head. In other words, for Turkish we will expect rules of the form XP → modifier X (for example, PP → NP P, NP → Adj N), and for Gaelic rules of the form XP → X modifier (for example, PP → P NP, NP → N Adj). In a dependency grammar, consistency will be reflected in the serialization rules: modifiers will either all precede or all follow their head. In either type of grammatical statement, the rules will capture a generalization about word order.

We might now reasonably ask two questions. What, if any, advantages might flow from consistency? Are languages actually consistent? As to the first question, a number of highly plausible possible advantages have been canvassed: unfortunately, none has been conclusively demonstrated. It might seem reasonable, for instance, that a consistent language is easier for children to acquire than an inconsistent one. This amounts to a claim that it is simpler for a child to learn a single rule for all modifiers (modify to the right, or the left as the case may be), rather than rules for each modifier. Unfortunately there seems no good evidence to suggest that English is more difficult to acquire than Turkish or Gaelic. A similar claim would be that a consistent language is easier for its speakers to produce and its hearers to process. That is, if hearers can expect modifiers consistently to precede heads (or the other way round) they will need only a single processing strategy rather than two. There seems no conclusive evidence for this either. Another hypothesis that has been advanced is that consistent languages are more 'stable' over time than inconsistent languages. In other words consistent languages should be less liable to word order changes than inconsistent languages. There is a corollary to this which is that inconsistent languages should, over time, become more consistent. There is, in fact, some evidence to support this hypothesis, since it does indeed seem to be the case that if a language changes, say, the order of the verb and object, then other changes are likely to follow in its train. Adpositions, for example, seem likely to follow the pattern. Here too, however, the evidence is inconclusive: some 'mixed' languages have been stable over long periods of time, and word order changes in one construction do not always entail consequential changes in others.

Although this is rather inconclusive, it does seem that there is something here that needs an explanation, since even if it is too strong a claim that certain typological features *must* cluster together, there certainly appears to be a very strong tendency for them to do so. It is to be hoped that future research will throw further light on this problem.

In this chapter we have been looking at a functional approach to language and shown some possible advantages of this approach. In the next chapter we will consider extending this functional approach to the description of the sentence. This will lead us to a consideration of connected texts rather than simply individual sentences.

8   Sentences in Texts

Mere talk to produce sentences, no matter how well formed or elegant the outcome, does not by itself constitute communication. Only when a move has elicited a response can we say communication is taking place.

(J. J. Gumperz)

Our primary interest in this book has been in the sentence, the traditional interest of the grammarian. We do not, however, usually encounter sentences in isolation, out of context, and we should end by looking briefly at some of the ways in which the structure of texts influences sentence structure. An examination of the structure of texts is an area of growing interest and importance, partly because of its intrinsic interest, and partly because it questions many of the assumptions of a view of language that concentrates on the sentence. It is also an area which attracts the attention of many disciplines other than linguistics, partly because the study of language in use has many practical applications.

'Discourse' or 'text' grammars really deserve a book to themselves and space dictates that we can do no more than take a brief look at some of the issues that they raise. We will, therefore, restrict ourselves to a consideration of two of the ways in which sentence structure is affected by discourse. We will first look at functional accounts of the sentence, and then turn briefly to some issues relating to word order. In both cases we shall see that we are led inexorably to a consideration of the use of language in contexts.

8.1 Sentence functions

In the preceding chapter we took a functional look at sentence constituents, distinguishing between formal categories like noun phrase and functional categories like subject and object. We have not hitherto paid much attention to the function that sentences themselves may fulfil, largely because we have been concentrating on the physical form of sentences in isolation and a consideration of sentence function must involve sentences in context. The sorts of descriptors we have applied to sentences hitherto have been categorizations like declarative, interrogative or imperative. Labels of this sort relate to the grammatical category of 'mood', and can be correlated with formal features of sentence construction irrespective of their context of use. By contrast a functional characterization of a sentence describes the kinds of communicative function that a sentence may fulfil in a particular context of use: whether it is used to make a statement, ask a question, issue a command or request and so on. An analysis in these latter terms is concerned with what is 'done' by the uttering of some particular sentence in a context, and is often referred to as a 'speech-act' analysis.

We saw in Chapter 7 that form and function often go hand in hand, and it is hardly surprising that this is also the case with mood and speech-act function: declarative sentences are often used to make statements, interrogatives to ask questions and imperatives to issue commands. We have also seen that form and function do not always have a one-to-one correspondence, and it will come as no surprise to find that this is also the case with the sentence. Each of the sentence forms mentioned above can, in context, fulfil a variety of functions. A declarative sentence, for instance, can be used to ask a question (*He's clever?*), or to issue a command (*All personnel will assemble on the deck at 0900 hours!*). In an appropriate context, a declarative sentence can also be used to make a 'promise', 'threat' or 'apology'. Indeed the 'same' sentence can, in different contexts, have quite different functions: *I shall leave all my money to the dogs' home* might be intended as a promise, a threat or a warning! The converse also holds, and the same function can be realized by a variety of formal sentence types: so the imperative *Open the door* and the declarative *I command you to open the door* can both function as commands.

There is, then, a clear difference in status between 'modal' descriptors like declarative and interrogative, which describe the form of sentences, and 'speech-act' descriptors like statement and question that describe their function. We will briefly examine each in turn. Mood, as we have seen, refers to formal characteristics of the sentence, independent of any particular context of use: a declarative sentence is declarative whatever its function, as in the examples in the previous paragraph. It follows, then, that a formal analysis of mood will need to recognize as many different moods as the facts of sentence construction dictate for the particular language in question, and these are usually rather limited in number. We have been working with three for English, but some other minor sentence types can also be identified. For example, sentences like *God save the queen* are sometimes described as being in the 'optative' mood. They have a subject expression and a verb in the 'base form': in this they differ from declaratives, which have a subject and a finite verb (cf. *God saves the queen*), and from imperatives, which also have a verb in the base form, but which lack a subject (cf. *Save the queen!*).

A speech-act analysis, by contrast, is concerned with the function of sentences in particular contexts of use. And since we call on language for a wide variety of purposes, it is hardly surprising that a large number of functions can be identified, many more than the number of moods. These functions range from very general notions like 'question' or 'statement' to more particular ones like 'apology', 'threat' or 'promise'. A functional analysis will, of course, still be interested in the way the function is realized, and the way function and form interact, but, as with the other functional approaches we looked at in Chapter 7, the primary concentration will be on function rather than form.

One of the things a functional analysis will be interested in is the conditions that govern the use of a sentence to perform a particular speech act in some context. The kind of conditions that will be of interest relate to the speaker's intentions in making an utterance and the hearer's expectations about these intentions. For example, when someone asks a question, we assume that the speaker does not know the answer, wishes to do so and thinks that the hearer might be able to provide it – otherwise why would a speaker ask questions and a hearer provide a helpful answer if he can? When someone makes an assertion, we assume that what is asserted is true, or that it is believed to be true, and that the speaker thinks that the hearer does not know the information – we don't expect people to lie, nor gratuitously to tell us things they think we already know! Manipulation of the various clauses in these conditions will allow us to make quite subtle distinctions between different kinds of speech acts. For example we can, in this way, identify different sorts of questions: in 'true questions' we may assume that all the conditions mentioned hold: in 'teachers' questions' we assume that the speaker does in fact know the answer, but that it is part of the teacher's role to check whether the pupil does too; in 'rhetorical questions' the speaker typically knows the answer before articulating the question and is certainly going to provide it, whether the hearer knows it or not!

An analysis of this kind will also interest itself in the appropriacy of a particular speech act to some context of use. This might be a physical context: it would be curious if I were to ask you to 'close the door' if the door is already shut and I knew it. It might be the social context: it is usually inappropriate in the classroom for the pupil to ask the teacher 'teachers' questions'. Or it might be the context of shared background knowledge and assumptions between speaker and hearer. A speech-act analysis, then, will want to involve a consideration of the speaker's intentions in making a particular utterance, of the hearer's perception of the speaker's intention, and of the appropriacy of an utterance to its context of use.

The question in which we are interested in this section is whether there is any possibility of bringing together a formal and a functional account of sentences. We can begin by making two points. The first is that sentences do not, as a general rule, carry outward signs of their speech-act function. If they did, it would hardly be possible to use them for a variety of functions. Consider, for example, a sentence like *John is kicking the ball*, and let us suppose that it may be said to express the proposition 'John is kicking the ball'. We can use the sentence as an assertion to convey the information that 'John is kicking the ball', information that might be true or false. We can also use it, in an appropriate context, to question the proposition that 'John is kicking the ball'. In neither case does the sentence *John is kicking the ball* bear any unambiguous outward sign that an assertion or a question is involved, and its status must therefore be inferred from the context. The second, related, point is that sentences do not normally describe the act that they themselves perform. It would, for example, be absurd to suppose that there is any sense in which the utterance of the words *John is kicking the ball* actually constitutes an act of 'John kicking the ball'.

There is, however, a class of sentences in which the speech-act function is overtly spelled out in the sentence itself and in which the utterance of the sentence does constitute the act it describes, and this is a useful point to begin a discussion of sentence function. For example, suppose this book were to carry the words *I dedicate this book to T. W. Bikehorn.* The function of such a sentence is actually to dedicate the book: the words do not describe a dedication, they actually are the dedication. With the example *John is kicking the ball*, the words themselves did not constitute an act of kicking, but in the dedication the words themselves do constitute the dedication. This difference corresponds to another difference: we cannot react to the examples in the same way. In uttering *John is kicking the ball* it is possible that the speaker is either correctly or incorrectly describing a situation: the sentence, in other words, is either true or false. Hence it would be appropriate to respond either *So he is* or *No he isn't*. Responses of this kind are, however, not appropriate to the dedication since it is not easy to see what it would mean for an act of dedication to be true or false: the response *No you don't* doesn't make sense. It is, however, possible for a dedication to be inappropriate, and hence 'misfire' – an author can dedicate his book to someone, because that is his right and the conventional way in which dedications of this kind work, but the reader clearly cannot dedicate the book in place of the author, and if he were to try, his attempt would misfire. Sentences like the dedication example have been called performative sentences, and verbs that describe speech acts in this way have been christened 'performative' verbs: performative because the uttering of the words constitutes a performance of the act in question.

We have been considering two general kinds of sentences: performative sentences, which carry overt signs of their speech-act function, and non-performative sentences, the majority of sentences, where the speech-act function has to be inferred from the context. It should, incidentally, also be pointed out that 'performative' verbs need not always be used performatively. In order to be used performatively, the performative verb must have a first person subject (the performer of the act), it must be in the present tense, and it must not be negative. When these conditions are not met then the verb is not used performatively: for example, *Keith Brown dedicated the book to T. W. Bikehorn* is not an act of dedication, but rather the report of an act, on a par with the example *John is kicking the ball* discussed above.

Now consider the pair of sentences:

I order you to open the door
Open the door

In terms of the discussion in the previous paragraph, the first sentence can reasonably be regarded as performative. Uttering the words will unambiguously constitute giving an order, and this is explicitly spelt out by the performative use of ORDER. Indeed, the words can hardly be construed in any other way. Parallel with the example of the dedication, the hearer may decline to obey the order (*No I won't open the door*), he can question the speaker's right to issue orders at all (*Don't you order me about!*), or he might question the contextual appropriacy of an order (*But it's already open*). He can, however, hardly deny that an order, expressed by the performative verb, has overtly been made, and in cases of this kind, the form of the sentence does show its functional status.

The second sentence, by comparison, is no more performative than our previous example about John kicking the ball. In some contexts the sentence would doubtless be understood as an order, but this interpretation derives from the context of utterance since the words themselves could be used in other functions in other contexts: they might, for instance, be used to question an order (*Open the door?*), or as a response (Qu: *What did he tell you to do?* Ans: *Open the door*).

That having been said, however, it is clear that there is a conventional relationship between the second, imperative, sentence and the issuing of an order. We might then ask whether this typical function at least could not be captured in a grammatical description. With this in view, it has been suggested that we could postulate an 'understood' abstract performative verb for the second sentence when it is intended as a command. Such an analysis, it might be argued, would capture the conventional relationship between mood and speech-act function, thus unifying form and function within a single description. In other words, why should we not, for analytical purposes, assume that the abstract structure of the second sentence is

(I ORDER YOU) you open the door

The bit in brackets represents the abstract analytical machinery, and to emphasize its abstract status it is recorded in capitals. If we are to adopt this type of analysis, then we will also want to extend the machinery to other kinds of sentences:

(I STATE TO YOU) the door is open
(I ASK YOU) is the door open

Analyses of this kind were promoted by the 'generative semanticists' (cf. 6.1) in the 1970s, and were called, for obvious reasons, 'performative analyses'.

Is there any point in such an analysis? To begin with, it is worth observing that the analysis of interrogative sentences in 6.2 can be thought of as being a step in this direction. In that section we proposed that all sentences should be equipped with an abstract 'Comp' node, and that this node should be filled with a feature [+/− *wh*]: [+*wh*], it will be recalled, marked the sentence as interrogative and, inter alia, 'triggered off' subject-auxiliary inversion. When we introduced this analysis in Chapter 5, the intention was to capture generalizations about mood, but it seems a short step to extend the notation to speech-act function by using an 'abstract interrogative' performative ASK (and analogously an abstract imperative, ORDER, and declarative, SAY), and then to introduce some notation to indicate speaker and hearer.

An analysis of this kind will in some obvious ways complicate a description of the sentence. For instance, and using the imperative as an example, if we assume a remote structure of the kind shown, then we will need to state in our description that the performative can either be realized by an actual performative verb (*I order you to* . . .) or that it must be deleted along with its subject and object (*Open the door*). Furthermore, when the abstract performative is ORDER, the subject of the embedded sentence must be identical to the object of the performative, i.e. *you*: we want to avoid structures like (*I ORDER YOU*) *for him to open the door*. We will also need machinery to ensure that when there is no overt performative in surface structure, the performative and the subject of the embedded sentence are deleted to yield the surface *Open the door*.

Although machinery of this sort complicates the description, there are some compensatory gains because the analysis offers a way of accounting for some distributional facts of sentence structure, and grammars are concerned to account for distributional facts. To take the imperative again as an example, the proposed derivation might be held to offer an 'explanation' of why imperatives have an 'understood' second person subject ((*You*), *open the door*): in the analysis they do in fact have such an understood subject. It might also account for the fact that imperatives only permit 'second person' reflexive forms – *Wash yourself!*, but not *Wash himself!*, *Wash myself!*: reflexives will agree with the subject of their sentence, and in the analysis this can only be YOU. It might also account for the fact that with expressions like HOLD ONE'S BREATH, where ONE is realized as a pronoun agreeing with the subject (*I held my breath*, but not *I held his breath*), we can only find second person pronouns in imperatives: *Hold your breath*, but not *Hold my breath*. Comparable arguments can be made for the other sentence types.

Superficially, then, this seems to be a not unattractive proposition, since it appears to offer a way of integrating an account of sentence function into a grammatical description. Intractable difficulties, however, begin to arise as soon as we try to extend this machinery to the frequent cases where the form-function relationship is less straightforward. Part of the problem is that whereas there are only a very limited number of distinct grammatical moods, we can with little difficulty discriminate between very large numbers of distinct speech-act functions.

We can appreciate the nature of the problem by a brief consideration of the analysis 'I ASK YOU', mentioned above. If 'I ASK YOU' is treated simply as a marker of interrogative mood, as in our original discussion of the feature [+/− *wh*] in 5.2, no particular difficulty arises since its task is to account for the syntactic features of interrogative sentences, like the inversion of subject and auxiliary. If, however, we also want to give 'I ASK YOU' an explicitly performative interpretation and treat it as a marker of the speech-act function of an utterance of the sentence, then all kinds of problems arise whenever form and function do not go hand in hand.

On the one hand we encounter the problem that any sentence, of whatever syntactic form, that is used as a question will need to have a marker of this kind in its underlying analysis to account for its function as a question. So, for example, if the sentence *John is kicking the ball* is used as a question, then it should include 'I ASK YOU' in its analysis in order to account for its speech-act function as a question. But if we do this, how do we then inhibit 'I ASK YOU' from triggering off the inversion transformation, when we do not want it to?

The converse of this problem is when an interrogative form is used in a non-question function. We have already briefly mentioned a case of this sort in 1.2 where we looked at the 'indirect' question *Can you open the door?* We noted there that the utterance of such a sentence is usually neither intended nor understood 'literally' as an enquiry about 'ability'. Rather, it is usually intended, and understood, as a 'request for action'. A performative analysis is now in a difficulty. If it follows the speech-act function with an analysis, say 'I REQUEST YOU' to stand for the 'request for action' performative, then we have a problem accounting for the syntactic form. If, on the other hand, it is given the analysis 'I ASK YOU', then there is the problem of accounting for the intended speech-act function.

One way out of the problem, and this is the solution offered by some 'generative semantic' performative analyses, is to suppose that such sentences actually have two performative verbs: one of which accounts for the speech-act function and the other the syntactic form. The last example, for instance, would have the two performatives, 'I ASK YOU AND I REQUEST YOU'. But this solution complicates matters even further since we now have to devise rules to get the surface forms right and ensure that one performative, 'I ASK YOU' perhaps, accounts for the interrogative form, and the other, 'I REQUEST YOU', accounts for the speech-act function.

For reasons of this sort a multiple performative analysis eventually proves to be more trouble than it is worth. There are two general types of problem. The first is the explosive growth of the rules needed to relate analyses of this kind to actual sentences. The reader will appreciate that even with the rather straightforward examples that we have been looking at, a great deal of derivational machinery will be needed. Complicating the analysis further will soon make the whole enterprise unwieldy. The second is that once we embark on this route, it is not clear where to stop. In context, speech acts can be extraordinarily indirect. It takes no great imagination to conceive of a context in which uttering *It's very cold in here!* is both intended and interpreted as a 'request' to 'shut the door'. It does not seem sensible to have a syntactic analysis in which this is overtly spelled out as part of the underlying structure of a sentence. Examples like those just mentioned seem to be more a matter of the 'implications' that a speaker intends his hearer to draw rather than something that is actually said. That is, in context the utterance of *It's very cold in here* does not actually state that the speaker wants the door closed, even though the hearer may correctly infer that this is what the speaker wants. The interpretation of a good deal of speech involves our ability to draw relevant implications, and one of the problems with the performative analysis is that it assumes too close a relationship between sentence form and function. Another is that it attempts to provide a structural, 'syntactic', solution to a problem that seems to be essentially 'pragmatic' since it is concerned with language use.

Its heyday is now over. It has been largely superseded by analyses in terms of discourse implicatures of a sort to which we will briefly return at the end of the section. It must, however, be said that the performative analysis drew attention to the often very subtle interrelationships between form and function. For instance, as we have noted previously, if we insert *please* into our example indirect question (*Can you please open the door*), then it seems to become uniquely a request for action and can no longer be treated as a literal enquiry about ability. Examples of this sort show that the form-function connection is intimate and not to be disregarded. Many such mysteries, to which performative analysis first drew attention, remain in search of a suitable explanation.

We should not leave the question of speech-act analyses without briefly mentioning an application of the notion to the study of text. This extension seems entirely appropriate since if speech-act analyses deal with the use of language in context then the study of text can hardly avoid this question since an analyst will be interested in the relationships between an utterance and those utterances that precede and follow. As straightforward examples, consider the fact that typically a greeting prompts a greeting in return, a question expects a response, a compliment invites thanks and so forth.

'Dyadic' relationships of this kind (question: response, compliment: thanks) are clearly not random associations, and this prompts us to ask whether there are not regular structural patterns of this kind superordinate to sentence structure which might yield to a functional analysis.

In highly structured situations this does indeed seem to be the case. Consider, for example, the kind of language found in the classroom. This is a situation in which particular 'roles' (teacher and pupil) are institutionalized and easily identifiable, and in which certain aspects of behaviour have become conventionalized. It is hardly surprising that this is reflected in the language used, and it is thus possible to identify certain types of sequences which, in a well-regulated classroom, have come to be mutually understood and accepted by the participants.

So, for example, in a lesson on 'telling the time', a teacher might ask a pupil *What's the time?* In this context both teacher and pupil know perfectly well that a 'teacher's question' is involved, that the teacher knows the time, and that the function of the question is not to find the answer itself, but to find out whether the pupil knows it. The context constrains possible responses. If the pupil responds correctly, the teacher is likely to accept the response as correct and perhaps add a comment like *Well done Jimmy*, or *Good*. This yields a structure: T(eacher): question – P(upil): response – T: accept and comment. If no answer is forthcoming, the teacher might attempt to prompt the pupil, or turn to another, perhaps yielding a structure T: question – P: no response – T: prompt or repeat question. If the answer is incorrect, the teacher might again attempt a prompt, or might supply the answer and ask for corroboration, perhaps a sequence like T: question – P: response – T: prompt – P: no response – T: supply answer and seek corroboration – P: confirmation. The reader is invited to call on his past experience to imagine the sort of verbal behaviour that is at issue, and it will soon be clear that the particular speech acts involved are not without influence on the language that is considered appropriate.

In highly structured situations, like classrooms, a speech-act analysis seems to lend itself rather well to an account of language of this kind, and analyses along these lines have been used to attempt to account for, inter alia, the structure of conversation, the language of the classroom, and interactions between doctors and their patients, both normal and pathological.

In less highly structured situations things are less predictable, and in order to make sense of interchanges in these circumstances we need some machinery to account for the way in which sentence function is computed. Suppose, for example, that I ask my daughter, *Has the cat been fed?* and she replies with another question, *Have you been to Safeways?*, how do I interpret this response? It is a commonplace of verbal interaction that we expect our interlocutor to be 'cooperative', to make an active attempt to understand what we say, and to make 'relevant' responses. How else would communication be possible? The normal convention is that a question provokes a reply, rather than another question, so, if I am to assume that she is being 'cooperative' in her reply, I must attempt to interpret her question as a relevant response to mine. To do this I must assume that we draw on a common fund of background knowledge: for instance, that the household normally buys its catfood at Safeways, and that my daughter is not normally responsible for its purchase. Given such shared knowledge, I can then perhaps infer the cat has not been fed because we are out of catfood. The process is open-ended: I can, if I care, go on to infer that my daughter wishes to imply that if I had been to Safeways we could now feed the cat, and if I happen to be feeling particularly neurotic at the time I might well choose to draw yet further implicatures, perhaps that my daughter declines responsibility for the cat's hunger, or wishes to shift it on to me, or whatever.

The example is deliberately overelaborate, but it will serve to illustrate the kind of thing that is at issue, and relates back to questions we first explored in Chapter 1. To make a full account of the way language is used to communicate we need to supplement any theory of sentence formation with a 'pragmatic' theory relating it to the way language is used. This theory will need to offer some account of what 'cooperative' behaviour consists of and how context and background knowledge are used to draw 'relevant' implications.

Perhaps the most influential recent proposals in this area derive from the work of Grice (1975) who proposes a set of 'maxims' which govern cooperative behaviour. These, in outline, are

Maxim of Quantity: be as informative as the situation requires, but no more informative than necessary.

Maxim of Quality: do not say what you believe to be false or that for which you lack adequate evidence.

Maxim of Relation: be relevant.

Maxim of Manner: avoid obscurity and ambiguity, be brief and orderly.

Maxims of this kind, as the name suggests, are very general, and there is no suggestion that they form a system of 'rules'. They might rather be regarded as a set of conventions or strategies governing maximally straightforward and cooperative behaviour. To pursue the ramifications of such an account would take us far out of our way, though it will doubtless be clear that any coherent account of discourse can hardly fail to include a well-articulated theory of conversational implicature.

8.2 Word order

When sentences are put together to form a text, the form of any particular sentence is usually influenced by that of its neighbours. This influence can take many forms. One, which we shall not have the space to consider, involves the pronominalization, or even the omission, of items previously mentioned: so we are more likely to find *When Kate comes in she feeds the cat*, or *Kate comes in and feeds the cat* rather than *When Kate comes in Kate feeds the cat* or *Kate comes in and Kate feeds the cat*. Another involves the choice of word order in particular sentences. For example, although active and passive sentences paraphrase each other, they do not always have the same distribution: we might, indeed, consider part of the function of the passive form to relate to the speaker's ability to choose to make a non-agentive NP subject, or to avoid mention of the agent altogether, or both. We would thus doubtless find it more natural to find a sentence like *John asked for the job and was given it* rather than, say, *John asked for the job and someone gave it to him*.

In both of these examples what seems to be at issue is the way in which the structure of a sentence is influenced by the way in which a speaker chooses to structure the information he wishes to present. This is clearly a question which relates to the structure of texts as a whole and one which we cannot hope to do more than touch upon. We shall, therefore, restrict ourselves to the consideration of two preliminary issues relating to word order within sentences – the choice of grammatical subject and the choice of the first constituent in the sentence. The identification of both is fairly uncontroversial, and the language offers a number of alternatives for each. Describing these alternatives is not particularly complicated. What is complicated, and controversial, is the question of why some particular item should be selected as subject or occur in first position. We will start with the easier matter.

The identification of the grammatical subject, as we saw in 8.1, concerns such matters as agreement between subject and verb and the relative order of NP and verb, the subject almost invariably preceding the verb. That having been said, a speaker clearly has some option as to what NP he will select as subject, and there are a number of syntactic and lexical means available to facilitate this.

An obvious syntactic means involves the choice of sentence structure. Given some proposition, the language has available a number of devices that enable a speaker to maintain the same functional relations between the verb and its various arguments, but to vary the order in which the arguments occur by different choices of subject NP. Active and passive have already been mentioned as an example of this. Another example is the formation of so-called 'pseudo cleft sentences'. Thus, corresponding to a simple sentence like *Harriet gave Victoria a pen for Christmas*, we can construct a set of 'pseudo cleft sentences' of the form *Harriet is the one who gave Victoria a pen for Christmas*, *Victoria is the one who Harriet gave a pen to at Christmas*, *A pen is what Harriet gave to Victoria at Christmas* and so on.

Lexical choice can also be a determinant of the grammatical subject, and English has a number of sets of lexical items which hardly differ in meaning, but which switch the order of their associated arguments. So, for example, *These houses belong to me: I own these houses*; *I sold that car to my brother: My brother bought that car from me*; *I am interested in antique furniture: Antique furniture interests me*. In this area syntax and lexicon interact in a complex way. There are a variety of other lexico-syntactic operations with a similar effect: *John kissed Mary*; *John gave Mary a kiss*; *Mary got a kiss from John*. It is not suggested that such alternants are complete paraphrases, and there are indeed small but subtle semantic differences between the various structures. But clearly, one of the things that is at issue is that the selection of subject may influence other aspects of sentence structure and lexical choice.

First position in the sentence, which we will refer to as the 'theme' of the sentence, is also a relatively straightforward matter. It clearly needs to be distinguished from subject since the subject need not necessarily be the theme, as we shall see from some of the examples below. As with subject formation, the language offers a variety of ways of thematizing a constituent. One involves the way in which sentence adverbs can occur at either the beginning or the end of a sentence. Thus related to a sentence like *Many people get drunk at Hogmanay in Scotland* (theme is *Many people*, which happens to be grammatical subject also), we find sentences like *In Scotland many people get drunk at Hogmanay* (theme is *In Scotland*), *At Hogmanay many people get drunk in Scotland* (theme is *At Hogmanay*). Another thematization process, usually known as 'topicalization', takes some constituent from a sentence and simply puts it at the beginning of the sentence, deriving structures like *That man, I thought I told you never to talk to*.

If we now ask why there should be this variety of syntactic options open to the speaker, we get into functional questions which concern how a speaker chooses to structure the information he wishes to convey. This is a vast subject and we will do no more than scratch its surface by offering two observations that show that, although there can be no simple correlation between word order and the way a speaker chooses to structure the information he wishes to convey, the two matters are intimately related.

The first is concerned with the notion of 'topic'. Sentences in isolation are sometimes said to have a 'topic comment' structure: the first noun phrase being taken to be the 'topic' of the sentence, and what follows to be a 'comment' on that topic. Thus we have noted that although active and passive sentences may both be related to the same proposition, an active sentence like *The farmer killed the ducklings* is typically construed as a comment on the activities of 'the farmer', and the corresponding passive, *The ducklings were killed by the farmer*, as a comment on the fate of 'the ducklings'.

While this may be true of sentences in isolation, it is not necessarily true of sentences in context. Consider a sentence like *Unicorns are white*. In the context of an implicit question 'Tell me something about unicorns', the example can indeed be held to have a 'topic comment' structure, since the question can be held to establish 'unicorns' as a topic. However, in the context of an implicit question, 'Give me an example of something that is white', which might be held to establish 'whiteness' as a topic, the example will need to be construed as having a 'comment topic' structure.

Examples of this sort, which multiply as soon as we begin to consider examples from text rather than invented sentences in isolation, suggest that we can only establish what a topic is by considering the sentence in relation to its context, and that topic need not correspond either with the grammatical subject or with the item that is thematized. That having been said, however, sentence structure and topic can sometimes coincide, notably in the topicalized sentences mentioned above.

The second functional notion which we will briefly mention is 'perspective'. If we define 'topic' as 'what the sentence is about' (this notion being derived from the structure of the text as a whole), then 'perspective' may be considered to be the point from which the topic is to be viewed in some particular sentence. We have already encountered an example of this when discussing quantified sentences in 6.1, where we noted the 'focusing' effect of word order. Another example is the different thematizations of the sentence *Many people get drunk in Scotland at Hogmanay* mentioned above. If the topic is 'drunkenness', then this can clearly be viewed from a variety of perspectives. We can, for instance, view the matter from a national perspective, in which case *In Scotland . . .* is a suitable way to phrase the sentence since it thematizes the nation; on the other hand if we were interested in a temporal perspective, *At New Year . . .* might be more appropriate.

We do not have the space to pursue matters of this sort any further. Even from this brief discussion, however, it will be clear that how a person chooses to structure the information he wishes to convey has an effect on the sentence forms he will use to convey it. Sentence structure does not exist in a vacuum, divorced from questions of sentence function. Both need to be taken into account if we wish to have a properly rounded account of the way sentences are used to convey meanings.

Epilogue

We have concentrated our attention on issues that arise in the description and modelling of syntactic matters, and even within this limited scope have not had the space to explore more than a few of the live issues in linguistics today: there can, however, be no doubt that it is alive and kicking. The fragmentation of the 'transformational paradigm', which we have looked at in Chapters 6 and 7, has opened up space for other theories of linguistic structure to flourish, and there is certainly no lack of competing theoretical positions. One of the advantages of this is that the field of syntax is no longer dominated by theories that concern themselves primarily with structural questions relating to sentences in isolation. Without losing interest in questions of structure, it has also opened itself to the serious consideration of a number of functional questions of a rather traditional kind, and has increasingly been interested in the relationship between the form of language and the use of language; in other words, the whole range of ways in which language can be used to convey meanings.

Further Reading

1. Language and Communication

The idea that the principal task of linguistics is to convey meanings has not always been held by all schools of linguistics. This was particularly true of the 'structuralists' who dominated American linguistics in the 1950s and 1960s. They often rather ostentatiously excluded the systematic study of meanings – cf. Bloomfield (1933) and any of the textbooks based on this approach, e.g. Gleason (1961). In its early days transformational grammar took a wary view of meanings too – see Chomsky (1957).

For psychologically oriented views of the nature of language see introductions to psycholinguistics, such as Aitchison (1983) or Clark and Clark (1977). For sociologically oriented views see introductions to sociolinguistics, such as Hudson (1980), Trudgill (1974a), and works like Firth (1957), Halliday (1973, 1978), Kress (1976). For views of language as an 'abstract calculus' see in particular writings on 'mathematical linguistics' like Wall (1972). For a particularly abstract view of language from a linguistic rather than a mathematical point of view, see for example Hjelmslev (1947). Useful and readable overviews of recent linguistic theory are Newmeyer (1980), Sampson (1980). A more detailed technical review of a number of current approaches to syntactic description and their relation to semantic descriptions is Moravcsik and Wirth (1980).

See Lyons (1977b) for a useful review of various views of different 'kinds of meaning'. Jakobson (1960) is a stimulating and very readable account of types of meanings.

For some discussion of language in the context of general semiotic theory see Chao (1968), Fromkin and Rodman (1974), Hinde (1972), Householder (1971), Sebeok (1977). Laver and Hutcheson (1972) is a useful collection of papers on conversational interaction.

On the relationship between language and knowledge of the world see Chomsky (1977a, 1982b), Smith and Wilson (1979), and for a rather different view Hudson (1980). Useful introductions to semantic structure include Leech (1971), Lyons (1977b), Palmer (1976). On phonological structure see Brown (1977), Fudge (1973).

On the use of language in texts see de Beaugrande (1980), Brown and Yule (1983), van Dijk (1977). On teaching 'communicative competence' see, for example, Widdowson (1978).

2. Models of Language

The issues of idealization, competence and performance etc. are much discussed in the literature. See, for example, Culler (1976), Derwing (1973), Katz (1972, 1981), Lyons (1977b), Matthews (1979), Sampson (1975), de Saussure (1916).

For discussion of the nature of explanations in linguistics see Botha (1973), Cohen (1976), Hornstein and Lightfoot (1981).

3. Words

There is a large literature on words, and most introductions (with the striking exception of introductions to transformational grammar) have something useful to say on the subject. 'Structuralist' introductions of the 1950s and 1960s like Gleason (1961, 1965), Hockett (1958), are still useful. Nida (1949) is a mine of analyses with examples from many languages. The terminological approach of this chapter owes much to Lyons (1968) and Matthews (1974).

A good brief introduction to different theoretical approaches to word formation is Matthews (1970). A useful historical account is Robins (1967). Adams (1973) and Marchand (1969) are useful and comprehensive accounts of word formation processes in English. Matthews (1974) and Bauer (1983) are both comprehensive recent theoretical studies. Until recently, transformational generative grammarians have treated those morphological operations that interested them within the syntax, e.g. Lees (1966), or, as part of the 'morphophonemic' component, cf. Chomsky and Halle (1968); more recently, and largely since Chomsky (1970), more serious attention has been paid to morphology, for example Aronoff (1976), Jackendoff (1975), and Selkirk (1982).

4. Sentences

There are many excellent introductions to the general principles of constituent structure analysis as outlined here: Allerton (1979), Brown and Miller (1980), Hockett (1958), Householder (1972 – a good collection of articles), Lyons (1968), Matthews (1981), Palmer (1971). Akmajian and Heny (1975), Bach (1974), Huddleston (1976), Koutsoudas (1966), Langacker (1972) are particularly cast in terms of a transformational approach. For an introduction to the more recent 'Xbar' approach see Radford (1981) and, for a more technical account, Jackendoff (1977). On the supposed inadequacies of phrase structure grammars see Bach (1974), Chomsky (1957), or Postal (1964). For contrary views see Gazdar (1982), Gazdar and Pullum (1982), Pullum and Gazdar (1982), Pulman (1983). Other, somewhat different, approaches to constituent structure include that taken by 'systemic' grammar, see Berry (1975, 1977), Hudson (1971, 1976), Kress (1976); and 'tagmemic' grammar, see Cook (1969) and Longacre (1964). For 'computational' approaches to parsing, which bear on these questions, see King (1983), Sparck Jones and Wilks (1983), Winograd (1983), Winston (1977).

5. Relations between Sentences

The account of sentence relatedness presented here is largely in terms of a 'standard theory' transformational grammar: the account does, however, borrow from later work where it seems sensible to do this, especially in connection with the relationship between syntax and semantics. Chomsky (1965), though an important work, is not an easy book to read, and many of the issues it addresses are now somewhat dated. The reader may find it sensible to approach Chomsky's work through general introductions like Langacker (1968), Lyons (1977a). Discussion and exemplification of the methodology of transformational grammar are to be found in many introductions like Akmajian and Heny (1975), Bach (1974), Burt (1971), Culicover (1976),

Keyser and Postal (1976), Soames and Perlmutter (1979): the theoretical position taken by these books is not uniform and reflects differences of emphasis among the authors and the way the theory has changed through time. Collections of papers in this mould include Jacobs and Rosenbaum (1970), Reibel and Schane (1969). A grammar of English largely in these terms and with extensive discussion of competing analyses is Stockwell (1973).

There are other ways to account for the same kinds of relationships: for a description of these matters within a 'systemic' framework see Halliday (1967–8), Kress (1976) or Winograd (1983); for an account within the 'tagmemic' framework see Cook (1969), Longacre (1964).

On the relationship between syntax and semantics see Allwood (1977), Kempson (1977), Leech (1971), Lyons (1977b), McCawley (1981). For a discussion specifically within the transformational framework see Fillmore and Langendoen (1971), Fodor (1977), Jackendoff (1972), Katz and Postal (1964).

On the distinction between deep and surface structure see Postal (1969). Smith and Wilson (1979) has a discussion on the 'reality' of deep structures. On universalist claims of transformational grammar see Bach (1965), Bach and Harms (1968), Smith and Wilson (1979). For some discussion of various psychological claims see Aitchison (1983), Derwing (1973), Fodor, Bever and Garret (1974), Greene (1972).

6. The Rise and Fall of Transformations

The developing nature of Chomsky's own views can be followed in, for example, Chomsky (1957, 1965, 1966, 1975, 1977a, 1980). Chomsky's most recent model is Chomsky (1981), which is hard to read and very technical. Chomsky (1982a) contains a brief overview. A useful introduction is Radford (1981).

For a view of the history of transformational grammar in the United States see Newmeyer (1980). Winograd (1983) contains a useful summary of developments in transformational grammar, and some of its developing problems.

Seuren (1974) is a useful collection of articles on generative semantics and has a good bibliography. The tone of the interchanges between the 'generative semanticists' and more 'mainline' transformational grammarians can be caught in some of the articles in Steinberg and Jacobovitz (1971); see also Chomsky (1977a).

For early work on morphological derivations see Lees (1966). The notion of enriching the lexicon at the expense of the transformational component dates from Chomsky (1970). See Radford (1981) for some discussion of this point, as of others in this chapter. Hoekstra, Hulst and Moortgat (1980), Moortgat, Hulst and Hoekstra (1981) contain a number of articles with a lexical approach and useful bibliographies.

Among the earliest investigators of constraints on rules is Chomsky himself, e.g. Chomsky (1973, 1977c). The work of Ross (1967) was very influential: parts are reprinted in Harman (1974). For traces see Chomsky (1975), Fiengo (1977).

On phrase structure grammars see Brame (1978, 1979), Gazdar (1981a, 1982), Pullum and Gazdar (1982). Gazdar (1981b) is an account of coordination in a phrase structure grammar.

7. Functional Relations

The classic work on dependency is Tesnière (1959). Matthews (1981) contains a good discussion. Allerton (1983), Dik (1978), Fink (1977), Leech (1976), Palmer (1974) are also worth reading, as are descriptive grammars like Jespersen (1909–49), Quirk *et al.* (1972).

Many different approaches to description have interested themselves in notions of 'case' – among them, though not necessarily from the same theoretical background, are Anderson (1971, 1977), Brown and Miller (1982), Chafe (1970), Fillmore (1968, 1970, 1971a, 1971b), Halliday (1967–8), Langendoen (1970), Longacre (1976), Nilsen (1972), Quirk *et al.* (1972). Fillmore (1970, 1971a, 1971b) are proposals to use 'case' information in lexical entries. Similar notions have also been influential in artificial intelligence, cf. Boden (1977), Schank and Abelson (1977).

On notions of subject and object see Jespersen (1909–49), Li (1976), and on relational grammar, articles in Cole and Sadock (1977), Moravcsik and Wirth (1980).

Work of the kind discussed here on language universals owes much to Greenberg (1966). See also Greenberg (1978), Hawkins (1980), Lehmann (1978), Li (1975). The data on the passive is taken from Perlmutter and Postal (1977) and that on Yidiny from Dixon (1980).

8. Sentences in Texts

On sentence functions see Austin (1962), Bach and Harnish (1979), Cole and Morgan (1975), Coulthard (1977), Grice (1975), Lyons (1977b), Ross (1970), Sadock (1974), Searle (1969, 1975), Sinclair and Coulthard (1975).

On word order see Brown and Miller (1980), Dik (1978), Halliday (1970), Halliday and Hasan (1976), Li (1976).

References

Adams, V. (1973). *An Introduction to Modern English Word Formation*. Longman.

Aitchison, J. (1983). *The Articulate Mammal*. Second edition. Hutchinson.

Akmajian, A. & Heny, F. W. (1975). *An Introduction to the Principles of Transformational Syntax*. MIT Press.

Allerton, D. J. (1979). *Essentials of Grammar: a consensus view of syntax and morphology*. Routledge & Kegan Paul.

Allerton, D. J. (1983). *Valency and the English Verb*. Academic Press.

Allwood, J., Andersson, L.-G. & Dahl, O. (1977). *Logic in Linguistics*. Cambridge University Press.

Anderson, J. M. (1971). *The Grammar of Case: towards a localistic theory*. Cambridge University Press.

Anderson, J. M. (1977). *On Case Grammar*. Croom Helm.

Aronoff, M. (1976). *Word Formation in Generative Grammar*. MIT Press.

Austin, J. L. (1962). *How to Do Things with Words*. Clarendon Press.

Bach, E. (1965). 'On some recurrent types of transformation'. In Georgetown University monograph series on *Language and Linguistics*, 18.

Bach, E. (1974). *Syntactic Theory*. Holt, Rinehart & Winston.

Bach, E. & Harms, R. (eds.) (1968). *Universals in Linguistic Theory*. Holt, Rinehart & Winston.

Bach, K. & Harnish, R. M. (1979). *Linguistic Communication and Speech Acts*. MIT Press.

Bauer, L. (1983). *English Word Formation*. Cambridge University Press.

de Beaugrande, R. (1980). *Text, Discourse and Process*. Longman.

Berry, M. (1975). *Introduction to Systemic Linguistics I: structures and systems*. Batsford.

Berry, M. (1977). *Introduction to Systemic Linguistics II: levels and links.* Batsford.

Bloomfield, L. (1933). *Language.* Holt, Rinehart & Winston.

Boden, M. (1977). *Artificial Intelligence and Natural Man.* Harvester Press.

Botha, R. (1973). *The Justification of Linguistic Hypotheses: a study of non-demonstrative inference in transformational grammar.* Mouton.

Brame, M. (1978). *Base Generated Syntax.* Noit Amrofer.

Brame, M. (1979). *Essays towards Realistic Syntax.* Noit Amrofer.

Brown, E. K. & Miller, J. (1980). *Syntax: a linguistic introduction to sentence structure.* Hutchinson.

Brown, E. K. & Miller, J. (1982). *Syntax: generative grammar.* Hutchinson.

Brown, G. (1977). *Listening to Spoken English.* Longman.

Brown, G. & Yule, G. (1983). *Discourse Analysis.* Cambridge University Press.

Burt, M. (1971). *From Deep to Surface.* MIT Press.

Chafe, W. L. (1970). *Meaning and the Structure of Language.* Chicago University Press.

Chao, Y. R. (1968). *Language and Symbolic Systems.* Cambridge University Press.

Chomsky, N. (1957). *Syntactic Structures.* Mouton.

Chomsky, N. (1965). *Aspects of the Theory of Syntax.* MIT Press.

Chomsky, N. (1966). *Language and Mind.* Harcourt, Brace, Jovanovich.

Chomsky, N. (1970). 'Remarks on nominalisations'. In Jacobs & Rosenbaum (1970).

Chomsky, N. (1973). 'Conditions on transformations'. In Andersen, S. & Kiparsky, P. (eds.). *A Festschrift for Morris Halle.* Holt, Rinehart & Winston.

Chomsky, N. (1975). *Reflections on Language.* Temple Smith.

Chomsky, N. (1977a). *Language and Responsibility.* Pantheon.

Chomsky, N. (1977b). *Essays on Form and Interpretation.* North Holland.

Chomsky, N. (1977c). 'On *wh-* movement'. In Culicover *et al. Formal Syntax.* Academic Press.

Chomsky, N. (1980). *Rules and Representations.* Columbia University Press.

Chomsky, N. (1981). *Lectures on Government and Binding.* Foris.

Chomsky, N. (1982a). *Some Concepts and Consequences of the Theory of Government and Binding.* MIT Press.

Chomsky, N. (1982b). *The Generative Enterprise: a discussion with Riny Huybregts and Hank van Riemsdijk.* Foris.

Chomsky, N. & Halle, M. (1968). *The Sound Pattern of English.* Harper & Row.

Clark, H. H. & Clark, E. V. (1977). *Psychology and Language: an introduction to psycholinguistics.* Harcourt, Brace, Jovanovich.

Cohen, D. (ed.) (1976). *Explaining Linguistic Phenomena.* Wiley.

Cole, P. & Morgan, J. L. (eds.) (1975). *Syntax and Semantics 3: speech acts.* Academic Press.

Cole, P. & Sadock, J. (eds.) (1977). *Syntax and Semantics 8: grammatical relations.* Academic Press.

Cook, W. A. (1969). *Introduction to Tagmemic Analysis.* Georgetown University Press.

Coulthard, M. (1977). *An Introduction to Discourse Analysis.* Longman.

Culicover, P. W. (1976). *Syntax.* Academic Press.

Culler, J. (1976). *Saussure.* Fontana.

Derwing, B. (1973). *Transformational Grammar as a Theory of Language Acquisition.* Cambridge University Press.

van Dijk, T. (1977). *Text and Context.* Longman.

Dik, S. C. (1978). *Functional Grammar.* Foris.

Dixon, R. M. W. (1972). *The Dyirbal Language of North Queensland.* Cambridge University Press.

Dixon, R. M. W. (1980). *The Languages of Australia.* Cambridge University Press.

Fiengo, R. (1977). 'On trace theory'. *Linguistic Inquiry*, 8.

Fillmore, C. J. (1968). 'The case for case'. In Bach & Harms (1968).

Fillmore, C. J. (1970). 'The grammar of hitting and breaking'. In Jacobs & Rosenbaum (1970).

Fillmore, C. J. (1971a). 'Verbs of judging'. In Fillmore & Langendoen (1971).

Fillmore, C. J. (1971b). 'Types of lexical information'. In Steinberg & Jacobovitz (1971).

Fillmore, C. J. & Langendoen, T. (eds.) (1971). *Studies in Linguistic Semantics*. Holt, Rinehart & Winston.

Fink, S. R. (1977). *Aspects of a Pedagogical Grammar Based on a Case Grammar and Valence Theory*. Niemeyer.

Firth, J. R. (1957). *Papers in Linguistics 1934–51*. Oxford University Press.

Fodor, J. D. (1977). *Semantics: theories of meaning in generative grammar*. T. Y. Crowell.

Fodor, J., Bever, T. & Garret, M. (1974). *The Psychology of Language*. McGraw Hill.

Fromkin, V. & Rodman, R. (1974). *An Introduction to Language*. Holt, Rinehart & Winston.

Fudge, E. C. (ed.) (1973). *Phonology*. Pelican.

Gazdar, G. (1981a). 'On syntactic categories'. *Philosophical Transactions (Series BR) of the Royal Society*, 295.

Gazdar, G. (1981b). 'Unbounded dependencies and co-ordinate structure'. *Linguistic Inquiry*, 12.

Gazdar, G. (1982). 'Phrase structure grammar'. In Jacobson & Pullum (1982).

Gazdar, G. & Pullum, G. K. (1982). *Generalised Phrase Structure Grammar: a theoretical synopsis*. Indiana University Linguistics Club.

Gleason, H. A. (1961). *Introduction to Descriptive Linguistics*. Holt Rinehart.

Gleason, H. A. (1965). *Linguistics and English Grammar*. Holt, Rinehart & Winston.

Greenberg, J. H. (1966). 'Some universals of grammar with particular reference to the order of meaningful elements'. In Greenberg, (ed.) (1966) *Universals of Language*. MIT Press.

Greenberg, J. H. (ed.) (1978). *Universals of Human Language*. 4 vols. Stanford University Press.

Greene, J. (1972). *Psycholinguistics: Chomsky and psychology*. Penguin.

Grice, P. (1975). 'Logic and conversation'. In Cole & Morgan (1975).

Gross, M. (1979). 'On the failure of generative grammar'. *Language*, 55.

Halliday, M. A. K. (1967–8). 'Notes on transitivity and theme in English'. *Journal of Linguistics*, 3, 4.

Halliday, M. A. K. (1970). 'Language structure and language function'. In Lyons (1970).

Halliday, M. A. K. (1973). *Explorations in the Functions of Language*. Arnold.

Halliday, M. A. K. (1978). *Language as Social Semiotic*. Arnold.

Halliday, M. A. K. & Hasan, R. (1976). *Cohesion in English*. Longman.

Harman, G. (ed.) (1974). *On Noam Chomsky: critical essays*. Anchor.

Hawkins, J. A. (1980). 'On implicational and distributional universals of word order'. *Journal of Linguistics*, 16.

Hinde, R. A. (ed.) (1972). *Non-verbal Communication*. Cambridge University Press.

Hjelmslev, L. (1947). *Prologomena to a Theory of Language*. Translated by F. J. Whitfield. University of Wisconsin Press.

Hockett, C. F. (1958). *A Course in Modern Linguistics*. Macmillan.

Hoekstra, T., Hulst, H.v.d. & Moortgat, M. (eds.) (1980). *Lexical Grammar*. Foris.

Hornstein, N. & Lightfoot, D. (1981). *Explanation in Linguistics*. Longman.

Householder, F. W. (1971). *Linguistic Speculations*. Cambridge University Press.

Householder, F. W. (ed.) (1972). *Syntactic Theory I: structuralist. Selected readings*. Penguin.

Huddleston, R. (1976). *An Introduction to English Transformational Syntax*. Longman.

Hudson, R. A. (1971). *English Complex Sentences: an introduction to systemic grammar*. North Holland.

Hudson, R. A. (1976). *Arguments for a Non-transformational Grammar*. University of Chicago Press.

Hudson, R. A. (1980). *Sociolinguistics*. Cambridge University Press.

Hymes, D. (1971a). 'Models of the interaction of language and social life'. In Gumperz, J. J. & Hymes, D. *Directions in Sociolinguistics*. Holt, Rinehart & Winston.

Hymes, D. (ed.) (1971b). *Pidginisation and Creolisation of Languages*. Cambridge University Press.

Jackendoff, R. (1972). *Semantic Interpretation in Generative Grammar*. MIT Press.

Jackendoff, R. (1975). 'Morphological and semantic regularities in the lexicon'. *Language*, 51.

Jackendoff, R. (1977). *Xbar Syntax: a study of phrase structure*. MIT Press.

Jacobs, R. & Rosenbaum, P. (1970). *Readings in English Transformational Grammar*. Ginn & Co.

Jacobson, P. & Pullum, G. (eds.) (1982). *The Nature of Syntactic Representations*. Reidel.

Jakobson, R. (1960). 'Linguistics and poetics'. In Sebeok (1960).

Jespersen, O. (1909–49). *A Modern English Grammar on Historical Principles*. Munksgaard.

Katz, J. J. (1972). *Semantic Theory*. Harper & Row.

Katz, J. J. (1981). *Language and Other Abstract Objects*. Blackwell.

Katz, J. J. & Postal, P. M. (1964). *An Integrated Theory of Linguistic Descriptions*. MIT Press.

Kempson, R. M. (1977). *Semantic Theory*. Cambridge University Press.

Keyser, S. J. & Postal, P. (1976). *Beginning English Grammar*. Harper & Row.

King, M. (1983). *Parsing Natural Language*. Academic Press.

Klima, E. & Bellugi, U. (1979). *The Signs of Language*. Harvard University Press.

Koutsoudas, C. A. (1966). *Writing Transformational Grammars*. McGraw Hill.

Kress, G. (ed.) (1976). *Halliday: system and function in language*. Oxford University Press.

Kruisinga, E. & Erades, P. A. (1911). *An English Grammar*. Nordhoof.

Kucera, H. & Francis, W. N. (1967). *A Computational Analysis of Present-day English*. Brown University Press.

Labov, W. (1972). *Sociolinguistic Patterns*. University of Pennsylvania Press.

Langacker, R. W. (1968). *Language and its Structure*. Harcourt, Brace & World.

Langacker, R. W. (1972). *Fundamentals of Linguistic Analysis*. Harcourt, Brace, Jovanovich.

Langendoen, D. T. (1970). *Essentials of English Grammar*. Holt, Rinehart & Winston.

Laver, J. & Hutcheson, S. (1972). *Communication in Face to Face Interaction*. Pelican.

Leech, G. N. (1971). *Semantics*. Penguin.

Leech, G. N. (1976). *Meaning and the English Verb*. Longman.

Lees, R. (1966). *The Grammar of English Nominalisations*. Mouton.

Lehmann, W. P. (1978). *Syntactic Typology*. Harcourt, Brace, Jovanovich.

Li, C. N. (ed.) (1975). *Word Order and Word Order Change*. University of Texas Press.

Li, C. N. (ed.) (1976). *Subject and Topic*. Academic Press.

Longacre, R. E. (1964). *Grammar Discovery Procedures: a field manual*. Mouton.

Longacre, R. E. (1976). *An Anatomy of Speech Notions*. Peter de Ridder Press.

Lyons, J. (1968). *Introduction to Theoretical Linguistics*. Cambridge University Press.

Lyons, J. (ed.) (1970). *New Horizons in Linguistics*. Pelican.

Lyons, J. (1972). 'Human language'. In Hinde (1972).

Lyons, J. (1977a). *Chomsky*. Fontana.

Lyons, J. (1977b). *Semantics*. 2 vols. Cambridge University Press.

Lyons, J. (1981). *Language and Linguistics*. Cambridge University Press.

McCawley, J. D. (1981). *Everything that linguists have always wanted to know about logic: but were ashamed to ask*. University of Chicago Press.

Marchand, H. (1969). *The Categories and Types of Present-day English Word-formation*. C. H. Beck.

Matthei, E. & Roeper, T. (1983). *Understanding and Producing Speech*. Fontana.

Matthews, P. H. (1970). 'Recent developments in morphology'. In Lyons (1970).

Matthews, P. H. (1974). *Morphology: an introduction to the theory of word structure*. Cambridge University Press.

Matthews, P. H. (1979). *Generative Grammar and Linguistic Competence*. Allen & Unwin.

Matthews, P. H. (1981). *Syntax*. Cambridge University Press.

Moortgat, M., Hulst, H.v.d. & Hoekstra, T. (eds.) (1981). *The Scope of Lexical Rules*. Foris.

Moravcsik, E. A. & Wirth, J. R. (1980). *Syntax and Semantics 13: current approaches to syntax*. Academic Press.

Newmeyer, F. (1980). *Linguistic Theory in America*. Academic Press.

Nida, E. A. (1949). *Morphology: the descriptive analysis of words*. University of Michigan Press.

Nilsen, D. F. L. (1972). *Towards a Semantic Specification of Deep Case*. Mouton.

Palmer, F. R. (1971). *Grammar*. Penguin.

Palmer, F. R. (1974). *The English Verb*. Longman.

Palmer, F. R. (1976). *Semantics, a New Outline*. Cambridge University Press.

Perlmutter, D. & Postal, P. (1977). 'Towards a universal characterisation of passivisation'. In *Proceedings of the third annual meeting of the Berkeley Linguistics Society*.

Postal, P. (1964). 'Limitations of phrase structure grammars'. In Fodor, J. A. & Katz, J. J. *The Structure of Language: readings in the philosophy of language*. Prentice Hall.

Postal, P. (1969). 'Underlying and superficial linguistic structure'. In Reibel & Schane (1969).

Postal, P. (1974). *Constituent Structure: a study of contemporary models of syntactic description*. Mouton.

Pullum, G. & Gazdar, G. (1982). 'Natural languages and context-free languages'. *Linguistics and Philosophy*, 4.

Pulman, S. (1983). 'Generalised phrase structure grammar'. In Sparck Jones & Wilks (1983).

Quirk, R. (1968). 'The survey of English usage'. In Quirk (1968). *Essays on the English Language: medieval and modern*. Longman.

Quirk, R., Greenbaum, S., Leech, G. N. & Svartvik, J. (1972). *A Grammar of Contemporary English*. Longman.

Radford, A. (1981). *Transformational Syntax*. Cambridge University Press.

Reibel, D. A. & Schane, S. E. (eds.) (1969). *Modern Studies in English: readings in transformational grammar*. Prentice Hall.

Robins, R. H. (1967). *A Short History of Linguistics*. Longman.

Ross, J. R. (1967). *Constraints on Variables in Syntax*. Indiana Linguistics Circle. Extracts appear in Harman (1974).

Ross, J. R. (1970). 'On declarative sentences'. In Jacobs & Rosenbaum (1970).

Sadock, J. (1974). *Towards a Linguistic Theory of Speech Acts*. Academic Press.

Sampson, G. (1975). *The Form of Language*. Weidenfeld & Nicolson.

Sampson, G. (1980). *Schools of Linguistics*. Hutchinson.

de Saussure, F. (1916). *Cours de linguistique générale*. Translated as *Course in General Linguistics*. Duckworth.

Schank, R. & Abelson, R. P. (1977). *Scripts, Plans, Goals and Understanding*. Erlbaum.

Scheurweghs, G. (1959). *Present-day English Syntax*. Longman.

Searle, J. R. (1969). *Speech Acts*. Cambridge University Press.

Searle, J. R. (1975). 'Indirect speech acts'. In Cole & Morgan (1975).

Sebeok, T. A. (ed.) (1960). *Style in Language*. MIT Press.

Sebeok, T. A. (1977). *How Animals Communicate*. Indiana University Press.

Selkirk, L. (1982). *The Syntax of Words*. MIT Press.

Seuren, P. A. M. (ed.) (1974). *Semantic Syntax*. Oxford University Press.

Sinclair, J. McH. & Coulthard, M. (1975). *Towards an Analysis of Discourse*. Oxford University Press.

Smith, N. & Wilson, D. (1979). *Modern Linguistics: the results of Chomsky's revolution*. Pelican.

Soames, S. & Perlmutter, D. M. (1979). *Syntactic Argumentation and the Structure of English*. University of California Press.

Spark Jones, K. & Wilks, Y. (eds.) (1983). *Automatic Natural Language Parsing*. Ellis Harwood.

Steinberg, D. & Jacobovitz, L. (eds.) (1971). *Semantics*. Cambridge University Press.

Stockwell, R. P. *et al.* (1973). *The Major Syntactic Structures of English*. Holt, Rinehart & Winston.

Tesnière, L. (1959). *Éléments de syntaxe structurale*. Klincksieck.

Trudgill, P. (1974a). *Sociolinguistics*. Pelican.

Trudgill, P. (1974b). *The Social Differentiation of English in Norwich*. Cambridge University Press.

Trudgill, P. (1978). *Sociolinguistic Patterns in British English*. Arnold.

Wall, R. (1972). *Introduction to Mathematical Linguistics*. Prentice Hall.

Widdowson, H. G. (1978). *Teaching Language as Communication*. Longman.

Winograd, T. (1983). *Language as a Cognitive Process. 1: syntax*. Addison Wesley.

Winston, P. H. (1977). *Artificial Intelligence*. MIT Press.

Wisser, F. Th. (1963–73). *An Historical Syntax of the English Language*. Brill.

Index

Index